Anthropology and Public Service

ANTHROPOLOGY AND PUBLIC SERVICE

The UK Experience

Edited by
Jeremy MacClancy

berghahn
NEW YORK · OXFORD
www.berghahnbooks.com

Published in 2017 by
Berghahn Books
www.berghahnbooks.com

© 2017, 2019 Jeremy MacClancy
First paperback edition published in 2019

All rights reserved. Except for the quotation of short passages
for the purposes of criticism and review, no part of this book
may be reproduced in any form or by any means, electronic or
mechanical, including photocopying, recording, or any information
storage and retrieval system now known or to be invented,
without written permission of the publisher.

Library of Congress Cataloging-in-Publication Data

Names: MacClancy, Jeremy, editor.
Title: Anthropology and public service : the UK experience / edited by Jeremy MacClancy.
Description: New York : Berghahn Books, 2017. | Includes bibliographical references and index.
Identifiers: LCCN 2016053589 (print) | LCCN 2016056858 (ebook) | ISBN 9781785334023 (hardback : alk. paper) | ISBN 9781785334030 (ebook)
Subjects: LCSH: Applied anthropology--Great Britain. | Anthropologists--Employment--Great Britain. | Political science--Anthropological aspects--Great Britain. | Civil service--Great Britain.
Classification: LCC GN397.7.G8 A67 2017 (print) | LCC GN397.7.G8 (ebook) | DDC 301.0941--dc23
LC record available at https://lccn.loc.gov/2016053589

British Library Cataloguing in Publication Data

A catalogue record for this book is available from the British Library

ISBN 978-1-78533-402-3 hardback
ISBN 978-1-78920-087-4 paperback
ISBN 978-1-78533-403-0 ebook

Contents

Preface	*Jeremy MacClancy*	vii
Chapter 1	Anthropology and Public Service *Jeremy MacClancy*	1
Chapter 2	On Her Majesty's Service (and Beyond): Anthropology's Contribution to an Unconventional Career *Mils Hills*	61
Chapter 3	You Can't Go Home Again: Anthropology, Displacement and the Work of Government *Benjamin R. Smith*	79
Chapter 4	Anthropology in the Closet: Contributions to Community Development and Local Government *Robert Gregory*	101
Chapter 5	Parading through the Peace Process: Anthropology, Governance and Crisis in Northern Ireland *Dominic Bryan and Neil Jarman*	123
Chapter 6	From Participant Observer to Observed Participant: A Prison Governor's Experience *Peter Bennett*	147
Chapter 7	Identity and Appropriation in Applied Health Research *Rachael Gooberman-Hill*	165
Afterword	An Endnote, About How to Begin *Jeremy MacClancy*	179
Index		185

Preface

The world turns, and anthropology with it. New theories come into vogue, tired ones are slowly forgotten. At the same time, events in the world may serially challenge academic anthropologists, pushing them to produce new ways to analyse and comment on the unforeseen yet already here. Given these circumstances, change within the discipline, whether gradual or revolutionary, is of our essence.

One dimension of that change is the increasing number of Anglophone anthropologists who do not take up permanent employment within universities. It has long been the case that some anthropologists with doctorates have chosen to take jobs as anthropologists beyond academia. For example, the USA-based Society for Applied Anthropology was founded in the early 1940s, and similar organisations started to arise in the UK from the 1970s on; within the last decade a host of books on varieties of applied anthropology have been produced by British publishers.

What is relatively new, at least within the UK, is the entry of anthropologists with experience of fieldwork into government service, at all levels: national, regional and local. The primary aim of this book is to investigate this activity and what its consequences might be for the future of the discipline. To my knowledge, this is the first time this domain has been broached and examined, let alone in a systematic manner.

The opening chapter has three main aims. First, I present the results of my interviews with as many Whitehall anthropologists as would agree to meet with me. We talked about the jobs they did, the ways in which they deploy anthropological methods in their workplaces, and of both the constraints and opportunities their positions offer. Second, I compare their work with that of the colonial anthropologists who were employed in British overseas territories in the first half of the last century. Third, I place the accounts and analysis given in the remaining chapters into the broader context of this collection.

The next chapter is written by an anthropologist who went from near-idyllic fieldwork in Mauritius to the Cabinet Office, one of a phalanx of young men and women sent in 'to shake things up'. From there he used his experience to set up a consultancy; recently he has returned to academia, this time in business studies. His knowledge of Civil Service ways has made him a fierce defender of anthropology within government, against academics who wish to keep their critical distance.

In Chapter 3 Ben Smith reflects on his transitions: from doctoral fieldwork among Aborigines, to applied work in the same area, to employment within an NGO mediating between the indigenes and the state, and finally his return to Britain and a post within the UK Border Agency. Among other questions, he asks whether he taught Aborigines how to think in state-appropriate terms, and whether he can balance both his present role and his sense of remaining an anthropologist.

Robert Gregory, who provides Chapter Four, is perhaps the most inspiring of all contributors to this book, for he is the only one who went straight from graduation to a job. Employed in community liaison within a Norfolk town council, he has adapted development anthropology, practised overseas, into 'backyard anthropology', practised in the UK. Moreover, he has done it so successfully his team wins national prizes and their methods are imitated elsewhere.

Working on government service might seem a mix of the intellectually engaging and the bureaucratic humdrum. In Chapter Five Dominic Bryan and Neil Jarman tell a very different tale. Based in Belfast, they acted repeatedly as advisors to the Northern Irish Government on ways to defuse tensions over Protestant parades. They admit some of their ideas worked, others not so well. But they recognize they were exciting tasks to be charged with.

The shift from Chapter Five to Six is one from monitoring outdoor demonstrations to managing the securely confined. In his chapter Peter Bennett ruminates over his time as governor of a series of prisons, especially Grendon Underwood, the first in Britain to be run as a therapeutic community. In some revealing comments, he also compares his doctoral fieldwork among a Hindu sect maligned as 'the Epicureans of India' with his experience running jails.

The final contributor is Rachael Gooberman-Hill, whose work straddles university and the National Health Service of the UK. She employs anthropological techniques in applied health research. In a very considered account of two research projects which she helped develop, she portrays how she modifies her anthropological style to dovetail with the desires of grant-giving bodies, while taking on board other modes from neighbouring fields of inquiry.

I finish with a brief endnote, a checklist for students of anthropology who are keen that their time at university enhances their chances of employment. It may also be of use to some teachers of our subject.

In sum, a rich mix covering key aspects of an important field of anthropological activity, which at present appears only set to grow further. Enjoy.

Jeremy MacClancy is Professor of Anthropology in the Department of Social Sciences, Oxford Brookes University. He is the founder-chairman of Chacolinks, a small, international charity that accompanies the indigenous Wichí of northern Argentina in the legal campaign to regain control of their ancestral lands.

Chapter 1

ANTHROPOLOGY AND PUBLIC SERVICE
Jeremy MacClancy

> An extremely valuable study would be one that compared the work of anthropologists for the colonial governments of yesteryear with that of anthropologists for governments today. My impression is that the work of the latter is considered insignificant by the governments and largely ignored or else the scholars are involved in tasks so superficial that their training is wasted.
>
> — S.R. Barrett, *The Rebirth of Anthropological Theory*

How wrong can you be!

*

In the UK these days the majority of social anthropologists who earn doctorates do not get jobs in university departments. Many go down one of a wide range of non-academic avenues: corporate anthropology (Suchman 2014), the media (Henley 2006), design anthropology (Drazin 2006), ethnographic consumer research, teaching in schools, non-governmental organisations (NGOs) (e.g. Survival International, Forest Peoples Programme) and a diversity of consultancies, among others.

In recent years, a small and rising percentage of those with doctorates have obtained, on the basis of their anthropological skills, positions in different sections of government. Here they can implement and help to create policy, whether at the national or municipal level. At times their potential influence on public life may be wide-ranging and profound. Yet almost nothing has been written on this recent, important development within anthropological practice. Hence the central aim of this book: to redress that imbalance, by documenting and drawing out the implications of this evolution for the discipline.

The topic is important not just because of the significance of the jobs these anthropologists come to hold. It is key because this move of practitioners into public service positions holds the very real potential to change the ways we conceive of anthropology in the round. Since the postwar period up until relatively recently, the most illustrious among British academic anthropologists acted as the national hegemons of the discipline. They had the authority to define its limits and its central aims. Advances in theory were the gold standard; anything else was of baser metal (Turton 1988: 145–46; MacClancy 2013). To use the language of that time, which today has a very dated ring, theoretical anthropology was 'pure', its applied counterpart 'impure'. This dire dichotomy had impoverishing consequences. One activity was to be looked up to as virtuous, a model for ambitious practitioners with an eye for the prestigious. The other activity, termed as tainted, was only engaged in out of necessity, by those who had not achieved enough to gain university posts. Landman, writing in the late 1970s, spoke of the persisting idea that applied work was 'the refuge of the less intelligent' (Landman 1978: 323). According to this discriminatory logic, tenured positions were for the front runners, extramural jobs for the also-rans. Why advertise your failure?

Perhaps the first fracture in this stereotyping vision of non-academic jobs as hidey-holes for the second-rate was the emergence of development studies as a scholastic endeavour in its own right. Indeed, anthropologists working in development played a key role in the creation and establishment of the discipline. They continue to do so. Another central factor came in the mid 1970s, with the end of university expansion and the first government cuts in tertiary education (Grillo 1985: 3; Riviere 2007: 8). The effect of these changes on the shape of anthropology as a whole did not become manifest for some time. University-based anthropologists were slowly made more and more aware of the number of fellow professionals outside academe, and then of the work they were doing. If the rise of taught postgraduate Masters courses is an indicator of their growing awareness, then the sub-fields of the discipline related to our theme which began to develop from this time on include, in rough order of emergence, medical anthropology, childhood studies, environmental conservation, refugee studies and migration studies.

Yet, for all these relatively minor developments, there has been, to my knowledge, no sustained work in the UK on anthropology in government, nor about the ways in which this new avenue might alter both how we conceive the point of our discipline and how we train students for life beyond the ivory towers. The fundamental pedagogy of undergraduate anthropology has changed surprisingly little. Thus, a supplementary aim of this book is to rattle that cage: to show the ways anthropologist-civil servants work, to investigate which skills they have exploited and which they have had to learn, and thus to suggest which abilities today's students may need to be trained in.

In this opening chapter I first examine the history of anthropologists in Her Majesty's Government, and then analyse the experience of contemporary anthropologist-civil servants in a variety of contexts. The other contributors to this volume discuss a range of ways in which anthropologists engage with public service in contemporary Britain: employment as an anthropologist, charged with community development, by a British town hall; working in the Ministry of Defence and the Cabinet Office; the consequences of moving from academic anthropology to prison governance or border control; providing anthropological advice to the government in Northern Ireland; leading research teams into health and healthcare to inform NHS policy and provision.

Our collective goal is not to cover every topic in this potentially broad and rich domain of activity. I had neither the time nor the opportunity to organise that. Instead I wished to provide a chance for a sustained scrutiny of what it means to be an anthropologist in government today, to see what generalisations we can and cannot make about our discipline and public service. For this practice is growing too much to be ignored any longer.

A little history

Anthropologists working with the British government is nothing new. Ever since practitioners began to turn their pursuit into a profession, there were anthropologists trying to persuade bureaucrats and politicians of its pragmatic value. Very occasionally, they succeeded.

The first attempts were long on promise, short on delivery. Victorian anthropologists, evolutionists to a man (and they were all men), argued the social utility of their practice in strictly Anglocentric terms: they wished to reinvigorate the British 'race', then perceived to be at grave risk of collective degeneration. Despite their efforts, however, they failed to impress politicians of the day. No grant was forthcoming (Stocking 1987: 266). Similarly, in the 1900s the Home Office 'certainly took note' of the work on racial degeneration by the Italian criminal anthropologist Cesare Lombroso, but its civil servants were ultimately unsympathetic to his widely known though controversial ideas. In 1906, for instance, an American follower of Lombroso encouraged the Home Office to imitate the US proposal to establish a laboratory for 'the study of the criminal and defective classes'. His offer of 'free advice' was declined (Pick 1989: 180–81).

A much longer-lived justification repeatedly deployed by anthropologists and their supporters was not aimed at home, but abroad: anthropology would help save the Empire from itself. They propounded that ignorance of others' ways led to a series of dire consequences: insouciant colonisers unwittingly provoked locals, wasted the benefits of costly expeditions and created political difficulties and complications that need not have arisen. Furthermore, some evolutionists and diffusionists were not so much concerned with homeland degeneration but with a much starker overseas worry: depopulation, disintegration, and even extinction of recently pacified peoples. Their message was clear. If colonial authorities did not take advantage of anthropological know-how, they could end up with no one to colonise (Kuklick 1991: 184). In the words of one diffusionist who conducted fieldwork in Melanesia:

> I was asking for skulls the other week and received the ironic reply, 'In a little while the white man will be able to take all ours'. (Deacon 1934: xix)

Perhaps the first academic to exploit the imperialist argument was the great Victorian scholar Max Müller. In 1891 he petitioned the government to produce a series of records on customs in the colonies. For all his eminence, Müller's plan 'expired in the pigeon-holes of the Colonial Office' (Müller 1891: 798). There were further attempts in the late 1890s, again argued on imperialist grounds, for the government to fund a Bureau of Ethnology, modelled on its very successful US counterpart. The responses, including one from the Prime Minister, Lord Salisbury, were supportive, but did not extend to the dedication of public funds (Urry 1993: ch. 5; Stocking 1996: 373). In 1903 Alfred Cort Haddon, in the name of the Anthropological Institute, together with a representative of the Folklore Society urged the Colonial Secretary, Joseph Chamberlain, to create a commission in South Africa to produce a complete ethnographic record, for the sake of efficient administration. The politician, however, thought the moment 'inopportune'. When a weightier delegation met with him two years later, his reply remained the same. In 1911 an even more formidable group of public dignitaries and academics approached the Prime Minister, now Herbert Asquith. But the response was, once again, empty-handed sympathy. A second approach to Asquith made in 1914 was stymied by the outbreak of war (Stocking 1996: 375–80).

Some well-placed colonial administrators, now retired in Britain, also banged the imperialist anthropology drum, to pedagogical end, with some success. Sir Herbert Risley, India's first Census Commissioner and president of the Royal Anthropological Institute in the early 1910s, used his presidential address to underline the need for colonial officers to learn local customs in order to avoid fomenting unrest (Risley 1911). At much the same time, Sir Richard Carnac Temple, former Chief Commissioner of the Andaman and Nicobar Islands, gave speeches throughout the UK urging the need for fledgling colonial administrators to receive university training in anthropology (Temple 1913, 1914a, 1914b). His campaign paid off, as a course that included anthropology was set up for trainee political officers destined for the Sudan. Furthermore, in 1914 Radcliffe-Brown, who had done fieldwork in the Andamans, was hired to give a course of lectures in the discipline at the University of Birmingham. From 1924 on, men selected for posts in tropical Africa had to take a year-long course at Oxford or Cambridge that includes anthropological instruction (Kuklick 1991: 196–97, 202; Stocking 1996: 378–79).

If central government offered nothing more than goodwill, specific colonial administrations were prepared to go much further. The Indian Civil Service is the outstanding early example here. The most prestigious overseas administration in the Empire, with the stiffest entrance requirements, its civil servants regarded themselves as a mandarin elite. Some fulfilled their brief by acting as imperial ethnographers; their goal was to both understand and ameliorate local ways. An early stimulus to systematic ethnography was the periodic censuses of the entire subcontinent, the first being held in the early 1870s. Then, in 1901, a Director of Ethnography was appointed, charged with the production of a comprehensive ethnographic survey that would result in a series of tribes and castes encyclopaedias. In the following decades some administrator-scholars also produced tribal ethnographies. While the best work on the censuses generated schemes of classification grounded on theoretical visions of the origin and development of the caste system, the tribal tomes were much closer in format to a synchronic functionalism. The anthropologist of India Chris Fuller argues that although some of their colonialist ethnography was exemplary, their work as a whole had little effect on metropolitan anthropology, for two reasons. First, the nature of their material did not dovetail with contemporary theoretical debates. Second, members of this selective intelligentsia did not think they had to prove their worth to study-bound anthropologists. Most of the references in their works are to one another, not to theoreticians back home (Fuller n.d.a, n.d.b).

On other continents, only a few, very senior administrators wished to advance colonial anthropology and had the authority to do so, for example Sir Hubert Murray in Papua, Lord Lugard in Nigeria and Sir Fredrick Gordon Guggisberg on the Gold Coast. In Africa the first person appointed as a designated government anthropologist was Northcote Thomas, in Nigeria in 1906. An undiplomatic individual, he disconcerted some of his superiors, who had him transferred to Sierra Leone in 1913, only to send him home two years later (Kuklick 1991:

199–201). After the war, the colonial administrations of the Gold Coast and Nigeria did employ some official government anthropologists, and also relieved some officials of usual duties for the sake of pursuing anthropological research. The Sudan government contracted first Charles Seligman then Edward Evans-Pritchard to carry out directed research on areas its administrators wanted studied. Further afield, in Melanesia, Murray took on a pair of anthropologists, sending one to the north of Papua, the other to its south. The return of world war in 1939 ended this activity. After the war it was only repractised very fitfully. Perhaps the last official appointee was Ioan Lewis who, in 1955, was given the title 'The Anthropologist', with his own one-man department, in British Somaliland. In reality, his august-sounding post was more a bureaucratic fiction for administrative convenience than a burdensome position with colonialist purpose (Lewis 1977: 229; 2003: 307).

The most noteworthy among this small number of interwar government anthropologists were R.S. Rattray, who studied the Ashante of the Gold Coast; C.K. Meek, who did fieldwork in both northern and southeast Nigeria; and F.E. Williams, who toured southern Papua. Although all three produced highly respected ethnographies, published by the most prestigious academic presses of their time, they are today virtually unknown except by regional specialists. Rattray has been classed as 'essentially a folklorist ethnographer', Meek's work became 'fashionable to denigrate' as but an example of anthropological subservience to colonial administration, while Williams' work, though of 'lasting scientific value', was 'unjustly neglected by his peers' (von Laue 1976: 53; Young 1990; Kirk-Greene 2004). Metropolitan anthropologists were disappointed that Rattray, once back home, did not produce 'something more theoretical', while much of Meek's ethnographies was too evolutionist and diffusionist in tone for the functionalist avant-garde (Machin 1998: 186). Even Williams' theoretical account of magic, which Stocking judges to be more sophisticated than that of his contemporary Bronislaw Malinowski (Stocking 1996: 391), was marginalised by British-based anthropologists then striving to cement their version of anthropology in home universities.

Both Rattray and Meek went on to teach anthropology at Oxford, Meek holding a university lectureship in the subject in the immediate postwar years. Although Stocking groups the two plus the Oxford-educated Williams as an 'Oxford School of government anthropology' (Stocking 1996: 387), both have been excluded from the oral history of the Institute of Social Anthropology at Oxford. I was a member of the Institute from 1976 to 1989, first as a student, later as a postdoctoral fellow, then as an occasional tutor. In those thirteen years, I listened to seemingly endless anecdotes about Radcliffe-Brown, Evans-Pritchard and other former members, both illustrious and not, of the department. But neither Meek nor Rattray was mentioned. Not once. When I asked Shirley Ardener, who came to Oxford in the late 1950s with her husband Edwin, what her recollection was, she agreed that Rattray and Meek were never mentioned in the Institute, even in those days (S. Ardener, pers. comm., May 2015). A younger colleague, associated with the department since 2004, reported to me that he had experienced exactly the same (P. Alexander, pers. comm., 5 January 2016).

If we take a broader view of the discipline, where a metropolitan academic's version of theoretical advance does not hold exclusive sway, the anthropological achievement of these government employees becomes starkly evident. Later anthropologists of Ashante extraction recognise Rattray's 'important contribution to knowledge' (Goody 1995: 205). His analysis of the disturbances caused by removal of the Golden Stool (the symbolically central Ashante throne of power) was repeatedly upheld as an exemplar of practical anthropology, while his plan for the realisation of indirect rule was ultimately implemented (Kuklick 1991: 228; Stocking 1996: 389). Meek 'represented for countless field administrators in inter-war Nigeria the *beau idéal* government anthropologist' (Kirk-Greene 2004). Williams made 'innumerable' informed recommendations to Murray: 'His greatest coup, perhaps, was to prevent the suppression of the "bull-roarer cult" in the Gulf of Papua' (Young 1990). Young's assessment of Williams' more specifically anthropological contribution is acute:

> While accepting in part the reigning doctrine of British functionalism, he had the practical experience to judge its limitations. For him, a culture was not an 'integrated system', but 'always ... to some extent a hotchpotch and a sorry tangle'. In his isolation from the academy Williams developed his own approach and addressed those issues he saw to be salient in the cultures he studied, rather than those which his academic colleagues deemed to be important. The result was a body of published work unusual in its ethnographic range, integrity and pragmatic focus. (Young 1990)

At Cambridge, anthropologist-mandarins scaled even greater heights than their counterparts in Oxford, yet today are still denigrated by historians of our subject. The first two incumbents of the Chair of Anthropology were both former members of the Indian Civil Service: T.C. Hodson, and J.H. Hutton. Both were accomplished ethnographers; as professors, they developed anthropology as a central subject in the curriculum for colonial cadets. Yet Stocking, because focused on anthropological theory and its contexts, sees their combined tenure at Cambridge as a time of stagnation, 'a long period of decline' (Stocking 1996: 430).

To give a specific areal example of the long-lasting effects of anthropology done by and for governments, on both colonial rule and subsequent anthropology, I here discuss a case from the South Pacific. In 1978, when I went to do doctoral fieldwork in the Anglo-French Condominium of the New Hebrides (now the independent republic of Vanuatu), I was surprised and pleased to see how many colonial officers in both the British and French administrations had read and discussed the ethnographies of the French government anthropologist Jean Guiart and of Michael Allen, whose 1950s fieldwork was partly funded and directed by the British Resident Commissioner of the archipelago. Also, while doing archival research in the 2000s, I found numerous references to their work in colonial officers' reports and correspondence (MacClancy 2007). In these colonial circumstances of genuine Western ignorance about local ways, the revelations provided by these anthropological publications were multiple, profound and of great worth to the colonisers. Furthermore, conversations with colleagues who also worked in the islands made clear to me that both Guiart and Allen had as well helped to set the anthropological agenda for their successors, which of course included me. Thus, in this sense of regionalist ethnography informed by and informing theory, the work of government anthropologists has been central for both administrators and academics.[1]

Overall, what this historical sketch suggests is twofold. First, the use of ethnography and the employment of anthropologists by colonial governments was patchy but productive, to the extent that any colonialist project can be so ranked. Second, within the greater scheme of things colonial, which after all had a long history and a global reach, anthropology played a relatively insignificant role; yet modern day interpretations of colonialism are so generally negative (and with good reason) that even this minor part within the imperialist project is still considered by many to be worth damning. One consequence is that, in Oxford anthropology at least, the contribution of colonial anthropologists has been airbrushed from institutional history; whatever positive impact they may have had is also swept away in the process. This raises a more general point: downplaying, depreciating or simply ignoring this variegated conjuncture only serves to skew contemporary understanding of the history of our discipline; at the same time, it threatens to blinker current conceptions of just how broadly anthropology can be conducted.

Anthropologists in the British Civil Service

So much for our past. What of today?

The workshop 'Anthropology beyond Academia' and subsequent seminar series at Oxford Brookes University, on which much of this book is based, included talks by several civil servants with doctorates in anthropology. Almost all of them, however, were later unable to write up their discussion: they were too busy; there is little kudos within their career path for academic papers; because of security concerns, most are far more restricted in what they can write than in what they can say. So I interviewed them and every other anthropologist I could find who had worked for a central government department and, in one case, for a county council. In all, I spoke with eleven, and failed to interview, despite repeated attempts, another two. I re-interviewed two, and sent all correspondents a draft of this chapter for their comments, to prevent gross misrepresentation. Three replied.

A few words on words, to prevent possible misunderstandings. First, all of the people I interviewed held doctorates in social anthropology bar one, who had a Masters degree. In the following I refer to all my interviewees as 'anthropologist-civil servants'. For the sake of lexical variety, I sometimes refer to them as 'anthropologist-functionaries'. One interviewee, who read a draft of this chapter, thought 'functionary' might be viewed as belittling in some way; that is not my intention at any time. Second, I uphold a plural vision of anthropology, one of anthropologies rather than of a singular version promoted by the hegemons of the moment (MacClancy 2013). A colleague who commented on a draft argued that I was yoking the incomparable: what academic anthropologists do is so different to the practice of anthropologist-civil servants that the latter should not be seen as anthropology. Similarly, Maia Green argues that anthropology is of little use to development projects because their knowledge-making practices are constituted by different agendas. She defines anthropology as the production of ethnography, grounded on the traditions of the lone fieldworker and the status of fieldwork (Green 2012: 44, 54). That portrayal can be easily classified as overly rigid and static. I regard the statements of both my colleague and Green as prescriptive delimitations of our pursuit, positioned declarations by the academically ensconced. On my reading of contemporary anthropology, it is far more productive to explore practice in both domains and see what is and might be common, rather than draw an arbitrary line between the two, for what can easily turn into self-interested ends. I fully accept that some readers may come to the same conclusion as my colleague and Green, and that my own pleas for the recognition of plurality can be seen as self-serving.

The long-maintained tradition within the Civil Service of sharing information only with those holding 'the need to know' means that all those interviewed only agreed to speak with me on grounds of anonymity. The only exceptions were the retired. One key limitation to my research was this total reliance on interviews. Given the nature of their jobs, I could not see any civil servant in situ. We met for coffee or a drink outside their offices; I did not even walk the corridors of power. My interviewees thus tended to speak to me about process, not content. Only civil servants working in international aid or the Ministry of Justice were relatively open about what they did, why, when, to what effect. Those in the Ministry of Defence or the Home Office were particularly tight-lipped (as far as I can judge, those in the latter tend to work on counterterrorism). One year, when I saw in the newspapers that an anthropologist acquaintance who chaired coordinating committees for the Cabinet Office had been awarded a CBE, I emailed my congratulations; I added that I presumed she could not tell me what she had received it for. She has yet to reply.

Malinowski famously defined anthropology as the study of what people say they do, what they do do, and how they justify the gap between the two. Here I cannot uphold this dictum, as I could not witness a single civil servant actually at work, interacting with colleagues. Of Malinowski's threefold division, I could only study the first. I am deeply aware that this lopsided style of research, my near-total reliance on interviews, and the lack of any participant observation by me of this bureaucratic world gravely limits my understanding of what is actually going on. The only area of Civil Service activity for which we have more rounded assessment is international development, thanks to the work done by anthropologists who entered that branch of government and then returned to academia, where they later analysed their experience, as reported below.

To help preserve the anonymity of my interviewees and to avoid any charge of sexist language, I only use female forms of personal pronouns, no matter the gender of the interviewee. The only exceptions occur when I quote from named publications by an anthropologist-civil servant.

In the following sections I first examine why two key ministries began to employ anthropologists (International Development, from the 1970s; Defence, from the 2000s) and what they did there. I then look, in order, at: the polemic raised by the prospect of military anthropology; the pleasures and downsides of my interviewees' jobs; the skills they have used, and those they have had to learn; and finally, their interactions, both positive and negative, with academic anthropologists.

International development

The branch of the British government concerned with international development was the first to start employing anthropologists in post-colonial times. Among government departments, it has also been the greatest employer of anthropologists.

The status and title of this sector within government has varied repeatedly over the last decades. Harold Wilson's Labour government of the late 1960s created the Ministry of Overseas Development (ODM). When the Conservatives came to power in 1970, the Ministry was renamed the Overseas Development Administration (ODA), a relatively self-contained unit within the Foreign and Commonwealth Office (FCO), with its own minister. Labour, back in power four years later, revived its status as an independent ministry. In 1979, with the Conservatives back in the saddle, overseas development was returned to the FCO, again as an identifiable unit and once again renamed the ODA. The Minister for Overseas Development was a minister of state within the FCO and did not hold a seat in the Cabinet. In 1997 the new Labour government reformed the unit into the Department for International Development (DfID), headed by a minister with a seat in the Cabinet. The feisty MP Claire Short was its first minister.

In the mid 1970s the ODA created the generic post of Social Development Advisors (SDAs). At the time, international development was primarily concerned with the formulation and successful execution of projects. The patent failure of several of these made the ODA realise that its expertise in domains such as economics, engineering, forestry, health and agriculture was insufficient. It needed to examine the social dimensions of projects as well. SDAs would study the social impact of projects and consult the people to be affected by them. At first their numbers rose very slowly: one was appointed in 1975, another in the early 1980s (Sean Conlin), a third in 1986. They were seen as 'an anomaly by most people' within the organisation. When one of the three criticised aspects of a project, she was viewed as 'a typical SDA with a negative attitude' (Eyben 2003: 881, n. 3, 882). These anthropologist SDAs had to argue the case, strongly, convincingly, if they wished to participate in the design of a project.

The SDAs were keen to promote a people-first agenda. In the language of one of them, they deployed five 'guerrilla strategies' to achieve that. First, they wanted to increase their number, so they stimulated demand. The 1986 appointee, adjudged an 'especially effective promoter and very good persuader' by one of her anthropologist colleagues (telephone interview, July 2013), proved particularly adept at working the system: 'Creating jobs required some political manoeuvring. I had to get a Head of Country programme to ask the Director of their region for new SDAs' for their programme (telephone interview, July 2013). The new recruit, once in place, would find a kaleidoscopic range of social issues in grave need of attention. They would then call for a second appointee, who in turn would be quickly overwhelmed by the volume of work and so call for a third.

Second, the SDAs appropriated agendas then emerging within the department as falling within their specific domain of expertise, e.g. gender, poverty, social exclusion. In particular, gender analysis became a key staple concern of the SDAs. Third, they promoted distinctive methods, e.g. the participatory and self-reflexive approaches originally championed by the development scholar Robert Chambers. The sum consequence of these strategies was that, when working on a project, the SDAs tended to focus on inequalities and fault lines within a developing nation. In other words, they disaggregated the components of a complex problem, as a way to find effective but nuanced solutions. In contrast, they viewed other professionals in DfID, trained in other disciplines, as lumping information together, instead of teasing it apart. These professionals were seen as aggregators of information, who all too often sought simple solutions to complex problems. According to at least one ex-SDA, economists in particular (most of whom were, moreover, macro-economists) tended to see a targeted country as comprising a homogenous population whose members would all develop equally. The same ex-SDA told me that once when she raised the topic of gender with a senior economist within the department, he replied, 'We're not concerned with inequality'.

Fourth, the SDAs worked to influence outside bodies. Gaining the approval of colleagues in the World Bank enabled the SDAs to challenge the otherwise dominant position of their economist counterparts in their UK department. To do this effectively, the anthropologists found they had also to learn some economics. Fifth, they entered into internal alliances: the SDAs, once armed with a little economics, began to work more closely with economists on the staff. This coming together benefitted both parties, as they shared the aim of taking power from the technical specialists. The trio also worked hard to persuade colleagues with overlapping interests to take on SDAs, for example those concerned with humanitarian issues or working within the UN section of the department.

These various empire-building efforts were so successful that by 1995 there were about seventy to eighty SDAs, though now including some from other disciplines. Their number was sufficiently impressive that when in the early 1990s Raymond Firth met a senior SDA at a meeting of the Association of Social Anthropologists (ASA), he thanked her for employing so many anthropologists. A further sign of the anthropologists' power-winning success came in 1995 with the appointment of one of the original trio as Chief SDA, with her own budget, a place within the senior management and independence from the Chief Economist (Eyben 2003, 2014). Twenty years' labour had finally won the anthropologists their own seat at the department's top table.

Recently retired SDAs, looking back over this period, remember fondly that most of the department's staff regarded themselves as on the left, committed to social reform. Moreover, they were pleased to be in a unit with such a reputation, one so clearly different in ethos from almost all other branches of Whitehall. And, within this already unusual department, anthropologists were regarded as particularly distinctive, at times even suspiciously so. One recalled being broached by a senior economist in the department, who bluntly asked her, 'What is it you do?' (Telephone interview July 2013) A second interviewee said that she and another female SDA were talked about within their department, as 'Those women!' 'What do they really do?'(Interview July 2013) She believed others coming from other disciplines were jealous because they were forced to recognise that the anthropologist SDAs got things done, yet where were their models? The anthropologists in the department were viewed as more politically radical than the economists, and were dubbed socialists or even 'reds under the bed' (interview, July 2013). In one revealing incident in the early 1990s, when the Thatcherite legacy was still very strong, the line manager of the Chief SDA took her aside to warn her that she had been heard talking about 'redistribution' and that she would be in trouble if she continued using that term. Generally, the anthropologists were thought 'oddballs'. These attitudes were not new: decades before, they were expressed about Northcote Thomas. In 1930 a colonial servant described him, in official correspondence, as

> a recognized maniac in many ways. He wore sandals, even in this country (*Nigeria*), lived on vegetables, and was generally a rum person.
>
> (*Residents did not want*) to have an object like that going about ... partly because he was calculated to bring a certain amount of discredit upon the white man's prestige. (Quoted in Lackner 1973: 135, emphasis in original)[2]

In the 1980s, one of the Permanent Secretaries in the department went so far as to dub its anthropologist employees 'the beard and sandals brigade', despite the fact that the majority were women. The spectre of the bearded lady?

SDAs, to be successful, had to transcend these dismissive stereotypes. They needed to be both 'technically very competent' and 'politically astute': to change the world, they had also to change the bureaucracy (Eyben 2003: 887). Conlin, writing in the mid 1980s, emphasised that anthropologists working within or for the ODA often failed to recognise both 'the great deal of institutional commitment' to projects and 'the great deal of emotional investment' in them by other SDAs (Conlin 1985: 82). He was blunt in stating that many anthropologists found it 'difficult to work in a team with other disciplines', while their claims to moral superiority bordered on the egregious:

> Anthropologists often seem to think they are the 'keepers of morality' and assume that no one else working in the field possesses the same fine moral sense. Apart from being very irritating to others, this attitude is often adopted even in the face of moral dilemmas which development poses. (Conlin 1985: 84)

As one of the original trio said to me, many SDAs were very good anthropologists while on field trips but not so perceptive once back in the London office. The ones who succeeded in climbing the hierarchy never forgot that.

Across the Civil Service, the ambience within the section for international development was seen as distinctive. Compared to other ministries, it was thought to do pretty much what it liked, and to be staffed by 'a bunch of lefties', who suffered fewer constraints than their homologues elsewhere in Whitehall. In the first decades of British government involvement in this sector, most of the staff, and not just the anthropologists, had already spent many years living and working in developing countries before being recruited. Even when there was a deliberate shift to employing younger staff instead of 'old colonials', the newcomers were still sent abroad for their first posting, 'to get mud on their boots'. These strong traditions of relative autonomy, fieldworking and research production meant the department felt like an unusual mix of development agency and Whitehall ministry.

In the early 2000s, the Permanent Secretary of the department thought it 'too much like a university', so set about change. About the same time the Chief SDA took a posting abroad: 'I was sick of management. It was boring. I wasn't doing anything more than just managing people' (telephone interview, July 2013). Her departure from London roughly coincided with the rise in the department of governance professionals, many trained in public administration.

This was part of the shift in DfID from investing in specific projects to creating partnerships with national governments. The rationale was that rather than attempt to implement particular initiatives to alleviate poverty, it was more productive to engage in restructuring governance: reducing the scope of state services, liberalising markets and increasing recognition for human rights. The priority of this approach, usually dubbed 'the new institutionalism' or 'neoliberal institutionalism', was 'to get the system right'. In this context, the models deployed by governance professionals of how the world works were considered more comprehensive and applicable than those used by anthropologists, sociologists or political scientists. As their leverage grew, the number of SDAs with doctorates in anthropology began to decline.

Today, old hands lament that the Department for International Development has become much more like a conventional branch of government and its anthropologists have to act like mainstream civil servants. These days most aid money is channelled directly to national governments, and the much-reduced number of site-specific local projects initiated by DfID are managed by local technical officers. No more need for muddy boots.

Defence

By the early 2000s sectors within the Ministry of Defence (MoD) had realised that the nature of armed conflict had changed. Modern wars were less and less likely to involve the mass deployment of tanks arrayed across an open battlefield. Instead they required a very different style of military involvement and were increasingly based in countries whose populations held radically distinct values and attitudes to common Western ones. It was a shift from 'Have we more firepower than them?' towards 'How do we influence?' Armed units stationed in contested zones had to learn, at one and the same time, how to withstand the enemy and how to win the support of locals not engaged in the conflict, no matter how difficult the troops might find it to distinguish, within the resident population, between adversary and non-adversary groups.

To assist its troops in developing the requisite skills in these novel theatres of war, the MoD, among other initiatives, began to recruit anthropologists. The first openings for them were in the Centre for Human Sciences within the Defence Evaluation and Research Agency, and slightly later in the Influence and Analysis Team within the Ministry's multidisciplinary research wing, the Defence Science and Technology Laboratory (DSTL), based in Farnborough, Hampshire. Only a small section of DSTL, in reality a large umbrella organisation, is dedicated to research in the social sciences, and within that small section anthropologists were greatly outnumbered by psychologists. Yet the anthropologists were received very positively and given great leeway. In their own words, in the MoD anthropology was 'the new black'; they were viewed as 'oddballs, the new kids on the block'. Their new workmates and superiors, who liked the idea of anthropology though they did not really know what it was, were very willing to listen to the anthropologists' ideas, to test them out and give them space. And this, as one interviewee pointed out, in an organisation which until then only did things like inventing jet engines.

Their job was not only surprisingly open-ended, but excitingly varied as well. If the overall shift, which they had been hired to assist in, was from assembling overwhelming firepower to winning hearts and minds, the central query the anthropologists had to pose repeatedly to their paymasters was, 'What do you want?' In other words, they needed their superiors to specify their overall objectives. Once specified, the anthropologists could begin to elucidate what were the 'bits' that could be used and what were the 'levers' that could be pulled in order to achieve those objectives.

These anthropologists, deeply trained in one discipline, had to learn quickly how to cooperate in interdisciplinary teams, using multi-methods approaches to solve pressing practical problems. They also had to research and produce reports on what they perceived as future problems the MoD would have to face. For instance, one had to carry out a literature review of the definitions of states vis-à-vis 'terrorist groups' and then sum up the results of her copious reading in a five-page report. At the end of every year, each would be asked, 'What are the problems you see on the horizon?', and would be expected to come up with an informative response no longer than one paragraph.

One new recruit found she had to play two roles. The first was very generic: helping the military to understand how people work. In her later article on this 'very successful' project, entitled 'More Tea and Fewer Messages', she states that she showed MoD officials and members of the armed forces how the application of sophisticated social scientific theories could help them in their everyday tasks, whether in Whitehall or Afghanistan. If abroad, the key idea was for them to engage with the local population. The underlying logic was along the lines of, 'If I build you a well, the chances of you giving me information rise'. She emphasised the importance of talking to people, as a way of building and consolidating trust (Tomlinson 2009). She also developed cultural assessment tools, a checklist of questions to help the military understand who they are living among. The questions focused on economics, politics, religion and even kinship, though the word itself was not used.

The new recruit's second role was more ethnographically specific: she had to learn a lot about particular countries, using her social scientific understanding of, for example, Afghanistan or Libya. Another anthropologist, recruited the year before, had developed a series of very brief, introductory notebooks on local cultural ways, such as non-verbal behaviour and gestures, in a further effort to prevent soldiers misunderstanding locals, or being misunderstood by them. I do not know how successfully these booklets were regarded or used by the troops.

One anthropologist-functionary made it clear to me that while some of what they presented to the officers might have seemed obvious, they were presenting it in such a way that their listeners could then talk about it later, to themselves and others. For instance, portraying a person's multiple identities as a diagram of overlapping petals gave the audience an image they could remember and transmit easily. It also helped the officers to realise and visualise their own tendencies to stereotype. In fact, the talk produced by this anthropologist about identity was so well received that she was asked to give it more than twenty-five times, to different groups.

The interdisciplinary group of social scientists within DSTL assembled a college of university academics in related fields curious to learn more of their Ministry-based colleagues' work. At periodic day meetings, members of the DSTL team showcased their aims and multi-methods, and then set their guests exercises to practise and assess the value of their approaches. The next outreach initiative to academia was staged by two anthropologists who had moved from DSTL to the MoD in Whitehall. There they held a pair of workshops for a clutch of invited academic colleagues, and one serving major, to discuss and comment upon their project to develop a statistically grounded cultural modelling programme. Although some of the invitees entertained doubts about the viability of the programme, they did reach consensus about the cultural categories to be employed. The workshops themselves were judged 'a great success' by one of the organisers, as the pair took their results to senior MoD staff, which led to the creation of one hundred new posts and 'people trained up in new ways' (interview, 15 June 2013).

The MoD anthropologists stressed to me their pleasure in coming to realise how bright and how open to discussion even the most senior officers could be. Indeed, the higher the rank, the better-read in anthropology they tended to be, because generals have drivers and can spend car journeys reading ethnographies. And they do.

Military anthropology

British anthropologist-functionaries are well aware of the work done by their colleagues in other governments. In particular, these UK anthropologists' engagement with the military was, in at least one key area, much influenced by the unfortunately good example of their US counterparts, whose approach provoked a sustained polemic, both in American anthropology and national media.

In the early 2000s the US Department of Defense began to create Human Terrain Teams (HTTs). The aim was to train mixed groups of anthropologists, other social scientists and area specialists in ways of gathering culturally sensitive information. They would then be embedded within military units on active service in zones of conflict, above all Iraq and Afghanistan. Although the HTT programme was closed down in 2015, its central ideas were morphed, rebranded and privatised that year. The use of anthropological practice and knowledge by the American military continues (González and Price 2015).[3]

Many US anthropologists and other academics soon spoke out against this new government initiative (e.g. González 2009, 2010; Lucas 2009; Network of Concerned Anthropologists [NCA] 2009; Price 2011), forcing the American Anthropological Association (AAA) into a lengthy debate about the ethics of the teams. Several HTT anthropologists were aware that some of their critics' arguments were well grounded. Although an HTT member might call herself a 'high-risk ethnographer' or be dubbed 'a uniformed anthropologist toting a gun', several admitted that the vaunted separation of assembling cultural information from gathering intelligence was extremely difficult to maintain: they could not know all the ends to which their information would be put (Gezari 2013: 45, 46, 94, 189). Moreover, in the eyes of its critics, this exploitation of anthropology for military ends besmirched the reputation of the discipline and threatened the physical security of fieldworkers. In 2007, after much deliberation, the Executive Board of the AAA publicly stated its disapproval of the programme (AAA 2007). At the same time, a select commission of the AAA recognised that the HTTs were but one part of the multiple modes of anthropologists' engagement with the military (see Fosher 2013; Fujimura 2013; Holmes-Eber 2013; Rubenstein 2013; Turnley 2013; Varhola 2013), and that even the most vocal of HTT critics were not categorically opposed to working with the military (Commission on the Engagement of Anthropology with the US Security and Intelligence Communities [CEAUSSIC] 2009). In the words of Sally Engle Merry, critical anthropologist of human rights:

> I'm not a fan of war, and I don't think war as a way to produce peace makes much sense. But I also think the military is in a very difficult box, and people are trying to do the right thing. I just wish we could find a way to use the knowledge anthropology can produce to bring these wars to an end. (Quoted in Gezari 2013: 126)

Anthropologists in the MoD were well aware of this debate, at the very least because they periodically conferred with their US counterparts, such as Montgomery McFate, who oversaw management of the HTTs. These civil servants recognised that some HTTs had done very good work, producing very detailed reports. In fact, they considered some of the work too detailed. However, to avoid reigniting the heated controversy generated in the AAA and mainstream American media, the anthropologist-functionaries decided to imitate a different US military mode of deploying the discipline. Instead of preparing anthropologists to work alongside troops on active duty, they suggested training officers in anthropology. In 2009, partly at the anthropologists' prompting, the MoD decided to set up a Defence Cultural Specialist Unit (DCSU), where selected officers could learn how to collect material in an anthropologically informed manner. The plan was that all its recruits would undergo a ten-week course in social sciences and 'influencing skills', as well as training in an Afghan language, before being deployed in Helmand, the southerly province of Afghanistan where the British Army operated. A NATO press release on the course specifies their role there:

> The specialists will help build a picture of Helmandi society for commanders in Task Force Helmand and battlegroups across the province to help them identify and understand issues relating to the local cultural, political, economic, social and historical environment to help commanders make better and more informed decisions. …
>
> The specialists will build on their existing language skills and cultural understanding by gathering local knowledge and fostering contacts at bazaars, *shuras* [consultative assemblies] and other places where local people gather.[4]

The intention was that the DCSU would have forty-two members, from any of the services, eight of them stationed in Afghanistan at any one time. Besides sending specialists into conflict zones, the Unit would also support cultural training in the wider military and other government departments. Its inaugural, truncated training course was attended not just by UK officers, but also by civil servants from the MoD, FCO, DfID and the Civil Service Stabilisation Unit.

Almost inevitably, one captain in the DCSU, who chose to live for a year with a unit of the Afghan Local Police, was compared with the legendary World War One ethnographer-spy, Lawrence of Arabia. As he himself put it:

> My job was to go into areas where we didn't have a lot of knowledge, to speak to the villagers and to train the local police officers.
> In these areas allegiances could change in a moment, everyone knew someone in the Taliban. I would lead these Afghan elements in engagements against the insurgents.
> Sharing a bed with Afghans wasn't the done thing, nobody else was doing that. I suppose I went a bit bush, especially with the really horrible beard.[5]

It is thought that several of those who complete this course and put it into military practice will themselves become academics on leaving the armed services. Despite repeated attempts, I have been unable to obtain any further information about the course they undergo.[6]

As the broader work of the DCSU suggests, it can be very difficult these days to isolate the work of the military from that of other divisions of government. For critics today, exclusive focus on the armed forces is hard to achieve. The expansion of 'joined-up thinking' and the establishment of a broad-based 'security agenda' has led to delegated members of the Ministry of Defence, the Foreign Office and DfID working together on the same committees, in Whitehall or the field, for the same ultimate ends. The only complaint from those in DfID about these meetings is that they tend to be regarded as the poor relation at the table. As one wag put it, 'Crumbs for bums?' (Interview July 2013)

For some, however, all is not rosy in this new, more 'humanised' vision within the British armed forces. A pair of feminist critics, for instance, have argued that although the avowed intention is to understand others and so enable transitions towards stability and security, they contend that their scrutiny of an MoD release reveals that it continues to uphold an instrumentalist approach to culture, which it regards as immutable and thus akin to 'race' (Duncanson and Cornish 2012: 163–65). At the very least, their work suggests that the DCSU has much work to do if it is to spread a modern anthropological approach through the MoD.

The skills they brought to the job, the ones they learnt on the job

Anthropology students are taught a range of skills. Those who go on to do fieldwork and write a thesis learn an even broader set. Of course, which skills turn out to be important for anthropologist-civil servants depends on the jobs they have to do. The range of those jobs can be remarkably diverse.

The skills my interviewees already had which proved of use in the Civil Service were: the ability to use a very wide, very varied evidence base ('very, very useful, that', said one); their interviewing skills; and their capacity to read and understand new material at reasonable speed (one admitted she could do that much faster than expected, so kept quiet about her ability). Studying anthropology had taught them to understand other cultures in 'an informed subtle way', while doctoral fieldwork had trained them to observe and record things very closely, and how to collate the amassed data into meaningful patterns. They had also learnt the importance of taking into account 'agents' visions of us and how that influenced their own actions'. Several emphasised anthropology's holistic approach, as opposed to the seemingly more narrow-visioned styles of those who came from other disciplines, where they had been trained to look solely at one aspect of a problem. One identified a tendency within the MoD and the Home Office to focus on individuals, such as important political figures; anthropologists, she said, could counter this, 'especially if it is exaggerated' (interview July 2013).

For some interviewees, cooperating on common tasks with graduates of other disciplines made them far more aware of just how distinctive their own skill-set was. One former member of the MoD said she had not realised what anthropology had given her until she had to work with other professionals, such as economists and political scientists. Work-based chats with them made her appreciate that she thought of groups in ways different to them.

The skills they had to learn make up a long list. I noticed the more successful tended to provide a more fulsome inventory. Most of the items they gave tend to fit under the twin rubrics of how to manage people and how to influence them. One said she learnt to be always cheerful and positive: 'Don't say "No"'. Unlike their American counterparts (Nolan 2013), most of those I interviewed said they did not 'network'. To them, that sounded too instrumental. Instead they emphasised the importance of getting to know the people they worked with, of respecting them, and in turn being respected. To gain and then hold colleagues' attention and respect, these fledgling civil servants had to learn, and learn quickly, how to be highly professional: in these contexts that meant being clear, down to earth, responsive, rigorous and able to deliver on time what was needed. They needed to learn to recognise what mattered, and what did not. In the words of one former functionary, one had 'to engage with the customer' (interview July 2013), clarifying what they needed before trying to deliver it.

As veterans of fieldwork, my interviewees knew the importance of learning the local language, building up good relations with 'stakeholders' on a common project, assessing where they fitted into the hierarchy, identifying when to interject and when to hold back: 'You pick your battlegrounds' (interview July 2013). Experienced ethnographers, they were well aware that they had to learn the model and the reality of the organisation now employing them. If they wanted to get anything done, interviewees had to know whom they could talk to, at what level. To get a decision made and then see it implemented, they had to 'sell' the idea, to the right people, by making them see its benefit. In the words of one, who had worked in the MoD, 'I was cutting things down to their essence for the colonel, at the same time taking into account "What kind of person is the colonel?"' (Interview July 2013) Another, in DfID, revealed that she influenced decisions by making friends with others at the same level as her in neighbouring sections of the Ministry, and then persuading them to push for the same change at much the same time. It usually worked, she said.

In the MoD, the anthropologist-functionaries also had to become confident in themselves, to be ready to challenge people. They were helped in this by the self-image of the Ministry as a 'learning organisation'. One interviewee in the MoD said they could tell even generals and other very high-ranking officers to their face that they were wrong, and if the anthropologists learnt how to do that without insulting them in the process, these senior military men would accept their correction. The top brass knew it was important for them to meet with academics, to develop and rethink their strategies. And sometimes they were prepared to pay the price of those encounters.

The anthropologists also had to learn how to work productively with others in teams. They emphasised how multidisciplinary these groups can be: economists, operational researchers (who model large systems), statisticians, social researchers, political scientists. As they have begun to ascend the Whitehall hierarchy, my interviewees have also had to learn how to delegate: they were no longer researchers but managers of research projects. One point all interviewees stated was that they had had to develop quantitative skills: 'Doing a PhD in social anthropology did not teach me about reliability, validity, or the need to number questionnaires'.[7]

The skills they learnt to cast aside included reading from the text when making a presentation and giving hour-long seminar papers: twenty-five minutes was the absolute maximum. They also had to avoid at all costs 'waffle' and esoteric prose. As one said, 'I now write in a pithy style, so that ministers can absorb information rapidly and make decisions: a two-page document; nothing more' (interview July 2013). It is notorious how far hidebound academics can stray in the opposite direction. Audrey Richards was famously told by a colonial official, 'Just half a sheet – just the salient facts' (Richards 1977: 178). To her, his remark exemplified the impatience of administrators. Today anthropologist-functionaries would regard it as yet another indicator of many academics' inability to be exact but still terse.

To learn how these skills might be employed in a concrete fashion, I asked one interviewee how policy is crafted. She replied that it was a very difficult question to answer as the process could be so complex, but she gave as a simplifying example the goal of the present government to reduce the number of immigrants. First, relevant ministries would be asked to review the existing legal parameters and how they might be changed. In this case, the ministries involved would be the Home Office, which oversees the police force, the FCO, which grants visas, and those concerned with the management of social services. Each would have to investigate the consequences for their department of any development of policy, by commissioning some of their civil servants to begin the process of finding out and evaluating the options. As this initiative moved closer to the formulation of a bill, a bill team would be formed, its membership drawn from the ministries most involved. Its task would be to shepherd the proposal through Parliament. The team leader would be charged to tour the ministries concerned, to discuss and solicit input for the legislation. The team would then assess the collated inputs, and produce a draft bill, to be discussed with and approved by their political superior. When the selected minister has to present the finished bill to the House of Commons, a senior member of the team stands in a nearby passageway. She makes notes on questions put by MPs and then has her commentary passed to the minister, so that he or she can respond in an apparently informed manner.

In an age of IT, this latter procedure sounds almost Victorian, on a par with the maintained tradition of printing Acts of Parliament on goatskin vellum.

Fun, fun, fun?

Upsides

So far the only other ministries to take on anthropologists are the Foreign Office, the Home Office, the Ministry of Justice and the Cabinet Office. In all four and in the MoD, outside of DSTL, my interviewees first worked primarily as researchers, carrying out research projects. If they proved good at that task, within a few years they could then progress to managing research projects. At this more senior level, they have to think up viable projects, bid for their funding within an internal competition and, if successful, usually oversee and coordinate the project through to its final report. For example, one anthropologist at the Ministry of Justice said she at first researched drug markets, assessing the effectiveness of police strategies to control the trade. She then started to design research projects and to commission others to carry out the projects, some of which could be quite large, for instance qualitative work on the criminal behaviour of drug traffickers, evaluating middle markets, and assessing police evaluation.[8]

Interviewees said they did not usually devote all their time to research or managing research projects. There were also rote tasks to perform, still intellectually challenging but with less range for their imagination and shorter-term targets. One said a very high proportion of their work was 'keeping the wheels of government turning': helping to formulate parliamentary questions, which have to be adjudged truthful and accurate, as well as commissioning research, assessing the reliability of relevant, already existing information, and providing ad hoc, urgent information to ministers. A second interviewee said that working out the most appropriate discourse for their superiors to use was another common task: 'I help politicians to find the right language in which to express issues to the people' (interview July 2013).

For the sake of their careers, it is important for these anthropologist-civil servants to gain broad experience. However, switching between ministries is much easier, I was told, than being promoted from research to project management. One interviewee stressed to me that it was important to control the alluring charms of research. If one wanted to move up, one had to move on. DfID is the exception: perhaps because of the commitment they show and satisfactions they gain while working in international development, no anthropologist, to my knowledge, who has entered that department has then left it for another ministry. Candidates for promotion are assessed via an evidence-based process: 'It's not enough to be shiny. One has to deliver high-quality products, to time, in accordance with the Civil Service Values' (interview July 2013). Ascent can be relatively rapid. One interviewee, who served in the MoD for four years, had, by the time she left, achieved an administrative grade that equated to the military rank of lieutenant-colonel.

Every civil servant I spoke to stressed the pleasures and satisfactions of their work. Some were energetically emphatic on this point. Only one looked back on her doctoral days with patent nostalgia: 'My PhD was fun. I miss that fun!' (Interview July 2013) Several interviewees underscored their keenness, on completing their doctorates, to apply their anthropological knowledge to public end; they did not wish to remain in academia all their working lives. Most had decided relatively early to get out of university and put their training to extramural use. One confessed how disappointed she had been, when a research student, that she had had to debate with her Oxford tutor why anthropology needed a point. To my interviewee the question was real; to the academic it was merely academic. As another interviewee put it, 'I am not here to indulge myself to write papers. I am here to help the people' (interview July 2013).

Some interviewees saw working for the Civil Service as a real opportunity to effect change, not just campaign for it. One, who worked for the MoD, said she 'saw the value of stimulating change from the inside' (interview July 2013). For instance, the first unit she worked in, DSTL, drew on social scientific understanding in order to develop influence and to advance the use of 'non-kinetic techniques', i.e. talking to people, not killing them.

Without exception, all of those who had worked in international development were particularly eloquent. 'I loved feeling I was making a difference, influencing processes and policy.' One former SDA said she was 'just curious about people. I liked a challenge, getting people to do what they hadn't considered or were not sure they wanted to do'. 'There are a lot of committed people in DfID. It has a very strong ethos. There is a great buzz.' (Interviews July 2013) A recent retiree from DfID stated:

> I am now writing a report on how to spend £80,000,000 on urban poverty in X [one of the poorest countries on earth]. Because of my experience, I have inordinate, unjustified leverage on projects. I know how to get money out of departments. I am continually surprised how easy it is to prise money out of people. (Interview, 27 June 2014)

Some spoke of the excitement at being so close to power, the seductiveness of being party, in however marginal a manner, to the making of grand decisions that might affect millions. One SDA mentioned the 'frisson' of being asked by a minister to speak with him or her about something. When Claire Short was Secretary of State for International Development, she held regular roundtable meetings where 'people would get angry or pleased with what you'd done. You felt very included, part of the decision-making process. It created quite a buzz' (interview July 2013).

Several said they liked the interdisciplinary dimension to their work; they found it exciting, having to work with psychologists, sociologists, political scientists and others. One called it 'fascinating'; she 'learnt loads'. She had worked for NGOs previously and had been somewhat frustrated with the range of her research work. To her surprise, the MoD, where she worked, stressed the need for continual learning: a refreshingly 'huge percentage of time was spent on training' (interview July 2013).

There can be important differences in ministry workstyles. I have already mentioned the distinctiveness of DfID. The FCO, as one of its members pointed out to me, is still regarded as the senior branch of the Civil Service. The Foreign Secretary is able to bring greater political pressure to bear than other ministers. He or she is granted greater freedom of comment, and that relative degree of liberty percolates down to his mandarins. Also, civil servants in the Home Office have to monitor the dissemination of extremist views solely within the UK, whether those views are imported or internally generated. In contrast, my interviewee added with a smile, those in the FCO working on similar themes get to make trips abroad.

Downsides

My interviewees, some of whom I have known for years, listed surprisingly few downsides to their jobs. One former SDA said the politics of the government of the day was a major constraint, which could prove frustrating. Come a post-electoral change of governing party, civil servants had to learn the development programme and set of priorities of their new ministers, what new tasks they would have to perform, and what initiatives they would have to drop, no matter how much work they might have done on them. Another interviewee frankly admitted that the work could at times be dull; she found the levels, spread and weight of bureaucracy dispiriting and frustrating. A third complained of how tightly her time was organised. While in DSTL, she had to account for every fifteen-minute slot of her workday.

A social scientist friend, who in the 1980s had done a series of consultancies for the Home Office, told me that, in her experience, if the released results of her commissioned work clashed with the stance of the government, her findings would be publicly dismissed, on television or the radio, by the relevant minister. In contrast, all my interviewees said that no work they had ever done was suppressed. One did confess that sometimes '[a] point of view didn't chime ... It can be disappointing if you see the rational and right path to take, and it's not taken' (interview July 2013). Another, who has since left the Civil Service, said her suggestions had never been ignored while she worked for a ministry. The only time any of her ideas had been disregarded was when she worked for an NGO.

Perhaps the apparent lack of suppression is because the more adept civil servants learn to censor themselves, before others get them to do it. One ex-member of DfID confessed that there was a continual tension in the Department for people like herself, between an anthropological point of view with its concerns about nuance and complexity, and the formulation of public policy, which requires quick and simple answers: 'But that's what politicians want. So we spent a lot of time suppressing our concerns. There's no space for doubt in public policy' (interview July 2013). This self-suppression can be particularly difficult for practitioners of a discipline like anthropology, which prides itself on reflexivity and ethnographic subtlety.

Only one of those I interviewed said that she had ever been asked to do something she considered unethical, and that was only once or twice, in the MoD. On both occasions, she said, she rethought the request in a way that made it ethical, to her satisfaction. The officers were pleased with her re-presentation of their task. As she put it, she had given the customer what they needed rather than what they wanted. Another interviewee, an ex-member of DSTL, stated that during her time with the unit she never felt the information she produced was used in ways she was not informed about. Indeed, one former anthropologist-functionary said the only time she had received demands to twist a report, they did not come from within the Civil Service but from representatives of a professional body being assessed by a regional government. When their initial pleas for a change in her assessment of them failed, they shouted directly to her face. She told me she refused to budge. I learnt of only one anthropologist-civil servant who resigned for ethical reasons. She left DfID on a matter of principle: she would not be party to a departmental decision to supply the Nepalese police with helicopters. She thought, very probably with good reason, that they would not just be used for emergency evacuations of the injured and endangered, but for hunting down the then-active Maoist insurgents as well.

Some of my interviewees considered there was no significant difference in the main ethical problems they faced, compared to those encountered by academic anthropologists and fieldworkers. The key questions were the same: who are you representing? What is the end result of one's information? One interviewee stressed that, contrary to the image held by critical outsiders, anthropologist-civil servants were in fact better protected ethically than academic anthropologists in their own sphere. On joining Whitehall, a recruit has to enter a contractual agreement to abide by the statutory Civil Service Code. As she said, 'This has legal bite. And I've seen stronger use of it in government than of the ASA guidelines in anthropology'.[9] (Interview July 2014) The Code is explicit about the duty of civil servants to raise any concerns they may have. It is equally clear about the consequences: 'If the matter cannot be resolved using the procedures set out above, and you feel you cannot carry out the instructions you have been given, you will have to resign from the Civil Service'. This may be seen as a strength or integral weakness of the Code. Compare the epilogue to the ASA guidelines: 'This statement of ideals does not impose a rigid set of rules backed by institutional sanctions, given the variations in both individuals' moral precepts and the conditions under which they work'.[10]

Recently, some anthropologist-civil servants from across government have gone further, and formed an informal group to discuss ethical issues and provide a structure to support colleagues who may feel they are being put under unduly difficult conditions. When I asked what clout this body, independent of ministerial structures, might have, one interviewee replied that if any collectively agreed statement by its members were disregarded, that 'would be at a cost' (interview July 2014). The group, in other words, acts as an informal lobby within governmental structures. I have been unable to learn more about the functioning of this group.

Depending on one's point of view, distance from academe might be included here as a further downside of becoming a civil servant. One former SDA said that when she gave seminars in departments of anthropology, audiences were on the whole excited by her work. But generally she learnt to steer clear of academics, as she found it too complicated to explain the various constraints she had to work around. She therefore came to find that most academic critiques of topics relevant to the department seemed very distant. She said there was an inside circle of academics, former colleagues in the Ministry, who understood their work and who collaborated productively with them. Those on the outside circle did not understand the way the Ministry functioned, and had different agendas and criteria. They were not given work.

The government's desire for secrecy, perhaps overdeveloped in the British case, was given as another change one had to get used to. This was especially felt by former academics used to living their subject all day. To one ex-MoD interviewee, one downside of her job was not being able to talk about it to outsiders, no matter how close they were. She added that she was a pacifist, who did not believe that killing people was the best way to resolve conflicts. But that was an opinion she had kept to herself, not shared with either friends or work colleagues. Another said it took several years to get used to the idea that one's labours ended at the end of the workday. Because her tasks were classified, she could take no documents whatsoever out of the Ministry building. While an academic, she had been used to working as late as she wanted, wherever she wanted. By the time of our interview, she no longer regarded this imposed limitation as restricting, but rather liberating.

Of course, committed civil servants can reinterpret apparent downsides in a positive manner, because they stress dedication to the ultimate aims of their work. Some interviewees, brought up in the questionable traditions of the 'solitary fieldworker' and of academics as 'lone stars', found the transition to teamwork particularly hard. One said she had to learn 'to let go' (interview July 2013): ideas and the resulting products did not belong to oneself, but to the team one was on. 'There's no copyright on your work', said another (interview July 2013). Some found this change in style liberating:

> Three months in, I realised my ego didn't matter. Such a different world to academia: there's no back-stabbing.
>
> When I was a postdoc at [a major London department], I was shocked, really shocked at how anthropologists behave towards one another.
>
> Here we give ideas freely. Careers are not dependent on those ideas. You are part of a team. We are very corporate here. (Interview July 2013)

One interviewee said that teamwork on a proposal was a collective endeavour in 'what'll wash', i.e. an exercise in language. The general attitude was that if their proposal was not accepted the first time, they would rephrase it in a different language the next time. As good anthropologists, they also learnt to comprehend the underlying logic of the armed forces. One recounted that in DSTL and the MoD, she and fellow anthropologists were constantly striving to unpick military assumptions. They learnt that some could be unpicked, but some not, or else they had to be approached in a different way 'because of political realities' (interview July 2013). None of my interviewees saw either strategy

– washing or unpicking – as a downside to their job. On the contrary, they saw them as enjoyable challenges. Ultimately, several confessed that what maintained their interest and their belief in their position was the ability to ask, at any point, 'What are we doing with the information we've gathered?' and being able to come up with an answer that satisfied them. They were using their skills 'to try to improve the situation' (interview July 2013).

A few interviewees complained about the sustained level of pressure in their workplace, and its potentially damaging consequences. One, a rising civil servant in the mid levels of the FCO, exemplified the point by detailing what she called 'a typical day' (interview July 2014):

> 8AM: hour-long meeting with a deputy director of an overall mission, who reported to the Director-General of the FCO (equivalent in rank to a Private Under-Secretary). They discuss how best to staff the mission. They need to get the right mix of skills at different levels and stay within budget.
>
> 9AM: a Training Department meeting with the lead person for one of the Ministry's diplomatic training courses. They discuss whether everything is properly organised and set up: e.g. actors would be used for role-playing exercises; were enough, and enough of the right kinds, booked? They also have to scrutinise whether the most appropriate exercises are being allotted to the different trainees. The two have to check that the course will test and develop the required skills: will it be a productive use of everyone's time?
>
> 9.40AM: she gives a ninety-minute class teaching 'Cultural Difference' to a dozen members of the FCO. She sketches the way the study of culture has been broached by anthropologists, sociologists and business analysts, who have researched multinationals as well as different organisations around the world. She shows how one can shift from theory to quotidian manifestation, e.g. in face-to-face meetings and unexpected events. The class overruns by ten minutes.
>
> 11.20AM: fifteen-minute tea break.
>
> 11.35AM: a forty-five-minute meeting with a new recruit whom she is mentoring and coaching. Concerns include: how is he finding his new job? What challenges is he finding? A military officer in his mid 30s, he is used to working within very clear parameters. My interviewee tries to get him used to taking independent initiatives; she suggests techniques he can use.
>
> 12.10PM: Lunch, with a small team she is working with on the second iteration of a new training course. They hammer out its future, discuss how it could be improved, and take note of feedback: 'Not too much theory please!'
>
> c. 1PM: back at her desk for an hour, she goes over the results of a cross-department plan. Over the previous eight months she had put to-

gether what a certain discipline could contribute to our understanding of a recognised danger to British society. Her sub-task for this plan is to facilitate a network of forty academics who were consulted on the question. (My interviewee stresses that an important side-dimension of her work is to facilitate the contribution of academics.)

2PM: she takes the report about the plan to a meeting with several Director-Generals and Directors who have already read it. They opine that the report is very interesting but too long: two pages would have been better. They ask how its implementation might impact on the FCO. What does it mean for posts and people? In the process, an initial discussion about the direction and future tasks for the FCO is turned into a question about the allocation of resources. The meeting has to end at 3PM, but at least another hour of work on it is needed. She will have to 'squeeze it out' of her schedule.

3PM: tea, with a junior colleague who wishes to talk about the use of social media by Daesh. She identifies the relevant experts and suggests he speak with them.

3.30PM: forty-minute discussion with a senior colleague about the development of policy towards an unstable African country.

4.10PM: discussion with some colleagues about three projects in which she is involved. All three have online data dimensions, and are concerned with ways for the FCO to make better use of its online presence. For example, one new programme has gone through its preliminary stages of development; they now need to probe its level of trustworthiness. The questions they ask include: are we holding it up to the right level of scrutiny? Can we make it more available? Will it be seen as UK government propaganda? They wish to reassure themselves that at the upper level there is due diligence, and at the lower level sufficient resources to run the programme successfully.

Later this week she will join a further meeting, with all those involved in this particular project: its manager; representatives of the various departments that contributed to its funding; academic liaison; two or three pilot users. The key question here will be whether the project is worth spending more money on, or whether the time has come to staunch the cash flow. As she put it, 'Is it time to cut, and cry "No more"'?

5.10PM: back to her desk for sixty to eighty minutes, to go through her emails. Only fifteen today; this is less than usual. But her online calendar, to which others have access, is full for the next three weeks. So colleagues tend to leave her alone, for the time being.

One email is a conversational thread, started by a colleague who describes a recent event and worries whether they reacted appropriately. My interviewee tries to reassure him: 'Don't worry. You did the right thing'.

Another email is a request for information: the department is gathering evidence about what they have done in countries X, Y and Z over the last eighteen months. They wish to know where departmental efforts have had the greatest impact or success. My interviewee parks this item;

maybe she will attend to it later. She quietly ponders why colleagues are asking others to do their work for them.

6.30PM: her average leaving time. Other days she might leave at 5PM, 7PM or at the worst 7.30PM.

Phew! As she said to me, 'Days are frantic at the moment'. She added that her daily schedule was more complex now compared to her time in DSTL. However, she noted that this was a common consequence of promotion, especially in the contemporary context of a government with fewer resources 'and more arses on it'. She said she had never seen colleagues taking long lunches; rather, they always felt under pressure. Expectations were rising, and levels of stress with them. Recently, for the first time in the fifteen or so years she had been in the Civil Service, she had started to notice that colleagues were having to take time off on medical grounds. Today's Whitehall is not for slouches.

Professional identity

All those I interviewed had been civil servants for several years at least, some for decades. A number were surprised at my question about whether they still thought of themselves as anthropologists. It was not something they usually considered. Perhaps my question was wrong-footed; I should not have used so concrete a term as 'identity'. Maybe they did not wish to appear rude to an anthropologist who had chosen to remain in a university.

As one interviewee pointed out, new entrants to the Civil Service come as either generalists or specialists. But if even an anthropologist with a doctorate enters as a specialist, she can still end up with a series of different identities, which matter in different ways. One retiree, who had spent much of her life in DfID, said she had blown hot and cold about being seen as an anthropologist, as being a development professional was a different, equally professional identity. An interviewee who had been a civil servant for over a decade classed herself as both an anthropologist and as a government researcher, but the latter was clearly more important in her day-to-day work. Another, who worked in international aid for twenty years, said whether one was an anthropologist or not, one still became a DfID bureaucrat with a particular Department-framed view of how the world, above all the aid world, worked. One interviewee looked uncomfortable at first, then replied that it had been important early on to be an anthropologist but her skill base had widened greatly since then: 'It can become a hindrance to be a specialist' (interview July 2013). If she were to come back to academia for a sabbatical, it would not be as an anthropologist, but an anthropologist-civil servant. Only one was emphatic about shedding that period of her past. She, who had worked first in international NGOs, then in the MoD, and now held a senior position in a charity with global scope, said that her professional identity as an anthropologist was by this stage completely irrelevant.

Others were much more positive about their anthropological background. One recent retiree from DfID said her identity as an SDA was central for her, and that was linked to her social anthropological training. Being an anthropologist was, she stated, 'important': 'Something about anthropology which gets into your blood. It sort of informs however you see things' (interview July 2013).

It was notable that this interviewee, who had a Masters but not a doctorate in anthropology, was very vague about what exactly she meant. Here, anthropology appeared to be more a personal banner than a specifiable intellectual practice. Another interviewee, who had started as a specialist but now regarded herself as a generalist, was emphatic: 'I'll always be an anthropologist' (interview July 2013). Although she had been in the Civil Service for more than a decade and a half, she stressed how important it was to her that she was still publishing and editing anthropology. Indeed, she was now more heavily involved in a particular international anthropological organisation than she had been when a postdoc.

Reactions from/to academic anthropologists

The very idea of working for the Civil Service can excite strong reactions, in favour or against, across a broad swathe of British academic anthropology. A lively section within the discipline is firmly opposed to any anthropological involvement whatsoever with the government, and especially with the military or associated bodies. They phrase their rejection primarily in ethical terms. These attitudes were starkly expressed in a mid 2000s debate.

In 2006 the FCO and the Economic and Social Research Council (ESRC) launched, in an exclusivist manner, an ill-considered joint research programme on 'Combating Terrorism by Countering Radicalisation'. The ESRC, it was said, was very keen for this initiative to prosper: it hoped it would be the first of many, linking its organisation and various ministries, and thus the sharing of budget provision. After much criticism, especially from anthropologists, a revised brief for the programme was issued. However, the ASA resolved that the initiative, whose results would inform UK counterterrorism policy overseas, was 'prejudicial to the position of all researchers working abroad, including those who have nothing to do with this Programme' (Minutes, ASA AGM, 12 April 2007). There was a real fear that the scheme could endanger anthropologists in the field. The Royal Anthropological Institute (RAI), after a particularly charged debate on the issue, finally decided to support and endorse the ASA resolution (Minutes, Council, RAI, 25 April 2007). In a comment on this debate (which I attended), the editor of *Anthropology Today* adjudged:

> Alarm bells ring for many academics when they are asked to work not so much broadly for the public good as on behalf of the ruling powers – whether in service of … particular public agencies, or for the government of the day and its international allies. Such engagement often entails pressure to modify our findings in the light of values that ought to be themselves the subject of in-depth research; the 'Combating terrorism' project is a case in point. (Houtman 2007: 2)

One civil servant considered that the poor handling of this initiative had been 'very damaging, as anthropologists kept away from the FCO' (interview July 2013). In contrast, another thought it did lead to some beneficial rethinking: what were better ways to commission independent academic work? How could the government clarify that it was asking for independent views? In her opinion, if the grant-holders felt muzzled, any exploratory programme would be a waste of money.

In an insightful review of this controversy, in which he played a minor but significant role, Jonathan Spencer demonstrated, with detailed examples, how difficult it is for a university-based academic to make informed ethical decisions when involved in the murky world of powerful government bodies (Spencer 2010). One question is whether that is sufficient reason for anthropologists to keep away from government. Professional opinion remains deeply divided. Skinner, who sees ethics as skilled practice rather than a universal code, agrees with the call for anthropologists to commit to 'the possibility of ethical uncertainty' (Harper and Corsín-Jiménez 2005: 11). For Spencer, 'The best we can hope for is not so much being "right" but simply being "less wrong" than the last time' (Spencer 2010: S298). Or, to précis Beckett: Fail. Try again. Fail better.

One dimension to this debate is the desire of politically active academics to retain their privileged position, however embattled or reduced it might be, as critical intellectuals. They wish to uphold the anti-war Quaker maxim, 'Speak truth to power', even if (for some, especially if) power is not listening. In sharp contrast, almost all of my civil servant interviewees displayed no moral qualms about the commitment they had made. For them, it was Hobson's choice whether to be an outsider critic or an insider attempting to steer policy. An ex-member of the MoD justified her position on the grounds that she was happy to provide more nuance and understanding about a relevant topic, especially if it led to less violence as an outcome. One may also question how politically aloof the tenured can be. In the chiding words of one who has worked for DfID, 'As anthropologists we must ... acknowledge that there is no anthropology outside politicised institutional settings, and that what we do as ethnographers and as anthropologists is always part of some sort of political agenda, even if this uncomfortable fact is often unacknowledged within anthropology' (Green 2006: 125). Her words were echoed by one interviewee who, after reading a draft of this chapter, gently reminded me, 'Any anthropological practice is embedded in the society you're in. For instance, Jeremy, your publishing this book is an exercise of power' (interview July 2014). She added that it was not just academics who could speak truth to power: civil servants could do it as well, and maybe to more effect, though that would never be made public.

This commitment to working within government led to occasional face-to-face conflict with their tenured counterparts. One interviewee pointed out to me that, compared to other academic specialists, such as political scientists, British anthropologists are much more cautious and suspicious about the government (see also Green 2006: 125). Another interviewee recounted that when she had given a seminar at the School of Oriental and African Studies (SOAS), she had had a 'tough ride', though overall she had 'enjoyed the interrogation': 'It helped me top up my academic integrity, kept me on my toes about things I'd become complacent about' (interview July 2013). Another was similarly understanding. She stressed to me the view that civil servants were supposed to be by necessity apolitical. In contrast, she considered that academics could 'confuse' their intellectual opinions with their political views. Such was life, she thought, up in the ivory towers. She felt better away from those turreted enclaves. Of course, her statement relies on a restricted notion of the political; critics could easily respond that joining the Civil Service is itself a political decision, while the ability of functionaries to steer, indeed at times to manipulate the decisions by their political masters is notorious. One reason for the great popularity of the BBC comedy series 'Yes, Minister', whose axis is this tension, was viewers' well-placed suspicion that what they saw was so close to the truth (Crissell 2002: 201). The writers of the series openly admitted being inspired by Richard Crossman's account of the battles he had, when a Cabinet Minister, with his Permanent Secretary, Dame Evelyn Sharp, whom he called a manipulator (Crossman 1975). In return, she branded him a bully (Bendixson and Platt 1992: 2; see also Watkins 1965).

Other interviewees had stronger, less positive comments about their erstwhile colleagues which, if true, do not reflect well on academic anthropologists. One functionary told me that a university-based acquaintance had insinuated strongly that it had been both brave and foolish of her to join the Civil Service. Another, blunter anthropologist told her, 'Your career is over'. My interviewee added that she had been gently but firmly pushed out of the anthropological organisation she had helped represent because its members did not want to be associated in any way with an anthropologist in the MoD. Another said to me she had never been so insulted by anyone as the times when she was abused by anthropologists because of her work in the MoD. She found their level of rudeness and personal abuse 'despicable', and it had led her to cancel her subscriptions to both the ASA and the RAI. She regarded the invective of her former fellow professionals as very non-analytical: 'They refused to understand what I was saying. They were not prepared to put aside prejudices. It was very disappointing' (interview July 2013). In his contribution to this book, Benjamin Smith pushes the argument further: he contends that if anthropologists are committed ethically to the pursuit of insights regarding others, they are in turn obliged to unpack their own biases. 'On that basis, I regard the disdain of many academic anthropologists towards those working for the government as not merely disappointing, but also as profoundly un-anthropological' (Chapter 2).

American anthropologists working in different branches of the US military have made similar comments about their academic colleagues. One argues that for university-based anthropologists to regard any interaction with the military 'as a priori polluting severely limits the value of what we can learn and what we can do to affect changes in policy and actions' (Rubenstein 2013: 131). Another laments that in the process of condemning the Human Terrain System, 'Many anthropologists just lump everyone who works for the military into one basket' (Holmes-Eber 2013: 51).[11] In an unexpected twist, a third sees training troops in our subject as a class-crossing way to spread the anthropological message:

> As a discipline we do not make anthropology particularly available to those who cannot afford a college education or who have to focus that education on something more likely to get them a job with only an undergraduate degree. Any time an anthropologist teaches military personnel, there is a good chance the instructor will be bridging a socioeconomic gap the discipline has done very little to close. (Fosher 2013: 99)

Several years ago, a few anthropologists within the MoD participated, with some Australian colleagues, in a panel on 'Anthropology and Government' at an international conference. One commenter from the floor accused them of exploiting their training for what was essentially simplification, stereotyping; she said she had turned down an invitation to contribute an entry on a particular unstable country to an encyclopaedia of nationalism because she was asked to write it in a certain way. One MoD anthropologist on the panel replied that she respected her decision but, in her place, would have made the opposite choice, 'Because if you're not contributing, you're abdicating responsibility'. When a British professor then argued that the MoD anthropologists were 'giving their skills over to an empowered government', he was asked what his research had done for people on the ground. He did not reply. The MoD panellists were surprised and pleased to receive (very unexpected) support from Australian anthropologists working on Aboriginal rights and in the country's health services. Also, another interviewee said members of the Society for Applied Anthropology, a US organisation, whom she had met at one of its gatherings, were 'a lot more welcoming' than academic members of the ASA (interview, 15 June 2013).

A third interviewee, in a different ministry, criticised her former colleagues' chosen disassociation and refusal to participate. She argued that although anthropologists were very good at thinking about, reflecting on or dealing with complex issues, they were also 'very snobby'. It was

> disgraceful [that] anthropology doesn't contribute more. For example the riots of a few years ago: who's working to understand them?
> There's a tension here. You need to maintain a critical distance to write ethnography. But without engaging directly with the society within which we live, anthropology will fail to renew its identity, including its global identity. If we're not prepared to live in the real world, we as a discipline become more irrelevant. (Interview July 2013)

My interviewees judged that this traditional posture of academic self-distancing is beginning to decline, at least in other social sciences, because of the increasing pressure from the UK research councils for university-based work to have 'impact', i.e. an observable effect on public life or policy.

My 'anti-snobby' interviewee considered academic anthropology 'interesting, like philosophy, but not very practical'. In the words of another, 'There are big problems in the world. We should be using our skills to try to improve the situation' (interview July 2013). Let me give a personal example: in the late 1990s the Director of the RAI asked me to edit a book demonstrating how anthropology could contribute to public understanding of contemporary social issues. The publishers chose to entitle the resulting book, *Exotic No More. Anthropology on the Front Lines* (MacClancy 2002). To my very great surprise, one UK reviewer assessed the book's aim as 'Thatcherite', because the vision of anthropology I put forward there was too pragmatically framed for his tastes. Instead he underlined how many anthropologists see their subject 'as a sister discipline to philosophy' (Stewart 2004: 384). Another, equally critical British reviewer regarded anthropology as 'a humanistic anti-discipline … as much a voyage of subjective discovery as it is grounded in some shared practices' (Hart 2004: 5). Clearly, while an increasing number who publish in academic journals are deeply concerned with extramural exigencies,[12] some anthropologists, at least in the UK, remain reluctant to dislodge the priority for the discipline of developing academically oriented theory. It appears that, to them, the generation of novel concepts and modes of explanation, unfettered by concerns in today's world, is what universities should do.

At base here, in the sharp difference of attitudes separating my interviewees from these critics, is a strong tension between conceptions of our pursuit. Some, such as my interviewees, wish to turn their anthropology to pragmatic benefit, whether near-immediate or more long term; they accept that prospect may come at the cost of self-limiting the range or depth of their criticism. Academic opponents of this position uphold the equally uplifting dream of the 'anti-discipline', where anthropology is meant to act more as a provocation to thought than as a prescription for it (Herzfeld 2001: xi). Within the broad church that we dub 'anthropology', this tension is as creative as it is constant (MacClancy 2013: 189). It is also as productive as it is resolvable, for pragmatic benefit and theoretical advance do not have to be mutually exclusive. They are not incompatible. Some reflexive applied anthropologists hope to merge the two by constructing a 'theory of practice'. To some that sounds overly ambitious and formal: better to interlace the two in a well-grounded process of praxis (Partridge 1985; Baba 2000; Hill 2000).[13] Within this scenario, concerns about putting anthropology to work need not be seen as threats to a theoretician's paradise. Eden is not endangered. To put this another way, some UK anthropologists choose to proclaim their discipline as the art of the unthinkable while their counterparts in the Civil Service view their job as the pursuit of the possible. They might both be right, and still well able to work together.

It is also necessary to mention here that reliable sources informed me that several British anthropologists (including some very senior figures) provide, when asked, anthropological advice, usually based on their regional expertise, to sections of the armed forces. Both for reasons of security and, I presume, of professional self-image, these periodic contacts between academic anthropology and the military are not openly discussed. In other words, just because there does not appear to be a single tenured anthropologist in the UK openly promoting the benefits of anthropologists consorting with the armed services, this does not mean that linking up does not occur, and on a regular basis.

Varieties of public service

So far I have concentrated on anthropologists working in Whitehall. Most of my interviewees are still there and thus, for several reasons, feel unable to write their own accounts. Although I have tried to generate generalisations about their practice, there is no model career path, perhaps because the modern incorporation of anthropologists into central government is still relatively new in the UK. Some join a ministry and stay there for decades; others hop from department to department at regular intervals; yet others enter, then leave within a few years.

What is already clear is that the experience of anthropologists engaged in public service is much broader and more diverse than just those who work for the central ministries of the British government, as the various contributors to this book demonstrate. Their personal accounts also serve to portray the life-course of some of today's anthropologists, as they have shifted back and forth between academia, NGOs and government work. Since the increasing privatisation of public service, driven by a neoliberal agenda, is steadily eroding the jobs-for-life tradition of the Civil Service, these repeated shifts in workplace are likely to become more and more the norm, not the exception. Perhaps the best contemporary image for the career trajectory of an up and coming anthropologist is not that of an elevator but a switchback or, worse, a roller coaster.

For university teachers and undergraduate readers, the chapter by Robert Gregory is perhaps the most inspiring. Directly on graduation, with nothing but an anthropology BA to his name, Gregory got a job with an NGO working with a borough council, was then taken on by the council, and he has moved up its town hall hierarchy ever since. He was first charged to work with Portuguese migrant workers in the town, then with young people, older people, an angry residents' association and so on. In each case, instead of hiring outside consultants, he has engaged directly with the population, finding out their points of view, what they want, and has then persuaded the council to fund locally desired initiatives, usually run by the locals themselves. By applying the methods of development studies in this Norfolk town, Gregory exemplifies, and his team wins prizes for, 'backyard anthropology'. His initiatives are rolled out as models for other troubled areas in the country, and even come in under budget. At the same time, he has to anthropologise with the state, interpreting Whitehall calls, such as 'boost participatory democracy', into local terms and later back-translating the results into Civil Service-speak. Also, he thinks it important and worthwhile to build the ethnographic skills of other council officers. Gregory's action-oriented anthropology takes a different form to academic undertakings. But this continually adaptive style of our discipline may well be one of its best futures.

A complementary example is the work of Ian Litton, Commissioning Implementation Lead for Warwickshire County Council. There he manages teams charged with implementing IT strategy in various branches of local administration. He has also done prize-winning work on how to coordinate approaches by local and central government to identity assurance.[14] For example, he researched ways for individuals to prove their identity online, facilitated by a customer-controlled network of trust between organisations. In our interview (19 February 2016), he said this work made him realise the 'slippery' nature of identity within British public life and how IT systems could manage that. In overseeing teamwork, he employs 'agile methods', which put value on communication, verbalising the unspoken, co-production and user priorities. In response to my questions, he considered that the most directly relevant lessons of his anthropology training at the University of St Andrews were to make him more aware, in particular, that there were multiple ways of interpreting the world, that people living in one locale may yet understand the same events in different ways, and that in order to create efficient systems one had to learn 'where people are coming from', i.e. the power of ethnography as a research method (e.g. Litton and Potter 1985; Potter and Litton 1985). Unlike my other interviewees, he could pinpoint the guiding line provided by one of his teachers: Ladislav Holy's transactionalist emphasis on the constitutive role of the individual in the ongoing creation of social life (e.g. Holy and Stuchlik 1983). It was also noteworthy how similarly the language and style of our discipline dovetailed with those of agile methods; indeed, the latter is sometimes called 'software anthropology', and may today adopt explicitly ethnographic dimensions.[15]

Dominic Bryan and Neil Jarman, both based in Northern Ireland, made a series of key interventions in the late 1990s to resolve repeated problems of public disorder, as they discuss in their chapter. Initially they engaged with politicians, then assisted in the development of law and the application of policy, and finally worked with those practically involved with the issues on the ground. Exploiting their ethnographic nous, they repeatedly pitched ideas, accepted that some did not work and then thought up more, in a constantly evolving context where anthropology met government practice in a lively dynamic, which at its best ascended spirally. Their experience also demonstrates the intellectual potential of international exchange, as they took their ideas to post-apartheid South Africa, brought others back and persuaded the government to test them. As they confess, these were heady times; their chapter shows how a pair of hardworking imaginative ethnographers can take advantage of rapidly expanding horizons to put their anthropology to public use. In the process they have persuaded initially sceptical civil servants of the value of fieldwork methods for the gathering of relevant data, which can in turn inform the formulation of policy.

Mils Hills's career history is easily the most vertiginous of all the contributors. He went from near-idyllic doctoral fieldwork in Mauritius via the MoD all the way up to the Cabinet Office, where he was directly answerable to the Prime Minister, before leaving to start his own consultancy, and then back to academia, this time in a Department of Business Studies. It is a remarkable example of an anthropologist who really was able 'to speak truth to power', especially since his words were 'much appreciated by some individuals' (Chapter 2). On the basis of his own experience, he is also very ready to take a stance that, he openly admits, some will find 'unacceptably provocative'. Hills defends in a feisty manner the full integration of anthropologists into government, and he criticises those against it who, in his terms, are self-marginalising our discipline. This debate, central to the themes of this book, is not one that is going to go away. We must learn to extract what we can from it.

Peter Bennett traces a seemingly different work-course from other contributors. His chapter is all the more illuminating for that. His trajectory goes from doctoral fieldwork among a particular Hindu sect in India to working in prisons, then governing them, only to return decades later to academia, directing a Centre for Prison Studies. His last ten years working for the British Government he spent governing Grendon, Britain's first prison run as a therapeutic community. It is both broadly praised and much researched. He assesses that his anthropological training had a threefold effect. First, it made him value and support ethnographic work on his own terrain. Second, it allowed him to transcend a misleading opposition of us vs. them, the staff vs. the inmates; instead he came to regard the prison as a social context where he had to comprehend the views, feelings and behaviours of all those with whom he worked. In other words, an informed empathy was key. Third, Bennett argues that he went from being a participant observer in his Indian days to a self-observing participant in a much studied environment; in Grendon, he was an actor meshed within the thick description of his own ethnography, which was in turn an ongoing exercise in generative reflexivity. Also, he makes it clear that his doctoral training stuck with him, and to productive end: 'I have often listened to the highly charged life-changing testimonies of Grendon prisoners and been reminded of the devotional outpourings of sectarian saints' (Chapter 6).

Benjamin Smith's career has embodied yet another sequence of shifts: from fieldwork to applied fieldwork while still studying for his doctorate; working as an NGO intermediary between the indigenes and the state (in this case, Australia); finally, working for the state, in the UK Border Agency. Instead of viewing a bureaucracy as an isolable organisation with its own culture, he takes a neo-Foucauldian turn, viewing government as processual, '(re)produced between particular practices that may not necessarily be formally understood as governmental ... diffuse in character', which categorise and steer those with whom its agents and procedures come into contact (Chapter 3). Thus, NGOs performing 'the work of government' both encompass indigenes within the state and train them in state-oriented subjectivities. As a civil servant he finds his training is particularly advantageous in helping to understand colleagues' interests and aims, building relationships with them and using that to develop and deliver successful policies. At the same time, he holds dear the anthropological generation of unexpected insights, however inconvenient they may be to the bureaucracy. He worries that his two aims of remaining an anthropologist 'at heart' and fulfilling the needs of his bureaucratic role are not always well aligned.

Rachael Gooberman-Hill, compared to the other contributors, takes a different but highly relevant tack, in a world where an increasing number of government services are being outsourced. These days the Department of Health of the British government explicitly encourages partnerships between universities and the National Health Service, to such an extent that many research-active staff hold contracts in both academia and the NHS. Gooberman-Hill details the development of two research projects; she headed one, and played an important role in the other. In her discussion of these projects, she shows how she both adapts her research style to meet the expectations of funders and appropriates the modes of other disciplines. Since in-depth fieldwork is too lengthy for NHS funders, she pares her anthropological methods to the bare essentials. Yet she continues to affirm flexibility as key to research, especially given the increasing codification of qualitative analysis. For her, one cost of this stripping down is having to keep quiet about the need for reflexivity and creativity. She concludes with a worry that continues to gnaw: what will be the eventual effects of ranking short-term observation as a valid substitute for longer-term fieldwork? Perhaps what some see as a threat to our disciplinary distinctiveness others will regard as an opportunity.

Anthropologies elsewhere

The British experience is distinctive. We should not expect otherwise. Just how anthropology has been conceived and deployed over time differs from one country to another, each with its own administrative elites, educational traditions and historical trajectory. A cross-national skim demonstrates the point.

Let us start with the USA. Some of its great urban universities have long-established reputations for applied versions of the discipline, and in World War Two many practitioners willingly adapted their skills to defeating the enemy. Also, the US is still the world's largest economy, with the life of its residents regulated and monitored by a broad extensive bureaucracy. Today the continued high production of anthropologists with doctorates combined with the shrinking market in tenured positions, plus the established custom of practitioners working with government, means that an increasing number work in a diversity of public offices at a variety of levels from the federal to the local. Nolan's recent *Handbook of Practicing Anthropology* gives an idea of this range and its outsourced equivalents. Among others, it includes contributions from a disaster anthropologist and several professional consultants, as well as chapters from those working in the World Bank, the Marine Corps and an assortment of federal agencies: medical, environmental, USAID and so on (Nolan 2013). The American Anthropological Association strives to further this shift by routinely holding workshops on how to gain a job in government (Fiske 2008: 124).

The demographic composition of a country may play a key role in this arena. For instance, in Mexico, whose 'national minorities' comprise over 20% of the population, anthropology has played a constitutive role in government since the revolution, over a hundred years ago. For decades, anthropologists working within or advising the national administration have helped to formulate and implement policy;

at first they advocated acculturation of indigenous groups, later their integration within an explicitly multicultural nation. Unlike its British or US counterparts, Mexican anthropology is not burdened by colonialist hangover or neocolonialist excesses. It continues to be a force for change, with its graduates broadly placed across diverse sections of government (Krotz 2006). Little wonder, then, that when the International Union of Anthropological and Ethnological Sciences (IUAES) held its quinquennial congress in Mexico City in 1993, the president of the country delivered its opening address.

Population size may also be a relevant factor. Norway has a population of only five million; its educated elite is correspondingly small. Within that privileged sector, the social sciences are very popular choices for university entrants; this was especially the case for anthropology during the decades when multiculturalism was in vogue. Postgraduates with extended field experience hold posts, some very senior, in a variety of government ministries (e.g. Justice, Health and Care Services, Fisheries, Defence, Environment, and the Foreign Office, whose portfolio includes international aid). Furthermore, many tenured anthropologists are ready and willing to participate in public debates about issues of the moment: the treatment of the Saami, the status of immigrants, the worth of aid and so on (Eriksen 2006, 2013; Howell 2010). Their words may have weight because it is quite possible for a minister and a public anthropologist to be old university friends; failing that, it is quite likely that his/her First Secretary is a social scientist. On top of that, some anthropology research students, on graduating, do not go into Civil Service, but politics. The leading example here is Hilde Frafjord Johnson: in 1991 she went straight from gaining her research degree to becoming a political advisor to the Prime Minister. Within six years, she was Minister for International Development, a post she held for most of the following decade.

In many countries outside the West, anthropologists do not disdain the application of their craft. Indeed, they may find it hard to justify any other form of their discipline. For instance, in Cameroon today applied anthropology is not marginalised but lauded, and its graduates choose to enter the policy-making apparatus of the state (Nkwi 2006). Elsewhere, politicians' felt need for control may stifle the local development of our discipline beyond the university walls. For example, in Turkey the intellectual repression of certain governments has led to an anthropology yet to gain a public voice or to participate in the making of national policy (Tandogan 2006). Today, China is perhaps the most discouraging case. There the making of money, preferably in vast amounts, is so highly valued that anthropology is deeply unattractive for most university entrants (Smart 2006); I have found no evidence of anthropologists working for its government.[16]

The point is clear. We cannot generalise easily from the British experience. Other countries have other styles. These all too brief examples at least give us an idea of the factors that might enable a public service anthropology, and help grant our graduates access to posts in officialdom. What we do not know, and would be good to find out, is whether government anthropologies differ distinctively across countries, and how, within each state, national anthropology and bureaucracy intermesh, productively or otherwise.

Government anthropology: the colonial and the contemporary

It would be good to comment on the epigraph given at the start of this chapter. But there are obstacles to a productive comparison.

First, anticolonial attitudes are now so pervasive that the rewriting of history can make it difficult to assess the contemporaneous attitudes of colonial anthropologists. It is crucial to remember here that colonialism was thought a civilising mission by many until the postwar decades. Lucy Mair, who held a Chair in Applied Anthropology at the London School of Economics, remembered, 'None of us ... held that colonial rule should come to an immediate end. Who did in those days? We thought it should give Africans a better deal' (Mair 1975: 192). In the 1970s Sir Raymond Firth chatted about this shift with a fledgling doctoral student, James Clifford:

> Firth thought the relations between anthropology and empire were more complex than some of the critics were suggesting. He shook his head in a mixture of pretended and real confusion. What happened? Not so long ago we were radicals. We thought of ourselves as critical intellectuals, advocates for the value of indigenous cultures, defenders of our people. Now, all of a sudden, we're handmaidens of empire! (Clifford 2013: 2)[17]

If, for a moment, we were able to push these concerns to one side, and attempt to assess identifiable benefits of colonial anthropology, our list would still not be long: a few interventions, already noted, where authors informed colonial policy and forestalled counterproductive actions by the authorities; a heightened appreciation, by ethnographer-administrators, of the complexity and sophistication of local ways; commissioned ethnographies that informed the approach of district officers and their superiors.

Second, I iterate the limitations of my own research, based on interviews, not grounded on fieldwork. The only hint I had of the disparity between what my interviewees say and what they do was the occasional lack of fit between the comments made by the anthropologist-civil servants I quizzed. For example, my interviewees tended to gently dismiss suggestions of ethical dilemmas in the workplace. If that were the case, however, it is strange they have felt the need to find space in their already over-full schedules to assemble an informal lobby for the upholding of Civil Service values.

My caveats expressed, what informative comparisons can be made between colonialist practice and that of today? Several differences are evident. First, the mission of the early government anthropologists was usually to produce ethnography or to conduct surveys. They were generators of data, to help dissipate Western ignorance of native customs. Their reports were meant, in usually vague ways, to inform colonial policy. Rarely was their work problem-focused; an exception was F.E. Williams' study, in the Papuan Gulf, of the 1920s modernisation movement, then termed the 'Vailala Madness', whose rebellious dimensions so disturbed the administration (Williams 1923). In contrast, today's breed of anthropologist-civil servants are not hired for ethnographic survey work, but much more specific ends. They are given posts because of particular research skills, as detailed above. Second, they cannot play the role of 'the lone ethnographer', a solitary intellectual gone heroically native, but have to be team players, in suits. Third, anthropologists in Whitehall work to exacting and usually short deadlines, if they wish policymakers to pluck the fruits of their research; colonial ethnographers were usually given a freer rein. Fourth, unlike their contracted predecessors, their positions are long term and they can contemplate the prospect of scaling a career hierarchy. The price of scrambling up that slope, however, is periodic monitoring, further training and sustained pressure on delivering the goods. If they choose to advance their careers, they have to produce, and keep on producing.

Fifth, if an anthropologist working within or with government wants to do research that leads to a direct development in policy, it is near essential that they be involved in the creation, commissioning and management of projects. Otherwise, it is all too easy to disregard their results. In a similar manner, outsiders who wish to inform policy have to ensure their work fits into clearly defined, actively pursued project aims. For it to make a difference, it is preferable that the outside research be commissioned. For instance, Charles Kirke, a military anthropologist and ex-serviceman, told me that in the early 2010s the MoD sought informed proposals for internal reform (interview July 2014). He persuaded his academic institution to fund his research into cross-cultural differences between the four services (Civil, Army, Royal Navy, RAF). Staff at the Ministry welcomed his report 'enthusiastically'. However, as far as he is aware, the policy recommendations of his self-generated research (Kirke 2012) were never acted upon.

What chance an anthropology of government?

If an anthropology of contemporary government does emerge, its research remit would have to include the making of policy and the workings of bureaucracy. However, there are problems with the study of both.

An identifiable anthropology of policy has arisen since the millennial turn; in the late 2000s, the association dedicated to it was the most rapidly growing section within the AAA. Its methods and findings, one of its protagonists claims, are 'potentially transformative for the discipline' (Shore 2012: 101). However, like my interviews for this opening chapter, a good number of these studies are hampered by lack of open access to their field site. Instead they tend to focus on the evolving logic of documentary process rather than the internal disputes constituting its production. Similarly, most anthropological studies of bureaucracy so far are either ethnographies of the interface between the public and the administrative, or critical exercises into the rationality of form-filling (e.g. Herzfeld 1991; Bernstein and Mertz 2011; Hoag 2011; Graeber 2015).

An anthropology of Aidland, the study of professionals in international development, promises to overcome some of the above shortcomings. Many of these studies are written by anthropologists who have worked in development, for or within government. David Mosse, in a survey of this material, examines how their ethnographies dissect the productive interactions of the ideological and the actual. Tales of integral compromise, they portray these organisations as informally structured by concealed politics, hidden incentives and careerist strategies, with insiders maintaining an ostensible commitment to collective representations of bureaucratic rationality and institutional mythology. In order to keep their posts and reproduce their organisational structures, they discipline both themselves and one another (Mosse 2011). Of course, much of this is the case for the ethnography of institutions in general: in each sub-world, practitioners box and cox to achieve particular ends; they speak a common language and together uphold a professional ideology. They know their jobs depend on it.

Intimations of all the above are scattered throughout this chapter, as some interviewees revealed to me a few of their cunning wiles and effective stratagems, honed by their doctoral experience: elucidating how best to fit in, by scrutinising what was model and what unspoken reality; their self-disciplining (no talk of 'redistribution'); whom to talk to about what, when, how ('What kind of person is the colonel?'); whom to ally with when, to get an initiative accepted; the 'guerrilla tactics' of SDAs in DfID ('You pick your battlefields') and so on. Veteran fieldworkers, they understood before they stepped into the corridors of power that Whitehall was constituted by social relations and appeals to a protective Civil Service Code. My interviewees and contributors to this book are also well aware that the team-based production of policy and other documents leads to a loss of nuance; Smith strives to accommodate unexpected ideas; Gooberman-Hill worries about keeping silent over the need for reflexivity and creativity. Their realist vision of their workplace is backed by the rare, critical report from academics about the day-to-day functioning of government. For example, a study led by the behavioural economist Michael Hallsworth, who at present works for the Behavioural Insights Team, which reports to the Cabinet, classified policy making in the British government as a messy process deeply resistant to reform (Hallsworth, Parker and Rutter 2011).

For several interviewees and contributors, government process is as constraining as it is enabling. This does not necessitate that it is at all times rigid, as some academics seem to suggest. For instance, Green portrays development interventions as inflexibly formulaic. Some interviewees told me a different story, of being given space to conduct new styles of qualitative research, of thinking up new ways to investigate issues. Despite the constraints, there remains space for winning creativity, innovative initiatives. Gregory's 'backyard anthropology' and Litton's 'software anthropology' were both awarded prizes and imitated by other councils. Bryan and Jarman's chapter is a list of ethnographically informed policy recommendations, mostly implemented, some successfully, some not. Hills was one of a small group of energetic, bright young men and women, deliberately brought into the Cabinet Office and other strategic parts of the civil, defence and security services, in order 'to shake things up', to foment culture change. He is explicit that his team had the power to speak truth to power, and for that to be much appreciated by some. A sceptic might claim that what Hills and some interviewees are recounting are just the consequences of a brief experimental moment in the long history of the Civil Service. Maybe; maybe not.

My brief list of examples of interviewees as informal workplace ethnographers is but a necklace of anecdotes. A well-grounded anthropology of government needs systematic studies of particular ministries or their sub-departments. Outside of DfID, however, the chances are that they won't be appearing soon, for two key reasons. First, the ends of government and the perceived need for secrecy effectively block most investigations by outsiders. This applies both to the present day and the recent past: in the UK, official documents are not publicly available for thirty years, and by that time the protagonists of past initiatives are usually either dead or assisted by a failing memory. In fact, death is no protection: the Cabinet tried to prevent posthumous publication of Crossman's diaries. The second reason for pessimism is equally patent. Doctoral fieldworkers are more observers than participants; normally, by the time they have learnt how to act, they are preparing to go home. In contrast, anthropologist-civil servants who choose to stay become more participants than observers, as Bennett noted of his time in the Prison Service. Open, critical analysis of their own workstyles then becomes too threatening to their own positions. When David Mosse wanted to publish a rounded ethnography of a long-term DfID project in which he had been involved, his government co-workers were energetic in trying to block its release: they feared for their jobs (Mosse 2005, 2006).

The goal of government ethnography is not impossible. There are other solutions. Some anthropologist-civil servants, on retiring or shifting sector, may consider returning to the discipline and providing us with subtle, reflexive analysis of the world they inhabited, and helped perpetuate. A glimmer of this comes in Bennett's chapter, where he gently chides the pair of researchers (one of them my wife) who analysed Grendon in stark Foucauldian terms. The reality of prison life, he argues, was much more nuanced. Also, Mosse gives two examples of revelatory texts by former participants: one a tale of heroic effort, the other a confessional tract of the damage done (Mosse 2011: 18). Eyben's reflexive account of her decades in development is a further example (Eyben 2014).

A further question has to be, who would these ethnographies of government be for? Why do they need to be written? My listed examples four paragraphs above demonstrate that my interviewees are very well aware of organisational realities. Similarly, Mosse notes that 'there is little external criticism of development practice that is not prefigured within expert communities' (Mosse 2011: 18). These facts suggest that ethnographies of government would have very little new to tell civil servants themselves. At this rate, the main audiences for these accounts would be fellow anthropologists (which some would see as a self-referential circle), interested outsiders, curious to see their suspicions confirmed, or students, especially those who wish to work in organisations. On this reading, the *raison d'être* for ethnographies of government appears manifold: to advance academic anthropological debate, to further the education of the already informed and to forewarn job-keen undergraduates of institutional realities. These books could thus be sited in a broad middle ground between exercises in cultural translation and formalisation of the pre-known. Once again, this book does not escape that classification.

Futures for anthropology

The employment of anthropologists by colonial governments was patchy but productive. Those were balmy times, when ethnographers could go off-station, alone, for months. In comparison, the work of today's anthropologist-civil servants is much more collaborative, their timelines are more limited and their results more pragmatically assessed. A few of my interviewees held to a self-flattering image of themselves as the awkward Johnny at a gathering of professionals. The accumulated evidence of this book suggests that, with increasing examples of successful bureaucratic practice, that view may be slowly changing. In the future, it is likely that 'Anthropology is the new black' will be seen as but a catchphrase of this transitional phase.

Anthropology may be currently fashionable in certain Whitehall corridors. That does not assure its continued future in the Civil Service. One of my interlocutors, who maintains links with the armed forces, told me of a recent meeting with a pair working in 'behavioural science' for elite military units. They had been exposed to some poor-quality anthropology, and so dismissed anthropological insight in summary fashion: 'Just stuff you can get from Wikipedia'. It is tempting to interpret their remarks as the petty rivalry of fellow professionals competing for the ear of government. Perhaps, but the challenge is still clear: anthropologists need to demonstrate, time and again, that they can add considerably more value than just data to be gleaned from online sources. Evidence in this book suggests they can do that, so far.

One concern repeatedly raised by some contributors and interviewees was the very nature of, and prospect for the discipline. Whither anthropology? Amidst much uncertainty about our subject, one thing that does seem clear is that, thanks partly to forces beyond our control, anthropology is shifting towards a more practice-oriented mode.

Despite the informed protests of some, the begrudging reluctance of more and the studied avoidance of far too many, anthropologists are increasingly obliged to justify the continued existence of the discipline in broadly pragmatic terms. However, in a recent counter-charge defending 'useless knowledge', Marilyn Strathern observes that the Department of Trade and Industry (DTI) recognises the key contribution the sciences, including the social sciences, make to the national economy; the DTI even acknowledges the importance within those domains of 'curiosity-driven research' (Strathern 2007: 100–101). But the ESRC, funded by the Department for Business, Innovation and Skills, which replaced the DTI, has made the potential 'impact' of proposed research an increasingly important criterion for judging the worthiness of grant applications. The seven-yearly government evaluation of university research employs a similar measure. Whatever one department might have proclaimed about the value of the apparently 'useless', the general research policy of the government points in a different direction. What to call this style of impact-oriented work? For some, 'applied anthropology' today sounds passé (Johnston 2012), tainted by colonialist or neocolonialist association (e.g. Scheper-Hughes and Bourgois 2004: 7–8), while its practitioners' desire for a 'theory of practice' can appear but a will o' the wisp. To an extent, the term is being pushed aside by 'engaged anthropology', which usually means taking an ethnographic focus to appalling ills of the contemporary world and then trying to make possible contributions towards their remedy (Low and Merry 2010). To the jaded, this change of nomenclature can be too reminiscent of the semantic game-playing notorious in academia. Instead of turf wars over terminology, it seems best to examine the range of their results and gauge their cumulative effects.

It also appears that we are moving towards a much more plural anthropology, one practised globally, where the hegemonic role of university departments is no longer unquestioned. It would be comforting to envision a scenario where tenured academics and extramural practitioners participated horizontally, not vertically, in networks of earth-wide proportions. Furthermore, our interests are not served by overly rigid characterisations of our discipline, where anthropology is said to be constituted by certain practices and not by others. These premature prescriptions are out of place in evolving contexts. Instead of propounding exclusionary definitions of anthropology, as though it were a bounded culture, it is more productive to perceive our discipline in social, relational terms (Strathern 2007: 96).

In these open-ended circumstances, where the theory vs. practice binary is damned as an outdated dichotomy, any attempt to predict, or worse to proclaim our future would be as vacuous as it would be pretentious. Watch this space?

Acknowledgements

I thank Rosalind Eyben, Pat Holden, Charles Kirke, Ian Litton, Mike Schulz, Kathryn Tomlinson and five other anthropologists, who wish to remain anonymous, for the interviews they generously agreed to, as well as those who gave seminars but then had no time for an interview. All interviewees were sent a draft of the chapter, to forestall gross misrepresentation and in a bid for ethical equity; some responded. My thanks to Patrick Alexander, Riall Nolan and an anonymous reviewer of the manuscript for their comments on an earlier draft; especial thanks to Chris McDonaugh for his critique. My gratitude also to Chris Hann, Signe Howell and Jaro Stacul for providing information about anthropology and public service in the Western countries in which they reside.

Jeremy MacClancy is Professor of Anthropology in the Department of Social Sciences, Oxford Brookes University. He is the founder-chairman of Chacolinks, a small, international charity that accompanies the indigenous Wichí of northern Argentina in the legal campaign to regain control of their ancestral lands.

Notes

1. The products of fieldworkers put in place by colonial governments may be similarly enduring. Evans-Pritchard's terminology of Nuer leaders and political segments came to be used by administrators in the Sudan when discussing modes of authority among the ethnic group. Indeed, at least until the 1980s, his nomenclature was 'still the basis of most administrative descriptions of Nuer politics' (Johnson 1982: 240).
2. For a more nuanced assessment of Thomas, see Basu (2016).
3. See also González (2015a, 2015b).
4. 'Military Specialists Aim to Improve Cultural Understanding', ISAF News, 1 April 2010. Retrieved 13 May 2014 from http://www.isaf.nato.int/article/news/military-specialists-aim-to-improve-cultural-understanding.html.
5. 'The NEW Lawrence of Arabia: Captain Who Lived among the Afghans and Led His Warriors to Victory over the Taliban Wins Medal Second Only to the VC', Mail Online, 6 October 2013. Retrieved 13 May 2014 from http://www.dailymail.co.uk/news/article-2446262/

The-NEW-Lawrence-Arabia-Captain-lived-Afghans-led-warriors-victory-Taliban-wins-medal-second-VC.html.
6. An ex-member of the MoD said the content and level of training in the course would be equivalent to that offered by a postgraduate certificate in general social sciences methods.
7. https://twitter.com/fishaflying, 13 December 2011. Retrieved 23 June 2013.
8. According to The Guardian, anthropologists work within the Research, Information, and Communications Unit (RICU) of the Home Office. RICU combats the online communications of ISIS by discreetly disseminating its own, counter-radicalisation messages 'at an industrial scale and pace' via newspapers, leafleting and social media (The Guardian, 2 May 2016. Retrieved 24 June 2016 from http://www.theguardian.com/politics/2016/may/02/inside-ricu-the-shadowy-propaganda-unit-inspired-by-the-cold-war). According to The Sunday Times, anthropologists also work within the Behavioural Insights Team, based in Thames House, headquarters of MI5, the counter-intelligence agency of the British Government. The team's 'main task ... is to establish whether people flagged as potential threats are "talkers" or "walkers" – those who simply boast or those who are preparing to act', ('MI5's mind readers help foil seven terrorist attacks', The Sunday Times 7 August 2016, p.16).
9 For the Civil Service code, see https://www.gov.uk/government/publications/civil-service-code/the-civil-service-code. Retrieved 17 February 2016.
10. http://www.theasa.org/ethics/guidelines.shtml. Retrieved 17 February 2016.
11. For examples of other ways in which the US armed forces make use of anthropology, see Wunderle (2006); and the special issues of the Military Intelligence Professional Bulletin devoted to 'Cultural Awareness', January–March 2010; 'Cross-cultural Competence', January–March 2011; 'Language and Cultural Competency', January–March 2012; 'Culture, Regional Expertise and Language', July–September 2014. All available at http://fas.org/irp/agency/army/mipb/.
12. The list here could be long. For example, in indigenous rights, they include the proponents of cultural critique and activist advocacy (e.g. Hale 2006; Shannon 2006). Medical anthropology is another obvious field in which most practitioners are focused on effecting change.
13. On the idea of internships where students are asked to produce theory from practice, see Beck and Maida (2013: 3). Also, Mosse has commented on how 'engagement with international development has encouraged reflection on the practice of anthropology itself' (Mosse 2013: 240).
14. The prizes were at the Real IT Awards 2014, winner in both the 'Security as Enabler' and 'Partnership' categories.
15. For example, J.T. Pedersen, 2010, 'Is it Agile or Software Anthropology', retrieved 22 February 2016 from http://www.jtpedersen.net/2010/03/09/is-it-agile-or-software-anthropology/; C. Yury, 2015, 'Breaking it Down: Integrating Agile Methods and Ethnographic

Praxis', retrieved 22 February 2016 from https://www.epicpeople.org/breaking-it-down-integrating-agile-methods-and-ethnographic-praxis/.
16. In Canada, I was informed that there are a few anthropologists employed at federal, provincial and other bureaucratic levels but there was no connection between the posts they hold and their training in the discipline (J. Stacul, pers. comm., 28 February 2016). In Germany, a few appear to have gone into international development, but very few, if any, into other domains of the public sector. Despite my enquiries, I was unable to obtain any information about anthropologists working in either the French or Spanish Civil Services.
17. For a similar attempt to reassess attitudes to the work done by the first Australian-trained anthropologists, who coordinated with the bureaucratic gatekeepers to Aboriginal societies, see Finlayson (2008).

References

American Anthropological Association (AAA). 2007. 'American Anthropological Association Executive Board Statement on the Human Terrain System Project'. Retrieved 12 May 2014 from http://www.aaanet.org/issues/policy-advocacy/statement-on-HTS.cfm.
Baba, M.L. 2000. 'Theories of Practice in Anthropology: A Critical Appraisal', *NAPA Bulletin* 18: 17–44.
Barrett, S.R. 1984. *The Rebirth of Anthropological Theory*. Toronto: University of Toronto Press.
Basu, P. 2016. 'N.W. Thomas and Colonial Anthropology in British West Africa: Reappraising a Cautionary Tale', *Journal of the Royal Anthropological Institute* 22(1): 84–107.
Beck, S., and C.A. Maida. 2013. 'Introduction. Toward Engaged Anthropology', in S. Beck and C.A. Maida (eds), *Toward Engaged Anthropology*. Oxford: Berghahn Books, pp. 1–14.
Bendixson, T., and J. Platt. 1992. *Milton Keynes. Image and Reality*. Cambridge: Granta.
Bernstein, A., and E. Mertz. 2011. 'Introduction. Bureaucracy: Ethnography of the State in Everyday Life', *PoLAR: Political and Legal Anthropology Review* 34(1): 6–10.
Clifford, J. 2013. *Returns. Becoming Indigenous in the Twenty-first Century*. Cambridge, MA: Harvard University Press
Commission on the Engagement of Anthropology with the US Security and Intelligence Communities (CEAUSSIC). 2009. 'Final Report on the Army's Human Terrain System Proof of Concept Program Submitted to the Executive Board of the American Anthropological Association October 14, 2009'. Retrieved 12 May 2014 from http://www.aaanet.org/cmtes/commissions/CEAUSSIC/upload/CEAUSSIC_HTS_Final_Report.pdf.
Conlin, S. 1985. 'Anthropological Advice in a Government Context', in R. Grillo and A. Rew (eds), *Social Anthropology and Development Policy*. ASA Monographs 23. London: Tavistock, pp. 73–87.

Crissell, A. 2002. *An Introductory History of British Broadcasting*, 2nd edn. London: Routledge.

Crossman, R.H.S. 1975. *Diaries of a Cabinet Minister. Vol. 1, Minister of Housing 1964–1966*. London: Hamish Hamilton.

Deacon, A.B. 1934. *Malekula. A Vanishing People in the New Hebrides*, ed. C.H. Wedgwood. London: G. Routledge & Sons.

Drazin, A. 2006. 'The Need to Engage with Non-ethnographic Research Methods: A Personal View', in S. Pink (ed.), *Applications of Anthropology. Professional Anthropology in the Twenty-first Century*. Oxford: Berghahn Books, pp. 90–108.

Duncanson, C., and H. Cornish. 2012. 'A Feminist Approach to Counterinsurgency', in P. Dixon (ed.), *The British Approach to Counterinsurgency: From Malaya and Northern Ireland to Iraq and Afghanistan*. Basingstoke: Palgrave Macmillan, pp. 147–72.

Eriksen, T.H. 2006. *Engaging Anthropology. The Case for a Public Presence*. Oxford: Berg.

Eriksen, T.H. 2013. 'Norwegian Anthropologists Study Minorities at Home: Political and Academic Agendas', in S. Beck and C.A. Maida (eds), *Toward Engaged Anthropology*. Oxford: Berghahn Books, pp. 36–54.

Eyben, R. 2003. 'Mainstreaming the Social Dimension into the Overseas Development Administration: A Partial History', *Journal of International Development* 15: 879–92.

Eyben, R. 2014. *International Aid and the Making of a Better World. Reflexive Practice*. Abingdon: Routledge.

Finlayson, J. 2008. 'Anthropology and the State: What Kind of Handmaiden?' (Abstract). Retrieved 24 March 2016 from http://www.nomadit.co.uk/asa/asa08/panels.php5?PanelID=409.

Fiske, S.J. 2008. 'Working for the Federal Government: Anthropology Careers', *NAPA Bulletin* 29: 110–30.

Fosher, K. 2013. 'Pebbles in the Headwaters. Working within Military Intelligence', in R.A. Rubenstein, K. Fosher and C. Fujimura (eds), *Practicing Military Anthropology. Beyond Expectations and Traditional Boundaries*. Sterling, VA: Kumarian, pp. 83–100.

Fujimura, C. 2013. '"Living the Dream": One Military Anthropologist's Initiation', in R.A. Rubenstein, K. Fosher and C. Fujimura (eds), *Practicing Military Anthropology. Beyond Expectations and Traditional Boundaries*. Sterling, VA: Kumarian, pp. 29–44.

Fuller, C.J. n.d.a. 'Occupation, Race and Hierarchy: Colonial Theories of Caste and Society in India, 1871–1947'. Unpublished manuscript.

Fuller, C.J. n.d.b. 'Anthropology, Sociology and the Ethnography of British India, c. 1870–1947'. Unpublished manuscript.

Gezari, V.M. 2013. *The Tender Soldier. A True Story of War and Sacrifice*. New York: Simon & Schuster.

González, R. 2009 *American Counterinsurgency: Human Science and the Human Terrain*. Chicago: Prickly Paradigm Press.

González, R. 2010. *Militarizing Culture*. Walnut Creek, CA: Left Coast Press.

González, R. 2015a. 'Seeing into Hearts and Minds. Part 1. The Pentagon's Quest for a "Social Radar"', *Anthropology Today* 31(3): 8–13.

González, R. 2015b. 'Seeing into Hearts and Minds. Part 2. "Big Data", Algorithms, and Computational Counterinsurgency', *Anthropology Today* 31(4): 13–18.

González, R., and D. Price. 2015. 'Remaking the Human Terrain: The US Military's Continuing Quest to Commandeer Culture', *Counterpunch*, 31 July. Retrieved 25 June 2016 from http://www.counterpunch.org/2015/07/31/remaking-the-human-terrain-the-us-militarys-continuing-quest-to-commandeer-culture/.

Goody, J. 1995. *The Expansive Moment. Anthropology in Britain and Africa 1918–1970*. Cambridge: Cambridge University Press.

Graeber, D. 2015. *The Utopia of Rules. On Technology, Stupidity, and the Secret Joys of Bureaucracy*. London: Melville House.

Green, M. 2006. 'Applying Anthropology in and to Development', in S. Pink (ed.), *Applications of Anthropology. Professional Anthropology in the Twenty-first Century*. Oxford: Berghahn Books, pp. 110–29.

Green, M. 2012. 'Framing and Escaping: Contrasting Aspects of Knowledge Work in International Development and Anthropology', in S. Venkatesan and T. Yarrow (eds), *Differentiating Development. Beyond an Anthropology of Critique*. Oxford: Berghahn Books, pp. 42–57.

Grillo, R. 1985. 'Applied Anthropology in the 1980s: Retrospect and Prospect', in R. Grillo and A. Rew (eds), *Social Anthropology and Development Policy*. ASA Monographs 23. London: Tavistock, pp. 1–36.

Hale, C.R. 2006. 'Activist Research v. Cultural Critique: Indigenous Land Rights and the Contradictions of Politically Engaged Anthropology', *Cultural Anthropology* 21(1): 96–120.

Hallsworth, M., with S. Parker and J. Rutter. 2011. *Policy Making in the Real World. Evidence and Analysis*. London: Institute for Government. Retrieved 16 February 2016 from http://www.instituteforgovernment.org.uk/sites/default/files/publications/Policy%20making%20in%20the%20real%20world.pdf.

Harper, I., and A. Corsín-Jiménez. 2005. 'Towards Interactive Professional Ethics', *Anthropology Today* 21(6): 10–12.

Hart, K. 2004. 'What Anthropologists Really Do', *Anthropology Today* 20(1): 3–5.

Henley, P. 2006. 'Anthropologists in Television: A Disappearing World?', in S. Pink (ed.), *Applications of Anthropology. Professional Anthropology in the Twenty-first Century*. Oxford: Berghahn Books, pp. 170–91.

Herzfeld, M. 1991. *The Social Production of Indifference: Exploring the Symbolic Roots of Western Bureaucracy*. Oxford: Berg.

Herzfeld, M. 2001. *Anthropology. Theoretical Practice in Culture and Society*. Oxford: Blackwell.

Hill, C.E. 2000. 'Strategic Issues for Rebuilding a Theory and Practice Synthesis', *National Association for the Practice of Anthropology (NAPA) Bulletin* 18: 1–16.

Hoag, C. 2011. 'Assembling Partial Perspectives: Thoughts on the Anthropology of Bureaucracy', *PoLAR: Political and Legal Anthropology Review* 34(1): 81–94.
Holmes-Eber, P. 2013. 'A Day in the Life of the Marine Corps Professor of Operational Culture', in R.A. Rubenstein, K. Fosher and C. Fujimura (eds), *Practicing Military Anthropology. Beyond Expectations and Traditional Boundaries.* Sterling, VA: Kumarian, pp. 45–63.
Holy, L., and M. Stuchlik. 1983. *Actions, Norms and Representations. Foundations of Anthropological Inquiry.* Cambridge: Cambridge University Press.
Houtman, G. 2007. 'Double or Quits', *Anthropology Today* 22(6): 1–3.
Howell, S. 2010. 'Norwegian Academic Anthropologists in Public Spaces'. *Current Anthropology* 51: S269–77.
Johnson, D. 1982. 'Evans-Pritchard, the Nuer, and the Sudan Political Service', *African Affairs* 81(323): 231–46.
Johnston, B.R. 2012. *Applied Anthropology.* Oxford Bibliographies in Anthropology. New York: Oxford University Press.
Kirk-Greene, A.H.M. 2004. 'Meek, Charles Kingsley (1885–1965)', in *Oxford Dictionary of National Biography.* Oxford University Press. Retrieved 29 April 2014 from http://www.oxforddnb.com/view/article/34974.
Kirke, C. 2012. 'Cross-cultural Issues in the Four Services'. Swindon: Defence Academy of the United Kingdom. Retrieved 24 March 2016 from http://www.da.mod.uk/Research-Publications/category/95/cross-cultural-issues-in-the-four-services-19032.
Krotz, E. 2006. 'Mexican Anthropology's Ongoing Search for Identity', in G.L. Ribeiro and A. Escobar (eds), *World Anthropologies. Disciplinary Transformations within Systems of Power.* Oxford: Berg, pp. 87–109.
Kuklick, H. 1991. *The Savage Within. The Social History of British Anthropology, 1885–1945.* Cambridge: Cambridge University Press.
Lackner, H. 1973. 'Colonial Administration and Social Anthropology: Eastern Nigeria 1920–1940', in T. Asad (ed.), *Anthropology and the Colonial Encounter.* London: Athlone, pp. 123–51.
Landman, R.H. 1978. 'Applied Anthropology in Post-colonial Britain: The Present and the Prospect', *Human Organization* 37(3): 323–27.
Lewis, I.M. 1977. 'Confessions of a "Government" Anthropologist', *Anthropological Forum* 4(2): 226–38.
Lewis, I.M. 2003. 'Adventures in Somali Anthropology', *Annales de l'Éthiopie* XIX(19): 307–21.
Litton, I., and J. Potter. 1985. 'Social Representation in the Ordinary Explanations of a "Riot"', *European Journal of Social Psychology* 15(4): 371–88.
Low, S., and S.E. Merry. 2010. 'Engaged Anthropology: Diversity and Dilemmas. An Introduction to Supplement 2', *Current Anthropology* 51(S2): S203–26.
Lucas, G.R. 2009. *Anthropologists in Arms. The Ethics of Military Anthropology.* Lanham, MD: Altamira.
MacClancy, J.V. (ed.). 2002. *Exotic No More. Anthropology on the Front Lines.* Chicago, IL: University of Chicago Press.
MacClancy, J.V. 2007. 'Nakomaha: A Counter-colonial Life and its Contexts. Anthropological Approaches to Biography', *Oceania* 77(2): 191–214.

MacClancy, J.V. 2013. *Anthropology in the Public Arena. Historical and Contemporary Contexts*. Oxford: Wiley-Blackwell.

Machin, N. 1998. '"Government Anthropologist". A Life of R.S. Rattray'. Canterbury: Centre for Social Anthropology and Computing, University of Kent at Canterbury. Retrieved 11 April 2014 from http://lucy.ukc.ac.uk/Machin/.

Mair, L. 1975. 'Anthropology and Colonial Policy', *African Affairs* 74(295): 191–95.

'MI5's mind readers help foil seven terrorist attacks', *The Sunday Times* 7 August 2016, p.16.

Mosse, D. 2005. *Cultivating Development. An Ethnography of Aid Policy and Practice*. London: Pluto.

Mosse, D. 2006. 'Anti-social Anthropology? Objectivity, Objection and the Ethnography of Public Policy and Professional Communities', *Journal of the Royal Anthropological Institute* 21(4): 935–56.

Mosse, D. 2011. 'Introduction: The Anthropology of Expertise and Professionals in International Development', in D. Mosse (ed.), *Adventures in Aidland. The Anthropology of Professionals in International Development*. Oxford: Berghahn Books, pp. 1–32.

Mosse, D. 2013. 'The Anthropology of International Development', *Annual Review of Anthropology 2013* (42): 227–46.

Müller, M. 1891. 'On the Work of Major J.W. Powell, Director of the US Ethnological Bureau', Report of the British Association for the Advancement of Science.

Network of Concerned Anthropologists (NCA). 2009. *The Counter-counterinsurgency Manual*. Chicago, IL: Prickly Paradigm Press.

Nkwi, P.N. 2006. 'Anthropology in a Postcolonial Africa: The Survival Debate', in G.L. Ribeiro and A. Escobar (eds), *World Anthropologies. Disciplinary Transformations within Systems of Power*. Oxford: Berg, pp. 157–78.

Nolan, Riall (ed.). 2013. *A Handbook of Practicing Anthropology*. Hoboken, NJ: Wiley.

Partridge, W.L. 1985. 'Toward a Theory of Practice', *American Behavioural Scientist* 29(2): 139–63.

Pick, D. 1989. *Faces of Degeneration. A European Disorder, c. 1848–c. 1918*. Cambridge: Cambridge University Press.

Potter, J., and I. Litton. 1985. 'Some Problems Underlying the Theory of Social Representations', *British Journal of Social Psychology* 24(2): 81–90.

Price, D. 2011. *Weaponizing Anthropology*. Petrolia, CA: Counterpunch.

Richards, A.I. 1977. 'The Colonial Office and Research', *Anthropological Forum* 4(2): 168–89.

Risley, H. 1911. 'The Methods of Ethnography', *Journal of the Royal Anthropological Institute* 41, January–June: 8–19.

Riviere, P.G. 2007. 'Introduction', in P.G. Riviere (ed.), *A History of Oxford Anthropology*. Oxford: Berghahn Books, pp. 1–20.

Rubenstein, R.A. 2013. 'Master Narratives, Retrospective Attribution, and Ritual Pollution in Anthropology's Engagements with the Military', in R.A. Rubenstein, K. Fosher and C. Fujimura (eds), *Practicing Military Anthropol-*

ogy. Beyond Expectations and Traditional Boundaries. Sterling, VA: Kumarian, pp. 119–33.

Scheper-Hughes, N., and P. Bourgois. 2004. 'Introduction: Making Sense of Violence', in N. Scheper-Hughes and P. Bourgois (eds), *Violence in War and Peace: An Anthology*. Malden, MA: Blackwell, pp. 2–31.

Shannon, S. 2006. 'At the Crossroads of Human Rights and Anthropology: Toward a Critically Engaged Activist Research', *American Anthropologist* 108(1): 66–76.

Shore, C. 2012. 'Anthropology and Public Policy', in R. Fardon, O. Harris, T. Marchand, M. Nuttall, C. Shore, V. Strang and R. Wilson (eds), *The Sage Handbook of Social Anthropology*, Vol. 1. London: Sage, pp. 89–105.

Smart, J. 2006. 'In Search of Anthropology in China: A Discipline Caught in a Web of Nation Building, Socialist Capitalism, and Globalization', in G.L. Ribeiro and A. Escobar (eds), *World Anthropologies. Disciplinary Transformations within Systems of Power*. Oxford: Berg, pp. 69–85.

Spencer, J. 2010. 'The Perils of Engagement: A Space for Anthropology in the Age of Security?', *Current Anthropology* 52(S2): S289–99.

Stewart, M. 2004. Review of MacClancy 2002, *Social Anthropology* 12(3): 382–84.

Stocking, G.W. 1987. *Victorian Anthropology*. New York: Free Press.

Stocking, G.W. 1996. *After Tylor. British Social Anthropology 1888–1951*. London: Athlone.

Strathern, M. 2007. 'Useful Knowledge', *Proceedings of the British Academy, 139, 2005 Lectures:* 73–109.

Suchman, L. 2014. 'Consuming Anthropology', in A. Barry and G. Born (eds), *Interdisciplinarity. Reconfigurations of the Social and Natural Sciences*. London: Routledge, pp. 141–60.

Tandogan, Z.G. 2006. 'Anthropology in Turkey: Impressions for an Overview', in A. Boskovic (ed.), *Other People's Anthropologies. Ethnographic Practice on the Margins*. Oxford: Berghahn Books, pp. 97–109.

Temple, R.C. 1913. 'Suggestions for a School of Applied Anthropology', *Man* 13: 185–92.

Temple, R.C. 1914a. *Anthropology as a Practical Science*. London: G.Bell & Sons.

Temple, R.C. 1914b. 'Anthropological Teaching in the Universities', *Man* 14: 57–72.

Tomlinson, K. 2009. 'Engaging with Local People: More Tea and Fewer Messages', in D. Davis and A.E.R. Woodcock (eds), *Cornwallis XIV: Analysis of Societal Conflict and Counterinsurgency*. The Cornwallis Group, pp. 295–309. Retrieved 6 March 2014 from http://www.TheCornwallisGroup.org. http://www.thecornwallisgroup.org/cornwallis_2009/19-Tomlinson-CXIV.pdf

Turnley, J.G. 2013. 'Pebbles in the Headwaters: Working within Military Intelligence', in R.A. Rubenstein, K. Fosher and C. Fujimura (eds), *Practicing Military Anthropology. Beyond Expectations and Traditional Boundaries*. Sterling, VA: Kumarian, pp. 65–82.

Turton, D. 1988. 'Anthropology and Development', in P.F. Leeson and M.M. Minogue (eds), *Perspectives on Development: Cross-disciplinary Themes in Development Studies*. Manchester: Manchester University Press, pp. 126–59.

Urry, J. 1993. *Before Social Anthropology. Essays on the History of British Anthropology*. Reading: Harwood Academic Publishers.

Varhola, C. 2013. 'Ethnicity and Shifting Identity. The Importance of Cultural Specialists in US Military Operations', in R.A. Rubenstein, K. Fosher and C. Fujimura (eds), *Practicing Military Anthropology. Beyond Expectations and Traditional Boundaries*. Sterling, VA: Kumarian, pp. 101–17.

Von Laue, T.H. 1976. 'Anthropology and Power: R.S. Rattray among the Ashanti', *African Affairs* 75(298): 33–54.

Watkins, A. 1965. 'Portrait. The Academic in Office', *The Spectator*, 29 October, p. 8. Retrieved 4 July 2016 from http://archive.spectator.co.uk/article/29th-october-1965/9/portrait.

Williams, F.E. 1923. *The Vailala Madness and the Destruction of Native Ceremonies in the Gulf Division*. Port Moresby: E.G. Baker, Government Printer.

Wunderle, W.D. 2006. *Through the Lens of Cultural Awareness: A Primer for US Armed Forces Deploying to Arab and Middle Eastern Countries*. Fort Leavenworth, KS: Combat Studies Institute Press.

Young, M.W. 1990. 'Williams, Francis Edgar (1893–1943)', in *Australian Dictionary of Biography*. Canberra: National Centre of Biography, Australian National University. Retrieved 29 April 2014 from http://adb.anu.edu.au/biography/williams-francis-edgar-9109/text16063.

Chapter 2

ON HER MAJESTY'S SERVICE (AND BEYOND)
Anthropology's Contribution to an Unconventional Career
Mils Hills

Introduction

This chapter sets out the author's unconventional career track and attempts to explain the degree to which his qualifications in anthropology have assisted him in gaining unique experience and expertise. Along the way, the controversies that this has created or debates that are touched upon receive comment. Finally, the author identifies a number of clusters of practice that he feels represent critical advantages that an anthropological training has given him and that others may also find useful in considering how to present their transferable skills as they move from graduate to employed status.

My background

It will be difficult to have sympathy for the bold conclusions that I present later in this chapter if the reader is not provided with at least a brief overview of the career path of the author. I gained my MA and PhD in Social Anthropology from the University of St Andrews. As one would expect from St Andrews, the key ethos that ran through my training was one of humanism, interpretativism, the interdisciplinary turn and empathy. My personal research interests were in the construction of identity, sense and worldview. I was committed to challenging orthodoxy, uncovering novel findings and communicating research outcomes in the most effective and necessarily experimental ways possible.

For my doctoral research I passed a very agreeable year living in Mauritius, getting to grips with the nature of the multiple complexities of identity there. Where others (cf. Eriksen 1998) had found Mauritians to be living in a seething cauldron of diversity with internecine conflict barely contained, this was in stark contrast to how I had previously experienced the island, albeit on a brief visit from a year's study abroad on the French Indian Ocean island of La Réunion. Keen to return and discover what was – for me – the truth about Mauritius, my PhD concluded that while there could be tensions from time to time between individuals and communities of varying ethnic/religious/other diversity, generally speaking people lived remarkably peaceable and pragmatically mutually respectful lives.

Having concluded my PhD, I was definitively opposed to entering into the lengthy waiting game for an academic post that was anything other than casual 'as and when' tutoring and occasional lecturing. It was time, I thought, to move away from the domain of commentating from a reserved position and engage with the real world. Fortuitously, as an avid reader of the Tuesday job adverts in *The Guardian* newspaper, I spotted a vacancy in a very applied domain. The post described a desire to recruit social scientists (sociologists, psychologists, anthropologists) to the research agency of the UK Ministry of Defence. After considering the possible perils of working in and around the military – hailing as I did from a peacenik, anti-military, anti-authority family background – I applied.

I was delighted to be invited to interview, at a site bristling with experimental antennae, radar systems and the like, and even more delighted to be successful with my application. I joined (in 1998) a small and unique team, mainly staffed by psychologists, rejoicing in working in a domain known as Information Warfare (IW). At that time a very highly classified activity, we worked to develop new, evidence-based approaches that would enhance our defence and other capabilities to influence the decision-making of others (leaders, groups, states) while protecting the clarity of decision-making of our own military and political structures. The key to success was to be able to merge technical wizardry with human science innovation.

Later rebranded as Information Operations (IO), these approaches have now become much more mainstream to the fundamental activities of military, intelligence and other organisations – from the level of the most junior soldier, sailor or airman/woman up. My task in this team, to which I later rose to be head, was to add cultural insight to the psychological analyses that were already undertaken. Given my interest in worldviews and identity, I set about finding ways in which we could understand emerging situations and exploit opportunities faster than adversaries. I was fascinated by the challenges and options raised by learning from asymmetric adversaries: protestors, terrorists and criminals who – with low budgets, free time and innovative approaches – could achieve significant effects. I led the development of software-based and purely intellectual techniques to interpret vast amounts of open source information enabling the complementing of classified intelligence.

With technical colleagues, I mapped the coming together of religious extremism, use of social networking and alternative financial transaction technologies before this became a commonplace. I particularly relished working with customers with real needs: there were ways in which robust thinking, rapid qualitative research and innovative approaches could deliver real military advantage. Rather than beginning with the assumption that any solution would take a minimum of five years and several hundreds of thousands of pounds of research budget, there were pragmatic and unconventional ways in which substantial benefit could be achieved.

This was an exciting and stimulating role, in an organisation where it was possible to get access to a wide range of complicated problems by dint of one's reputation as a problem solver unafraid of dealing with people from very different technical or customer backgrounds. As my time with the organisation continued, I sought out multidisciplinary projects where, by fusing a deep appreciation of the human sciences with an equally deep understanding of what technology could offer, entirely new thoughts occurred to members of both 'soft' and 'hard' scientific communities. The era of 'socio-technical security' was in full swing.

Having been the first anthropologist to be recruited to the Ministry of Defence (MoD) – there are now a good deal more in the MoD, let alone across government – I found my skills sought after in the design and establishment of an entirely new unit in the Cabinet Office. Government, at the most strategic levels, had found itself embarrassed and largely powerless in the face of a range of events against which it had had no warning. A strike among fire officers, a series of floods, an outbreak of foot and mouth disease and an incredibly dangerous fuel crisis – against a backdrop of the terrorist attack on New York's Twin Towers – led to the recognition that there was a major gap at the heart of government's awareness, preparedness and reflexes. A new structure was needed: lean and pragmatic, it was to be charged with detecting potential crises and to work with partners and stakeholders across and outside of government to either avoid or mitigate the negative effects of such crises.

In other words, early warning of the potential of a hazard and a summation of the potential implications was required. The Cabinet Office, through the mechanisms of the nascent Civil Contingencies Secretariat (CCS), would brief the Prime Minister, through the Permanent Secretary and Security and Intelligence Co-ordinator, and ensure that appropriate measures were put in place across the silos of civil service departments.

The scale of culture change implied here was significant. The Cabinet Office reached out across its communications and other functions to pull in expertise to rapidly develop and deploy this capability. I was fortunate enough to be involved in both the design and then operation of the CCS as government accelerated the closing of the strategic gap identified where ill fortune, natural disasters, criminals, terrorists and hostile states could create pernicious and quite possibly irrecoverable effects. National resilience as a concept came to shape the *raison d'être* of the CCS.

It became apparent through exposure to both strategic and departmental plans and witnessing exercises, reviews of documents, near misses and actual emergencies that there was a major problem with the resilience of government and key partners. Plans, policies and procedures were extensively drafted and redrafted; often tested and re-tested – but when it came to their suitability to real world events, they were found to be absolutely wanting. A small team formed, of which I was one of three members. We developed a fast, hard-hitting and evidence-based technique by which we could research and test any issue. On behalf of the Cabinet Office and with the force of the Prime Minister's authority behind us, we identified - and individuals volunteered - plans, policies, draft legislation and nightmare scenarios that would benefit from having our distinctive approach lavished on them. At speed and with an intensely academic rigour, we would assess the quality of the logic of plans, the reliability of assumptions given, the credibility of the sequence of events anticipated and the availability of critical resources (information, technical expertise). We would speak with key people directly or otherwise implicated in the plan or process and compare their understandings with everyone else's. We would draft scenario-driven exercises that would be opportunities to showcase the effectiveness of a plan or policy – but only if the plan or policy was capable of meeting the requirements which it stated it could deliver.

In most cases, plans and policies failed very early in a test and in spectacular fashion. This was not because the questions asked were too tough, rather that the approach taken to planning was one which very puzzlingly seemed to lure otherwise smart people into believing that they were capable of incredible feats or that 'muddling through' was a safe and appropriate management technique. The assumptions made, the lack of any hope of complicated sequences of events happening in the ways assumed – these and many other basic and fundamental problems made our services much sought after. For as well as finding any gaps or weaknesses, we would also demonstrate integral strength in plans and teams as well as provide key logical and other support in repairing plans, policies and procedures found to be wanting.

This form of 'telling truth to power' was much appreciated by some individuals, departments and agencies who as an inherent value preferred and wanted to know the actual state of preparations. As the team slimmed down, I was commissioned to work with the intelligence agencies, the Prime Minister's Private Office at 10 Downing Street, the Governor and his Executive Team at the Bank of England, the national strategic crisis management facility (COBR) and elsewhere.

Having become convinced of the commercial possibilities of the unique approaches to testing of plans and policies, in 2005 a colleague and I established a small consultancy. We continued offering the same services and were re-engaged by many of the same clients. In addition, we won contracts with commercial organisations where we used proprietary techniques to investigate, analyse and exercise risk control and management plans and processes. Typically, we would review documentation, test plans, develop semi-structured interview scripts and also gain the confidence of employees to, for example, uncover entirely uncontrolled risks, review near misses in a forensic manner and ensure that critical services could be provided even under crisis conditions. Our work led to the direct saving of contracts, income and reputation, potentially to the tune of hundreds of millions of pounds that would have been lost in the event of an emergency.

With the catastrophic collapse of the consultancy market in 2010, I was fortunate enough to be able to transfer my expertise back into the university sector. After a couple of temporary positions, I joined Northampton Business School in 2012. Here, I lead a number of modules at both undergraduate and postgraduate levels, leveraging my experience in government and commerce.

Fighting the self-marginalisation of anthropology

This chapter continues a polemic first committed to print in 2006 (Hills 2006), where I summarised my somewhat unusual career and presented something of a 'call to arms' for fellow anthropologists to explore the possibilities of working in novel employment contexts. This publication, as well as the verbal expressions of earlier and later versions of the paper, proved somewhat controversial. Established elders criticised my professional work – often inelegantly – as being unethical. It is not appropriate, ran the charge, for anthropologists to work with liberal democratic governments, their militaries and intelligence agencies. This is collusion with oppressive, coercive and imperial power. It is wrong and not only should it be condemned – it should be prevented.

Around this time a campaign began led by the (largely self-anointed) guardians of the discipline's ethics to stridently develop an ethical code that would restrict the freedoms of anthropologists. This continued a thread which I discovered that a Joseph Jorgensen had contributed to as long ago as 1971, where he wrote of the need to agree upon and enforce 'ethical standards' (1971: 321). Given the sensitivity of anthropologists (and social scientists more generally) to the potential of the abuse of power intimately connected with the capacity to enforce things on others, this seems rather odd.

Roll forward to the twenty-first century and, in the minutes of the 2007 Annual General Meeting of the Association of Social Anthropologists of the UK and Commonwealth (ASA), we find a response to a written submission that I had made to the ongoing debate about the relevance and justice of 'the discipline' deciding what jobs its members could or should have. The background to this was major UK government investment in a research programme into radicalisation and violence, which spurred a large number of social science faculties to seek to prevent their graduates working directly or otherwise with governments. The minutes record that:

> JG [John Gledhill, ASA chair] has also received correspondence from Mils Hills who does not agree [that anthropologists should abstain from such activities], arguing that we are throwing away an opportunity to work with government. JG noted that his position starts from the premise that the UK government has a duty to protect its citizens from terrorist attack, through intervention in other countries. However, we are not arguing that anthropologists should not inform policy, but that tying research directly to interventionist policy abroad is objectionable. (ASA 2007)

In the United States, the point was reached whereby (relying entirely on media reports and their own prejudices),

> In 2007, the Executive Board of the AAA [American Anthropological Association] determined HTS [Human Terrain Systems – a US defence programme to improve military and related operations by understanding local cultures] to be 'an unacceptable application of anthropological expertise'. [Later], the AAA commission found that HTS 'can no longer be considered a legitimate professional exercise of anthropology' given the incompatibility of HTS with disciplinary ethics and practice. (https://sites.google.com/site/concernedanthropologists/home)

The view of the elders of the discipline in the UK, then, is that it is fine to 'inform policy' in government (and presumably business), but that if these policies are in any way connected to actions overseas, then this is beyond the pale. Does this mean that anthropologists should cease to become involved in development and aid? One wonders. Isn't aid 'interventionist' by definition? But we know what the ASA really means. It has been decided by the ASA that military, intelligence and even perhaps diplomatic work overseas is unethical and objectionable. And there is no conditionality here: no recognition that, say, interventions to avoid humanitarian catastrophe (e.g. by overthrowing a genocidal regime) would be exceptionally permitted.

The word 'interventionist' stands here for something quite different: a political stance that opposes military actions and anything related to them (e.g. defence diplomacy, covert intelligence activity, diplomatic channels). And yet these operations are how liberal democratic states pursue statecraft – this is how we maintain our security: economic, political, military, diplomatic, reputational. This is what states do. It may be unpalatable to some, mysterious to others, unknown to still more, but the exercise of force and influence, the construction of alliances and coalitions is the means by which states achieve their ends, assure their survival and gather friends. The ASA itself takes its non-interventionist stance to an extreme by, for example, refusing to engage with complaints about the conduct of their member anthropologists. Their ethical guidelines state that: 'The ASA does not adjudicate claims regarding unethical behaviour. Rather than intervening, the ASA can act as a forum for discussion among parties to a disagreement over ethics' (ASA 2011: 3). This seems strange. Surely a membership body seeking to impose quality standards on its members precisely *should* adjudicate claims – especially if these arise from aggrieved research subjects? And especially so again if ethical breaches are so obviously detectable by the discipline's guardians?

The ethical guidelines continue to state that:

> Being cognisant of the consequence of one's research activities is particularly relevant when anthropologists consulting for governments, multi-national corporations, invading armies and the military do not prioritise the rights and interests of the local population and in cases where the ostensible aims of the intervention might reasonably be questioned by critical and reflective social scientists. (ASA 2011: 9)

There are problems with this bald statement. Firstly, the term 'invading armies' is provocative. What could be described as 'invasions' by Western militaries and their allies are driven by law and policy – they are designed to achieve a strategic aim, they are not the invasion and occupation of sovereign territory for colonisation by rich Western powers. Secondly, very few military interventions are the preserve of *armies* – joint operations use all three services (army, navy, air forces). Thirdly, who says that anthropologists working for governments, businesses and the military (to say nothing of the intelligence services) do not 'prioritise the rights and interests of the local population'? This may be a fair assumption for many, but it is an un-evidenced assumption nonetheless. And, in counterpoint, given the myriad of completely pointless and often self-defeating humanitarian projects around the world, how can they be defended? The tomato canning factory built in rural Africa that required more water than local resources could supply. The aid interventions that encouraged people to leave their land and become dependent on handouts. The assignment of projects to wealthy and powerful leaders who found yet another tool with which to oppress their subjects. These are all indefensible.

It strikes me that the push to prevent anthropologists who wish to be members of the ASA (or the US equivalent) from working with their own governments in any position of influence is a powerful example of *cultural relativism* and it works because those endorsing it share a *common conspiratorial worldview* about, for instance, the reasons that lie behind the exercise of military and intelligence force by Western liberal democracies.

The cultural relativism in the debate I am confounding here is around the view that it is always wrong to intervene in the affairs of others, except in specific situations of anthropological concern such as the building of a dam in an area occupied by tribespeople. Bloody conflicts over resources, the slaughter of individuals based solely on their ethnicity or other identity, the slavery of generations of families in caste-like systems – all of these forms of life should not suffer intervention other than in the form of fact-finding tours, of attempts to bring people together to generate their own solutions. Or, in the words of the ASA, 'The ASA is committed to conflict resolution through cross-cultural understanding' (ASA 2007).

So even when the rights of some people are being brutally affected, no position should be taken, no intervention made or considered? Those who are the subject of attack are somehow to be encouraged to understand their oppressors? This position may be a morally defensible one to those who believe it; it is just not one that sits with my aspirational view that the Universal Declaration of Human Rights should apply to all. In short, my moral perspective is that those who undertake the oppression, enslavement, torture, genocide and mutilation of others should absolutely expect intervention. Indeed, early and effective intervention should be demanded by the global community of nations.

The ASA's view of intervention by Western states is that it is coercive, exploitative and imperialist. There are motives to intervention which are to do with naked power and aggression. Again, a perfectly defensible stance – but a political one. Having worked inside the UK government during the planning and execution of armed action against the Iraqi regime of Saddam Hussein, underpinned by United Nations Resolution 1441, my take is a rather different one. Indeed, my opinion is based on an understanding of a concept which most anthropologists – and no fault should necessarily be attached to this – would be unaware of: that of strategic deception.

I understand that Saddam Hussein may well not have had a massive capability in terms of Weapons of Mass Destruction (WMD). He had, however, extensively used chemical agents to commit genocide on Kurdish Iraqis and war crimes against Iranian forces. Hussein did understand and effectively exploit the doctrine of strategic deception. Here, doctrine comprises the 'fundamental principles that guide how … military forces conduct their actions'.[1] Saddam Hussein, heavily influenced by and with a system designed by Soviet/Warsaw Pact advisors, understood that deception is:

> a critical tool when attempting to maintain the element of surprise, a principle of war. … The former Soviet Union used deception in support of every level of operation: tactical, operational, and strategic. Their political slant encouraged them to deceive potential adversaries in ways that traditional western values do not promote. (Butts 1999: 1)

Military (intelligence, diplomatic) deception can occur in several forms. The variant that Hussein used was that of the *display*. A display may include one or more of the following:

- Simulations are projections of objects or systems that do not actually exist.
- Disguises are altered objects made to look like something else.
- Portrayals are presentations of units or activities to represent non-existent units or activities. Although considered acts in themselves, portrayals usually include disguises and simulations (United States Army 1994: A7).

As Butts and others note, deception plans contain five elements: objective, target, story, plan and events (Butts 1999: 15). The success of Hussein, it seems to me, was to construct all of the relevant components that would demonstrate to his local – especially Iranian – and other adversaries that he had a functioning WMD programme *even if he hadn't quite or still got it.* This, then, is the ultimate success of a strategic deception: you possess a track record of having developed and used illegal weapons; you have procured materiel that one would need to develop and maintain a WMD programme that encompassed nuclear (or at least radiological), biological and chemical weapons; you have recently undertaken unpredictable acts of violent invasion (Kuwait); you support violent extremist movements in the region and elsewhere; you hold vehicles that have been reported by confidential sources as being mobile weapons laboratories, and so on.

In short, whether or not Hussein had a fully functioning, weaponised WMD capability, he generated a *display* to convince specific audiences within and outside his country that that was exactly what was in existence. Given the gravity with which the possession of WMDs must be treated, it is hardly surprising that the strategic deception worked. Unfortunately, it did not work in the way Hussein and his elite assumed – that there would be leverage in being feared and assumed to have WMDs. Instead, the regime found itself subject to punishing sanctions, pressure and finally overwhelming military might from a coalition of nations operating to a UN Resolution which itself was created in response to the breaching of the ceasefire conditions accepted by Iraq after its expulsion from Kuwait in 1991.

As a friend – much more sighted on these issues than me – puts it, Hussein's problem was that he was trying to simultaneously strategically deceive Iran that he *did have WMD as a deterrent*, while trying to convince the West that he had *dismantled his capability and lost his interest in WMD* (to which there was some truth) (T. Hardie-Forsyth, pers. comm., 30 November 2012). Unfortunately for Hussein, strategic deception is not really a technique that can be compartmentalised. If something looks like a concealed WMD programme, shows all technical indications of being so, is surrounded by secrecy, disinformation and incoherent explanations and produces positive samples for precursor agents and cultures, then it is not unreasonable to conclude that what is actually a fake WMD programme is real. Again, the stakes are so high and the evidence of Hussein's prior enthusiasm to hold and use increasingly sophisticated chemical weapons irrefutable that assuming that the programme was fake was a risk that could not be taken by Western powers. In essence, the culture of the Iraqi regime was one that had encouraged and endorsed the research, development, testing, weaponisation and battlefield/genocidal use of WMD. In anthropological terms, Hussein sought to generate in others a worldview that he both held (and would use) WMDs *and* that he no longer had (and could not use) WMDs.

When anthropological commentators criticise 'invading armies and the military' for their ill consideration of local populations (ASA 2011 *op. cit.*), they cannot be aware that the military themselves, in this case in the United States, even if they fell short in the 2003 Iraq conflict, are fully committed to building the capacity to understand and function effectively in complex cultural contexts. In particular, they have to deal with the challenge of operating in situations where engaging and supporting the local populace may be an integral part of, for example, stabilisation operations that prevent the reoccupation of territory by forces such as the Taliban:

> The Army operates with and among other cultures, engaging adaptive enemies where indigenous populations, varying cultures, divergent politics, and wholly different religions intersect. This requires developing Soldiers who understand that *the context of the problem matters* and that their understanding of the non-military world of foreign societies and cultures be broadened. *Soldiers and leaders need to learn general cultural skills* that may be applied to any environment as well as just-in-time information that is specific to their area of operations. (TRADOC 2011: 11, emphasis added)

Of course, the common conspiratorial worldview differs from the participant-observer's account of strategic deception as a key driver for the Gulf conflict of 2004 presented above. Here, invasions, wars and sinister global activities of public and private sector organisations combine. This is a worldview that assumes a shared anti-imperialist view among anthropologists. Writing on the ASA's *Globalog*, for example, Nancy Lindisfarne (otherwise a contributor to publications of the Socialist Workers Party) writes of an unbroken continuum linking petition-signing anthropologists with the Taliban:

> Resistance to American, and rival, imperialisms takes many forms – from anthropologists who sign the pledge against counter-insurgency, to the activists fighting Coke and the Narmada Dam in India, the thousands of Chinese who are fighting forced homelessness in the run up to the Olympics, Chechen fighters and the Taliban and Iraqis who have resisted occupation so strongly that the US is losing in both these wars. (Lindisfarne 2008)

Of course it is vitally important that in all nations there is a vibrant competition between political ideas and ideologies. Lindisfarne and her fellow travellers contribute to the necessary diversity of opinion that enriches disciplines, debates and discourses. However, *privileging* these accounts of the world does not give anthropology any prestige; indeed, it serves to marginalise it as a discipline, as a force, as a brand. This, it seems to me, is a terrible shame. The 'navel gazing' for which we are famed is a great disincentive for engagement. The discipline's credibility and reputation are compromised by the actions of those who hijack ethical and other debates with their own political perspectives.

Indeed, Fassin (2008, cited in Caduff 2011: 467) concludes that 'moral indignation has become a major resource in the choice of topics to be studied, in particular among younger researchers or students, with the obvious risk of confusion between anthropological interpretation and moral evaluation'. We might usefully add from the analysis of the ASA and AAA above that 'moral indignation' is now leading to confusion over where the dividing line between political stance and impinging on others' personal freedom lies.

Anthropological training, and the type of people the discipline attracts, naturally produces a very broad variety of graduates. Those who continue to practice – in one form or another – anthropological techniques should be able to do so in the service of selling soap powder, understanding the human factors of investment decisions, advising intelligence agencies … or whatever else they wish to do with their careers. It will and should have to be up to individuals to adjudicate whether their activities are 'moral' or 'ethical' or not. The mechanisms of, for example, the International Laws of War and national legislation presumably constrain the activities of all but the most covert operatives, so there is little need for moral panic or righteous indignation that overflow into the development of controls on individuals' career choices.

On this note, I will devote the rest of this chapter to exploring what I believe to be – based on my career experience – some of the particular and peculiar strengths of anthropology and why it should still appeal as a subject to be studied at university and as a degree/advanced degree in candidates invited for interview for a wide range of jobs. In summary: what do I think some of the Unique Selling Points of anthropology are?

My Unique Selling Points of anthropology

As far as I am concerned, the need for a confident and expansionist spirit among the anthropological community remains. The challenges – whether seen from my current position in a business school, in speaking with colleagues working in the cyber and conventional security worlds and in sympathy with governments attempting to manage complex crises – that are faced by profit-focused and public good-driven organisations, by humanitarian agencies and intelligence agencies can all benefit from an injection of anthropological insight. But how can we begin to establish how that insight can be characterised? What are its vital characteristics? What is in the portfolio of techniques and tools that can add value to any commercial or social enterprise? In the following section, I will expand on findings I have previously made about how anthropology has served me well. Anthropology has equipped me with a distinctive approach and personal qualities that have made me (relatively) widely employable – whether as a junior civil servant, national head of a defence research capability, a key component of a Cabinet Office unit, a founding partner of a risk consultancy or a lecturer in a business school.

Sociability

The ability to (when it really counts) achieve high and genuine levels of sociability cannot be overstated as an advantage, whether one works as a consultant or within and across an organisation. Although some have (entertainingly) dismissed anthropologists' key skill as being that of sociability, the fact remains that this is not the devastating blow that it could be because being sociable is actually an uncommon skill. Most of my achievements in private consultancy and work within government have been underpinned by access to information that would otherwise be impossible to acquire had I not been able to socialise with people. Being able to foster trust and confidence, effective in building meaningful connections with individuals (especially those who may be members of 'difficult' stakeholder communities), in maintaining strong ties of emotional intelligence (EQ), I believe that anthropology has given me the ability to engage with a very wide range of audiences and customers. The quality of information that I have been able to source was unparalleled – vital, contained within organisations but unknowable to those who worked within them in conventional ways. I uncovered, for example, massive risks to commercial contracts; exposures to incredible reputational risk; total dependence on obsolete technology; uncovered 'near misses' from which nothing had been learnt and real crises that had not been shared with strategic and legally-liable levels of management.

Cultural translation

C.P. Snow originally noted the existence of the two cultures of intellectual endeavour in a lecture given in 1959 (Snow 2012). They haven't gone away. Indeed, in some ways the boundary between them is more ossified than before. Anthropology, being about cultural translation, has much to offer in mediating across that boundary membrane, to promote positive osmosis. In addition, because anthropology is about making sense of the ways in which people speak and write about their worlds, our familiarity and ingenuity in looking at and using metaphors and other devices can serve cross-cultural communication well. Whereas previously – in the aforementioned 1996 paper from which the previous sentences are taken – I had emphasised the role of anthropologists like myself as usefully being translators between scientific and non-scientific communities, or between various sub-communities *within* the world of science, more recently I have come to realise that another critical way in which I translated between communities was between the managed and the managers; the strategic and the operational. So, for example, by rigorously enforcing anonymity, I was able to represent (or advocate for) the managed to the managers. Where, for instance, undesirable (but to the anthropologist understandable) cultural and political obstacles existed in a company which mitigated against the upward reporting of major concerns (e.g. a known, uncontrolled risk). Here, again, only possible because of the irrefutable guarantee of anonymity and profiting from having generated intense trust and confidence with my informants, my anthropological training enabled me to show to senior managers that what was thought to be a reliable process was/had been/nearly was compromised. In addition, I would communicate the valuable learning point that the cultural/political values of the organisation needed to change such that information of this level of criticality (to multi-billion pound contract delivery) was actively sought and acted upon, and that to be able to rely on the supply of such information, new processes needed to be implemented.

Achieving the understanding of others

As I wrote in 2006, there is inherent value in what we find and in how we interpret and communicate those findings, adding rich, contextual insight where 'understanding is not of words or even of sentences and single statements, but is the communication of another way of understanding things about the world' (Overing 1985: 20). Whether we are involved in the formulation of domestic policy, or inputting guidance to overseas policy (e.g. defence, international development), we can assist policy- and decision-makers in understanding the worldview of others. Not least, this can avoid costly pitfalls that would otherwise occur in the real world. I would argue that the lesson to learn from blunders in military, commercial and humanitarian activities is that there is far more that anthropologists could contribute in the way of solutions than has so far been exploited. For example, in creating situations where narratives of assumptions are gathered, I repeatedly identified huge differences in understandings/assumptions of actions expected in emergency plans between individuals and groups charged with formal responsibilities in those plans. This is important *per se*, and especially so if a plan itself integrates or depends on the outputs of other plans/processes (e.g. a group emergency response that needs to be triggered by a business unit emergency response).

Empathy

As a civil servant or as a consultant, the conventional way of undertaking work is to service the commissioning client's need(s). Although this of course does have to be done, I argue that my career would not have been possible without being trained in the need to and means of empathising with the challenges, realities and dilemmas of, for instance, junior staff in an organisation. However, rather than just commentating on this, I have been able to harness this understanding with the ability to (at least) make recommendations to the client about the sense of addressing the plight of individuals. So, while it may be attempting to agree with senior management that the unhelpful or downright dangerous behaviours of grassroots-level employees need to cease, one adds real value by seeking to understand and communicate how a seemingly irrational and potentially lethal (commercially and otherwise) set of behaviours could emerge from the (mis)directed actions of well-intentioned and actually rational employees who, no doubt, are deeply convinced that what they are doing is right, legal, appropriate and would be endorsed by their bosses. This strikes me as a hugely important element of the possibility that anthropology offers in terms of 'speaking truth to power'. In seeking, for example, to achieve positive culture change in reducing risky work practices, an employer has (at least) two options: (a) engage a 'specialist' company to communicate the need to change, and enforce this policy with sanctions, and (b) understand, swiftly, how people have come to be in a position where their behaviour may, say, be putting their lives, the existential survival of the company and even the liberty of senior management legally responsible for corporate manslaughter on the line. With the second option, there is the prospect of developing pragmatic options to engage with staff to adapt their behaviour, not least by understanding why, typically, workaround solutions get generated by employees struggling to cope with situations where they need to invent solutions to the 'Heath Robinson' style of organisational dysfunction.

Laser-like quality assurance

Fassin states that we anthropologists deploy our discomfort as a heuristic and continue to 'question the values and judgments that underlie our work' (cited in Caduff 2011: 470). I agree. The constant and laser-like ability that we have to constantly challenge our assumptions, models and concepts can make us our own harshest critics. And this is a good thing, if one is in the competitive space of consultancy or of divining a career path that is less conventional than graduate, teach and write, retire. It is in stark contrast to, for example, conventional management consultants who are trained in an 'off the shelf' house process, which they endlessly reapply until it changes or they leave. No doubt other – natural science – disciplines are or have the potential to be equally self-critical, but I have consistently applied a very high level of self-critical reflection on the process, concepts and assumptions that I have deployed.

In conclusion

As this chapter is revisited ahead of moving to press, news coverage is suffused with reports of ever more horrific behaviour by Islamic State (IS), alongside the ongoing decay of fragile states, the continued existence of slavery, emerging resource shortages and occasional breakouts of pandemic human disease. In short, substantial populations of the world are either at risk from or continue to suffer from unjust and unfair forces limiting their freedoms and prospects. Alongside this, governments and their militaries in the West continue to welcome fresh ideas and approaches to help ensure that countries become more resilient to stresses caused by resource shortages, economic and political turbulence and the efforts of others to deliberately destabilise. Anthropologists are pushing on an open door if they have practical ideas to offer.

This chapter will be found by some to be unacceptably provocative. In reality, all I have done is report on how I understand anthropology can contribute to the charting of an individual's career in ways they can and should be best placed to choose. The decisions I have taken and the work I have done have all been informed by my approach to anthropology and an active hunger to 'make a positive difference' to any challenge that has come my way. I have also sought to robustly defend the observation that others must have no role in deciding what is ethical for other practitioners to do, in the way in which, for example, the ASA has blended some (probably minoritarian) political prejudice with apparent ethical concern. Finally, I have set out some of the key strengths which I think anthropology has bestowed on me. There are others, no doubt.

I can think of no more appropriate way to conclude than to express my deepest appreciation for the truly life-changing and career-enabling education and ethics that I received at the University of St Andrews in the lecture halls and seminar rooms of Professor Nigel Rapport, the late David Riches and Sandor Hervey. I am so grateful. To the customers, employers and stakeholders I have had the pleasure and pain of working with, many thanks too.

Mils Hills is Associate Professor of Risk, Resilience and Corporate Security at the University of Northampton. Graduating with a PhD in Social Anthropology from the University of St Andrews and appointed as the UK government's first 'security anthropologist', he has led research, consultancy and teaching activities in the public, private and higher education sectors for almost twenty years.

Note

1. Ministry of Defence, Joint Strategic and Operational Doctrine, retrieved 27 November 2012 from http://www.mod.uk/DefenceInternet/MicroSite/DCDC/OurTeams/JointStrategicAndOperationalDoctrine.htm.

References

Association of Social Anthropologists of the UK and Commonwealth (ASA). 2007. Minutes of the Annual General Meeting, held at London Metropolitan University 1–2.30 pm, 12 April. Retrieved 27 November 2012 from http://www.theasa.org/downloads/minutes/abm/abm07minutes.pdf.
Association of Social Anthropologists of the UK and Commonwealth (ASA). 2011. 'Ethical Guidelines for Good Research Practice'. Retrieved 27 November 2012 from http://www.theasa.org/downloads/ASA%20ethics%20guidelines%202011.pdf.
Butts, G.K. 1999. 'Russian Deception Operations: Another Tool for the Kit Bag'. Fort Leavenworth, KA: School of Advanced Military Studies, United States Army Command and General Staff College. Retrieved 27 November 2012 from http://www.dtic.mil/cgi-bin/GetTRDoc?AD=ADA370313.
Caduff, C. 2011. 'Anthropology's Ethics: Moral Positionalism, Cultural Relativism, and Critical Analysis, *Anthropological Theory* 11(4): 465–80.

Eriksen, T.H. 1998. *Common Denominators: Ethnicity, Nation-building and Compromise in Mauritius*. Oxford: Berg.

Hills, M. 2006. 'Anthropology at the Centre: Reflections on Research, Policy, Guidance and Decision Support', in S. Pink (ed.), *Applications of Anthropology: Professional Anthropology in the Twenty-first Century*. Oxford: Berghahn Books, 130–144.

Jorgensen, J.G. 1971. 'On Ethics and Anthropology', *Current Anthropology* 12(3): 321–334.

Lindisfarne, N. 2008. 'Charlie Wilson's War', *ASA Globalog*. Retrieved 27 November 2012 from http://blog.theasa.org/?cat=37.

Overing, J. (ed.). 1985. *Reason and Morality*, ASA Monographs 24. London: Tavistock Publications.

Snow, C.P. 2012. *The Two Cultures*, Cambridge: Cambridge University Press.

TRADOC. 2011. 'The US Army Learning Concept for 2015', Department of the Army, TRADOC Pam 525-8-2, January. Retrieved 27 November 2012 from http://www.tradoc.army.mil/tpubs/pams/tp525-8-2.pdf.

United States Army. 1994. 'Psychological Operations Techniques and Procedures', Field Manual, Appendix A, Deception Operations. Retrieved 26 November 2012 from http://library.enlisted.info/field-manuals/series-3/FM33-1-1/APPA.PDF.

Chapter 3

YOU CAN'T GO HOME AGAIN
Anthropology, Displacement and the Work of Government
Benjamin R. Smith

Displacement has always been part of the human life course. But it is an ever more pervasive aspect for most of those living in the 'late modern West' and for the majority of those living elsewhere as well. In the novel from which I take my title, Thomas Wolfe gestures towards these intertwined displacements – those that have always shaped our life paths, and those induced by broader global changes. As Wolfe suggests, these displacements leave each of us unable to go 'back home' not only to our family, childhood and places from our past, but also to 'the old forms and systems of things which once seemed everlasting but which are changing all the time' (Wolfe [1940] 1998: 666).

Those who have undergone the traditional anthropological rite of passage experience a further displacement from the forms and systems of things we once took for granted. Many who have gone through doctoral fieldwork have accommodated the resulting displacement through their membership of a professional anthropological community. But others experience yet further displacement by moving on from anthropology to find work elsewhere.

Six years after moving from academia to the Civil Service, I set out in this chapter some reflections on my own transit through applied anthropology to government social research and policymaking. Through these reflections, I try to understand how my anthropological background has shaped my experience of new kinds of work.[1]

My main concerns in this chapter include the ways in which anthropological training may or may not prepare anthropologists for the kinds of work they find themselves undertaking. I also consider whether my own experience beyond the academy might indicate something more general about the relationship between anthropology and the 'work of government'.[2] This leads me to reflect upon what the application of anthropology might mean in practice. I develop these reflections both in relation to my previous applied anthropological work and my later work 'within' government as a social researcher and policymaker. At first glance, my applied anthropological work may appear less related to the forms of public service that are the principal concern of this collection than my more recent work in the Civil Service (if we take public service to imply the work of government). But this presumption is complicated by the ways in which the distinction between work 'inside' and 'outside' of government is not as simple as one might think – a point I also take up below.

In attempting to understand the relationship between anthropology and the work of government, I further argue that both the possibilities and the limits of applied anthropological work flow, in part, from the marginality of the anthropological practitioner. In seeking to understand this marginality and its relation to my own professional practice, I draw on James Weiner's (2001: 151) underscoring of the inseparability of anthropology's methodology and subject matter, an observation that points to the way in which anthropology is simultaneously a social practice and a social science.

Lastly, in considering the new skills I have had to learn beyond the academy, I link the nature, possibilities and limits of anthropology to my experience of applied practice and work in the Civil Service. The affective dimension of such experiences can be particularly telling for anthropologists, including those who have 'left' the discipline. In particular, I suggest that affective experiences can help us to recognise the points at which other (non-anthropological) modes of practice exist in tension with an underlying anthropological ethos.[3] In the context of a shift from anthropology to public service, this affective dimension also sheds light on the trajectory of the anthropologist as he or she moves into a new role. My presumption here, of course, is that whatever else they may become, the former anthropologist nevertheless continues to experience new roles anthropologically.

Anthropology and the work of government

At the outset, it seems useful to say something about my understanding of both anthropology and government. In his introduction to this volume, MacClancy recalls Malinowski's account of anthropology's threefold character, which sees the anthropologist attend simultaneously to what his or her respondents 'say they do, what they [actually] do, and how they justify the gap between the two'.

Like MacClancy, I think Malinowski's definition remains apposite. However, I believe it also misses a vital aspect of our discipline and its practice. Alongside its focus on an ethnographic understanding of our respondents, I consider anthropology now (and indeed in the 1930s) to be essentially reflexive. As such, it sheds a comparative and particularising light on our own ways of thinking and doing, either explicitly or implicitly. Moreover, as anthropology has itself become globalised, drawing in practitioners from non-Western backgrounds, this reflexive and comparative aspect has become ever more important. Anthropologists need to be aware of where they are speaking from, not only to avoid the ever-present risk of ethnocentrism, but also in order to develop effective interdisciplinary conversations. Beyond such conversations, and those with our respondents, the failure to sufficiently acknowledge and develop this reflexive and comparative dimension also hampers healthy dialogue with those 'ex' anthropologists now working in public service.

Like other integral aspects of anthropological practice, I understand the reflexive aspect of anthropology to be vested in an underlying disciplinary ethos. Broader and deeper than ethics, 'ethos' refers to the distinguishing character, sentiment, moral nature or guiding beliefs of a person, group or institution.[4] I see the anthropological ethos as an often unconscious orientation taken on by those of us who have trained as anthropologists, particularly where we have undertaken postgraduate training based on immersive fieldwork. As such, the anthropological ethos is primarily a particular form of subjectivity rather than a set of conscious anthropological values, although such values, including our professional ethics, stem from it.[5]

This ethos is vested in anthropology's general situation as a social science, as well as the disciplinary history of anthropological relationships with respondents.[6] I consider the academic aspect of our ethos to have been somewhat weakened in recent years, as anthropology has sought to justify its existence vis-à-vis those with whom we work in the field. Needless to say, our engagement with postcolonial critiques of anthropology has been both valid and essential, not least in our efforts to resolve questions regarding rights of representation. But the cost of this engagement appears to have been a weakening of anthropologists' overarching commitment to impartial enquiry. I do not believe this is a price anthropology can afford to pay, however difficult it may be to resolve the tensions between our academic concerns and our respondents' worldviews and projects.

Such tensions remind us that the practice of anthropology should displace us not only from our own previous certitudes, but also from simple endorsement of the values and beliefs of those with whom we work. Properly practised, anthropology leads to the double experience of displacement that led Lévi-Strauss to describe anthropology as a *technique du dépaysement* ([1963] 1977: 117, 118–19). This double displacement is not incidental; it lies at the heart of our professional efficacy.[7]

Before moving on to discuss my own experience of working beyond anthropology, I should also briefly outline my understanding of government. In common with other recent anthropological accounts (e.g. Aretxaga 2003; Scott 1998; Shore and Wright 1997; Trouillot 2001), as well as the work of Foucault (e.g. [1982] 1983), I do not limit government to its formal apparatus. Rather, I see government (or 'the state'; also 'policy') as having a profoundly processual character, being (re)produced through particular practices that may not necessarily be formally understood as governmental; as such, I understand government to be more diffuse in character than might normally be the case. There is a marked disjuncture between this view and what might be called the 'folk theory of government'. The latter perspective sees government as an entity distinct from everyday lifeworlds even as it acts upon them, imposing itself through laws, regulations and formal state agents, e.g. the police, welfare officers, civil servants and so on. Contrary to this view, recent social or sociocultural accounts, including my own (Smith 2008a, 2008b), tend to understand government as inhering in a broader set of practices, values and orientations – both formal and informal – that involve the governed as much as those who govern them.

This latter understanding of government is of considerable importance for anthropology in general, and appears not to have had the impact that it should have had within the discipline. For academic anthropologists, this has meant a paucity of accounts of the saturation of the state within the local, and of the interaction of local social fields with the various forms of governmental action that press upon them (Shore and Wright 1997: 12–14). For applied anthropologists, the failure to take on board this more diffuse understanding of government risks a lack of awareness of one's positionality, with profound implications for applied work; even those forms of applied or activist anthropology that might be considered to be 'against the state' may, in fact, do far more to extend the forms and logics that embed the state in other people's lives than we may realise or wish to admit.

Training and trajectory

'You can't go home again' is a maxim that could be applied to anyone who has gone through what Margaret Mead called the anthropological 'puberty ritual' of first fieldwork and the return to the academy (Wafer

1996: 271). In my case this experience and its accompanying sense of displacement and growth have been followed by a subsequent move away from the academy and into the UK's Civil Service. If the ritual passage usually moves through stages of separation, transition and re-incorporation (van Gennep 1961) – with fieldwork constituting anthropology's liminal phase – then my own trajectory has been compounded by further transitions of role and milieu. This has added a sense of displacement from anthropology to the inherently anthropological sense of displacement that preceded it.

My professional trajectory began with undergraduate and initial doctoral studies at the London School of Economics. This led to a decision to undertake fieldwork on an Aboriginal 'outstation movement' in remote northeast Australia, analysing contemporary patterns of spatial mobility and the social significance of place. At that time (the mid 1990s), many commentators – including policymakers and NGOs as well as anthropologists – understood outstation movements to involve a 'return to homelands' by Aboriginal people. This supposed return followed prior, forced movements to centralised settlements after the colonial dispossession of Aboriginal lands.

My research suggested that things were more complicated (e.g. Smith 2002, 2004, 2008a). Most of the people I worked with were as committed to maintaining their connections to the larger central settlements to which their families had been relocated as they were to living on their putative homelands (despite endemic social problems in the larger settlements). Moreover, rather than marking a shift away from white control to an 'Aboriginal domain' in the bush, the outstation movement I worked on was deeply shaped by the intercultural social field in which my Aboriginal respondents were situated. This intercultural aspect was apparent, for instance, in Aboriginal engagement with government and non-governmental development projects at the outstations and the resources associated with them. These realisations led me to move beyond simple social and cultural distinctions (e.g. 'Aboriginal'/'mainstream') in an attempt to better understand the complexities apparent in my respondents' day-to-day lives.

Over time my own anthropological practice also became more complicated. While completing my doctoral research, I began working as an applied anthropologist on a number of indigenous land claims and development projects. I undertook this work alongside my academic work, despite the misgivings of my supervisor.[8] Although it was based on further fieldwork, this applied work necessarily involved learning how to work to particular governmental and organisational criteria – for example, producing expert reports that addressed the evidentiary requirements of the state or federal legislation that underpinned Aboriginal land claims.

This shift in practice was also accompanied by an academic relocation, leading to a subsequent shift in the focus of my research. Following the completion of my PhD, and after a brief (and unsuccessful) interlude working as a staff anthropologist for a regional Aboriginal organisation, I spent six years working in the Australian National University's Centre for Aboriginal Economic Policy Research (CAEPR).[9] My position as a CAEPR postdoctoral and research fellow saw me writing policy discussion papers alongside academic articles and consultancy reports. I also convened a Masters course in applied anthropology. Despite significantly increasing my workload, this proved to be a fairly productive period. In particular, it spurred me to reflect academically on my applied practice, analysing the social effects of land claims in particular communities (see Smith and Morphy 2007; Smith 2008b).

But while the opportunities for reflexivity mostly offset the strain of moving between academic and applied work, I felt increasingly uncomfortable about my work on land claims. This was so despite the catharsis offered by my reflexive academic engagement with claim work, the access to the field provided by applied projects and the sense that land claim work was a use of my skills (and presence) that my respondents considered to be beneficial. My discomfort increased when I moved away from the region in which I had conducted my doctoral fieldwork to begin work on land claims with Aboriginal groups elsewhere.

The first real instance of this discomfort occurred during the six months I spent working with the regional Aboriginal organisation that employed me prior to my move to CAEPR. While I was used to working in local Aboriginal communities and had worked alongside similar organisations previously, that experience had not prepared me for working within an organisation of this kind. The organisation's principal role was to broker Aboriginal people's engagement with land claims and linked negotiations with non-governmental stakeholders (e.g. mining companies; the development of a gas pipeline). This meant that my own role as a staff anthropologist included the facilitation of assertions of customary Aboriginal interests in land and associated resources, including supporting decisions about which Aboriginal people did and did not have a stake in a particular instance and what rights they might reasonably assert. This work involved formal and informal meetings with groups of putative 'traditional owners' who were often involved in protracted disputes over the nature of customary land tenure in a given area, the commissioning and assessment of reports by anthropological and other consultants, and playing a leading role in meetings and negotiations between our Aboriginal clients and the governmental and non-governmental organisations looking to progress 'business' on their land.

My involvement with this work left me feeling that I was caught in a marginal space between local Aboriginal families and a supposedly representative Aboriginal organisation. On the one hand, I felt compelled to orient myself with my Aboriginal clients, many of whom deeply distrusted the organisation I was employed by. However, my lack of previous or ongoing substantial engagement with them meant there was little of the trust or familiarity I had established with respondents in other contexts – a situation further complicated by endemic disputes between Aboriginal families across the region. Such an orientation also risked undercutting my obligations to my employers. But I also found it difficult to align myself with an organisation whose policy was predominantly set by an executive dominated by mostly non-indigenous lawyers and senior managers, and which (necessarily) sought simple solutions to complex social and political issues.[10] These tensions led to a deeply uncomfortable period, during which neither my employers nor I were satisfied with how I positioned myself with regard to my role. Thankfully this period was brought to an end by the offer of a postdoctoral fellowship.[11]

Although I failed to realise it at the time, the strong sense of marginality I experienced while working in this organisation was not simply a matter of a lack of personal 'fit'. In retrospect, I believe that my experience of disjuncture can be explained by the problems anthropology poses for those – including anthropologists themselves – who seek to utilise anthropological expertise in practical projects. I think that these problems are broadly threefold. They stem, firstly, from the dense, context-specific and not necessarily convenient (or easily applicable) understandings that flow from anthropological work. These problems are also linked to the relational practice through which anthropological understanding is established. Lastly (and paradoxically, given the simultaneous importance of anthropological relationality), these problems are profoundly tied to the marginality and singularity of the anthropological subject position. These problems came rapidly to the fore during my period of employment at the organisation that had employed me as a staff anthropologist.

Despite their seemingly non-governmental character, I have come to understand organisations of the kind I worked for and the forms of recognition of indigenous ties to land that they broker to be aspects of the work of government constitutive of the late-modern state. Such organisations (and the applied anthropology undertaken on their behalf) not only further encompass Aboriginal people within state formations; they also unavoidably embed state-oriented ways of acting and thinking within the day-to-day lives of Aboriginal people (Smith 2008b).

The work of government is particularly evident in the anthropological production of expert reports that identify particular groups (e.g. 'clans', 'tribes') as holding interests in clearly delineated areas of land, establish the customary bases for these interests and set out what particular rights and interests should be granted or recognised within the 'mainstream' legislative framework through which a land claim is being determined. Such reports enable the 'recognition' of indigenous systems of land tenure within the prevailing social and legal system (see Povinelli 2002; Smith and Morphy 2007; Weiner 2003).

Over time – and as I undertook my own research on the social effects of land claims – it became apparent that the accounts of local organisation in expert reports were not simply anthropological or legal constructions distinct from local Aboriginal practice. Rather, the 'thin simplifications' (Scott 1998) set out in these reports, and the broader legal and governmental processes that utilised them, were folding back into local practice and thus becoming part of the social reality of local communities. For example, these accounts led to the legal incorporation of formal landholding groups or new local Aboriginal organisations established to exercise newly granted rights in land. This folding back has transformed the ways in which many Aboriginal Australians exercise their proprietary interests. This has affected Aboriginal people's relations both with the state and with non-indigenous interests; it has also affected relationships between Aboriginal people themselves, despite the common presumption of distinct Aboriginal domains continuing to exist beyond the ambit of the state.[12] As such, it became evident to me that my applied work was inextricably tied to the way in which the state comes into being through a combination of external 'subjection' and internal 'subjectification' in particular social fields (Shore and Wright 1997: 9) – that is to say my work was, in effect, substantively deepening the grip of state within my respondents' lives.

Even where anthropologists are willing to work within the state's parameters, anthropology's relationship with the work of government is not necessarily an easy one. My own experience in Australia suggests that anthropological practice is often at odds with the requirements of those who commission applied work. This may be the case even where anthropological efforts are focused on meeting requirements apparently abstracted from local social life, e.g. the evidential requirements of a land claim process. Here, and more generally, the specificity of anthropological descriptions and analyses and the surfeit of detail and lack of generalisability this entails tend to present problems. Typically, ethnographic specificity will need be ironed out or cut down to provide a focused account in line with the requirements of a particular applied process or project.[13] Even where this is accomplished successfully, this process of simplification is likely to leave the anthropologist unsatisfied.

Anthropologists' interpersonal engagements with respondents may also pose difficulties for applied projects. In particular, these engagements tend to immerse us in local politics. They may also draw us into respondents' complaints about the processes and organisations with which we are engaged beyond the local community. In Aboriginal land claim work, this can result in a tension between the expectations of those organisations formally commissioning and directing a land claim process and those of local Aboriginal people who, understandably, presume anthropologists are 'working for them'.

These discrepancies between anthropological practice and the requirements of a given process require a workable compromise between collapsing the project that the anthropologist has been commissioned to deliver and alienating those subject to that project. Given the anthropological tendency towards split loyalties in such situations, it is no surprise that lawyers are the professionals who dominate Aboriginal land claim processes and the organisations that manage them, while anthropologists remain marginal to both.

In my Australian work, the tensions between the work of anthropology and the work of government were often apparent. This was particularly true in situations in which I had long-running ties with the Aboriginal groups involved in a land claim. Nevertheless, in some cases the two forms of work did not prove completely irreconcilable. In at least some instances I was able to bring together my knowledge of Aboriginal social practices, an understanding of the legal processes in which I was engaged, and relatively good relationships with both claimants and those managing land claims. This allowed me to produce accounts of Aboriginal social organisation that were not overly reifying, allowing some space for the fluidity of Aboriginal social and political life within the new social forms introduced into local lifeworlds by land claim processes.

Elsewhere, however, my experience of land claim work was less positive. Over time, case law in Australia has led to an increasingly restrictive, formulaic and legally dominated approach to 'recognition' of Aboriginal rights and interests. Despite the opportunities for observing state formation in action – and hopefully mitigating some of its worst excesses – I felt that enough was enough. In combination with questions about the sustainability of my academic position and the birth of my son, my growing dissatisfaction with land claim work led me to a decision to return to the UK.

The anthropologist as civil servant

In the UK, the slog of academic job applications, a longstanding ambivalence about lecturing and the unfamiliar experience of writing while halfway around the world from my field site all led to my becoming increasingly uncertain about an academic career. Casting around for other options, I came across a recruitment campaign for Government Social Researchers and decided to apply.[14] Somewhat to my surprise, I found the recruitment process fairly enjoyable. In part, this was because it touched on aspects of my previous applied work that I had found satisfying. These included project management, working in multidisciplinary teams and finding ways to resolve real life problems. During the 'competency-based' Civil Service recruitment process, I realised that my enjoyment of these aspects of my previous work had allowed me to develop a set of useful (and saleable) professional skills beyond social analysis, or even policy evaluation.

After a brief spell in a 'pool' of successful GSR applicants, I found myself in my first Civil Service job, heading up the European and international research team in the UK Border Agency's Analysis, Research and Knowledge Management Directorate ('ARK'). The principal work of my team proved engaging, although there was little substantive social research involved. Instead I found myself overseeing the production of reports on various aspects of the UK's migration and asylum policy, leading on the UK's engagement with the Brussels-based European Migration Network, working with policymakers to identify and meet their information and analytic needs and coordinating a national network of academics and NGO researchers working on migration issues.[15] While other colleagues within my new directorate were undertaking or commissioning original social research, I quickly realised that much of that work was radically removed from the kinds of qualitative social research with which I was most comfortable. Instead, the focus of their research was predominantly quantitative, and focused on surveys or statistical information.[16] Even where the approach of ARK's work was more qualitative (e.g. an interview-based evaluation of the integration of deaf migrants – see Parr, Bashir and Robinson 2010), the methodology was necessarily more constrained and time-limited than in the work I had undertaken previously, even during my applied consultancy projects. Over time, I understood better why there are relatively few Government Social Researchers with an anthropological background, even though GSR staff have a wide range of social science backgrounds, with many holding Masters degrees or doctorates.[17]

Despite this, I found my new role interesting and energising. There was a certain satisfaction to be found in the production of clear, concise reports that were potentially of use both within and outside of government. And my role as the lead for the UK's National Contact Point for the European Migration Network, which develops cross-EU comparisons of national migration, asylum and border policies, provided an opportunity to come to grips not only with policymaking in the UK, but also the wider European governmental and political context. My work also allowed me to gain an understanding of the state from the 'inside'. (Indeed, the opportunity to develop such an understanding was one of the factors that attracted me to the Civil Service in the first place, given my earlier academic research on the state and government.)

I also gained considerable satisfaction from my engagements with external research colleagues, including organising conference-style events to bring together external experts and migration policymakers. The challenges of management, of decision-making and of reshaping the work of my team and its relationship to the wider department also proved stimulating. Even the requirement to continually demonstrate the 'value added' by my team's work at a time of austerity proved to be oddly satisfying.

However, after a period in GSR, I became increasingly interested in the work undertaken by policy colleagues. This interest was driven by my growing sense that the skills of a qualitative researcher were better suited to a policy role, at least within the Home Office. Government Social Researchers are generally focused on more quantitative approaches; this focus is also expected by their policy 'customers'.[18] Building on contacts I had made in the course of the previous sixteen months, I took the opportunity of a colleague's maternity leave to move across to my current policy role.

After twelve years of applied and academic research in Aboriginal Australia and a brief stint working as a Government Social Researcher, I now find myself leading the Home Office's EU Migration Policy and Strategy team. My principal focus is the UK's engagement with the EU on migration, border and asylum policy. In day-to-day terms this means working with other policymakers and operational leads to develop a coherent set of positions on the EU's migration policies and their impacts on the UK, drafting briefings and speaking notes for ministerial and senior officials' meetings in Brussels, representing the UK in official-level EU working groups involved in the agreement of new policy, overseeing the development of strategy for negotiations with European and other international partners and coordinating the government's engagement with European institutions (e.g. the European Council and the European Commission) and other member states. This work has put me at the intersection of two sensitive policy areas – migration and Europe – and given me the opportunity to help develop the EU's policy response to irregular migration during a period of intense political and humanitarian concern.[19]

Anthropological limits

My more recent move through Government Social Research to policymaking sheds further light on the character and limits of anthropological practice, whether academic or applied, and the effects of an underlying anthropological ethos on our work beyond the discipline.

In my case, my career trajectory has necessitated developing a range of skills beyond those associated with the core practices of academic anthropology. These include developing policy, operating as part of a complex bureaucracy (and its associated hierarchy) and managerial and administrative skills.[20] My career has also required me to adjust to the inherent limits of my own anthropological and academic orientation. This has led to me having to unlearn some of what had become almost 'second nature' in order to succeed within the Civil Service.

In particular, I have had to learn to curtail written and oral reflection on a given question, both when briefing senior officials and in exchanges with peers. That is not to say such reflections are not useful (they often are). But they tend to irritate colleagues who are strongly inclined towards concise, direct and needs-focused exchanges and so need to be managed carefully. It is not uncommon for one or another colleague of mine to remark that a particular view is 'academic' – a response tinged with both mild disapproval and, perhaps, a twinge of insecurity. Certainly, ministers and senior officials tend to give short shrift to what are seen as woolly or overly speculative approaches.

As a manager, I have also had to adjust to delegating work to others (despite having had some experience of team working as a consultant) and not being able to be expert on all the issues my team are working on. Here I have had to overcome the habitual autonomy of the anthropologist, and the academic and fieldworker's customary expertise, in order to develop effective working methods.

But my previous anthropological work has also left me well equipped to take on some of the challenges of my current role. For instance, my academic background has left me with a relatively well-developed ability to prepare policy-relevant documents and give oral presentations (although, as already noted, I have had to learn to make these less academic in style and inclination). Anthropological writing has definitely left me equipped to work with narrative, the principal rhetorical tool of the policymaker and an integral aspect of any successful negotiation.

I also believe my anthropological background has provided me with a particular advantage in building relationships and networks, and using these to develop and deliver successful policies. Unlike many of my colleagues, who tend towards what is commonly labelled as a 'silo mentality' (i.e. insular working, focused on a team, directorate or department's own interests), my tendency is to build relationships with interested others and to seek to understand their interests and aims. The importance of this kind of working is continually emphasised in the contemporary Civil Service, but cuts against the cultural grain nevertheless. As well as building relationships, my anthropologically influenced approach also helps me to get to grips with a particular policy question by taking on the views of experts and stakeholders. While expert views can play badly in the 'strategic centre' of a government department ('too much detail', 'not demonstrating a "can do" attitude'), they are vital to developing effective policy and intra-departmental, cross-government or international partnerships. I have little doubt that this is an area in which my anthropological ethos leaves me better placed than many of my peers.

Like anthropology, the Civil Service has a form of professional subjectivity at its heart that underpins a particular body of skills and their practical development. In the case of both professions, this inherent manner of thinking and acting is developed primarily through an extended apprenticeship. For anthropologists this means fieldwork and mentoring by one's supervisor, alongside a deepening appreciation of the work of one's forebears. For civil servants this apprenticeship involves the gradual accrual of competence and an underlying process of enculturation as one works one's way up through a series of positions within and between departments. This process of advancement is strongly focused on a growing understanding of the challenges and working methods of the managerial grades above one's own (as well as the requirements of ministers and the broader political environment[21]), with such an understanding acting as a precursor to promotion.

If anthropologists work best as marginal observers of a social field, policymakers are positioned somewhat differently. They (we!) are aware of their role in reshaping the social, steered by the mandate and objectives of their political masters. However, they tend to operate at several degrees of remove from the social fields on which their policies operate (see Scott 1998). As such, while policy sets out desired outcomes and the principal means through which these should be pursued, it relies upon a set of operational mechanisms to deliver these. These mechanisms extend through intra- and inter-departmental relationships, down to local interventions by public servants and others implementing a given policy. This implementation chain unavoidably introduces a range of indeterminacies and unintended consequences.[22]

For civil servants, like anthropologists, there are matters of ethos and ethics at play through all of this. The indeterminacies of policy commence with the relationship between ministers of state and the civil servants charged with turning the bare bones of their political mandate into more fully developed and implemented policies. This creates a fair amount of leeway, in some cases allowing for significant deviation from ministers' original intentions. Such deviation may be unintended or intentional. Civil servants' ethic of public service notwithstanding, the scope for elaboration necessarily afforded to policymakers and those implementing government policies tests the notion of an unpoliticised, unelected Civil Service simply delivering the government's programme.

This quotidian aspect of government also tests the claims civil servants make about themselves, recalling Malinowski's distinction between 'what they say' and 'what they do' and how the gap between the two is accounted for. Like any large and complex social field, the formal institutions of government are constituted in a series of locales, including the various departments, directorates and teams at its putative 'heart' or 'centre' and periphery, and the networks established between these. The day-to-day interactions necessary to undertake the work of government are as socially and culturally constituted as those within any other social field, riddled with personal projects and interpersonal politics. As an Australian colleague and former public servant once noted, apropos of my academic work on the state in Aboriginal Australia, despite being fundamentally constitutive of the state, on its 'inside' government is in many ways as acephalous as any traditional Aboriginal lifeworld.[23]

Seeing the Civil Service as operating through a particular body of practices, themselves based on an underlying ethos, sheds further light on the experience of those who have moved into this profession from elsewhere. Such a move does not simply involve an adjustment to a new field of practice with its own norms, values and language. It may well also involve friction between these norms and values and one's own, previously established modes of thinking and acting.

The persistence of a particularly anthropological ethos, its limitations within a different professional setting and the affective aspect of the resulting experience of personal disjuncture from one's new milieu have all been apparent in my own move to the Civil Service. For example, I see a distinct difference between my own approach to a meeting or policy discussion and that of many of my colleagues. As middle ranking and senior civil servants with many years' experience of policy-making,[24] they are more forthright in asserting their own positions, and confident in their opinions, decisions and handling of policy questions. For the most part, they seek to lead, or strongly shape the situations in which they participate. I am increasingly aware that my own approach is marked by a different, more hesitant and reflective style of thinking and interpersonal orientation that can leave the role of a policymaker feeling like an ill-fitting suit.

Other interactions bring home how my professional personhood continues to be reshaped by my non-anthropological engagements. Working with the network of external experts – some of them anthropologists – while leading UK Border Agency's European and international research team made it clear to me that I had rapidly taken on something of the ethos of my new profession. While many of these external colleagues were content to occupy what Andrew Garner, a fellow ex-anthropologist, calls the 'position of eternal comment',[25] I found myself more than occasionally frustrated with the limited applicability of much of their research in a policy context. I also struggled with the apparently unfocused character of many of their interventions in exchanges with policymakers, and their lack of awareness both of the factors shaping policymakers' positions and how their analytic interventions might best inform or constructively criticise these.[26]

This disjuncture between anthropologists and policymakers is closely linked to an anthropological and broader academic disdain regarding those colleagues employed within government departments and agencies. MacClancy (this volume) notes the way in which 'ex' anthropologists working in the public service may experience themselves as being shunned by those who have remained in the academy. I have certainly noticed this from time to time and I have experienced a measure of unease on the part of academic colleagues more generally, even where my exchanges with them have been relatively fruitful.

A degree of ambivalence was already apparent among some of my academic colleagues when I was working on Aboriginal land claims. At that time, I suspect that reaction was due to the fact that, while my consultancy work marked a shift away from 'pure' academic work, it simultaneously justified undertaking anthropological research through its focus on achieving 'concrete outcomes' for those I was working with.

For that reason, I have noted with interest the growing focus of academic anthropologists on work that has 'impact', alongside the growth of a self-identifying 'activist anthropology'. The need to demonstrate impact is doubtless related to the changing character of research grants. But it seems to me that both of these developments also involve a deeply felt need for anthropology to 'do' something beyond participating in and observing others' communities for academic purposes. Certainly, I have noticed that applied work has provided some measure of relief for colleagues who have become deeply uncertain of the ethical defensibility of their work.

Despite my own applied background, I remain concerned about these disciplinary developments. In part this is because they seem to mark an unwillingness to commit to anthropology as a good in and of itself. Of course, the 'applied' and 'activist' turns both respond to an ethical need; it feels increasingly important to justify our existence to those who fund our research (the putative 'taxpayer' in particular), as well as to those who accommodate us and lend themselves to our scrutiny. But I worry that these developments simultaneously mark a shrinking away from anthropology as an academic project. In my view, the sine qua non of that project is to pursue the insights offered through the ethnographic method and the development of anthropological theory, however irrelevant or even inconvenient these insights may prove to our interlocutors. Similarly, a properly 'applied' anthropology must hold to its inconvenient insights as best it can, however difficult that may prove in practice.

If anthropology involves an ethical commitment to the pursuit of its insights regarding others, this also implies a reflexive obligation for anthropologists to unpack their own biases. On that basis, I regard the disdain of many academic anthropologists towards those working for the government as not merely disappointing, but also as profoundly un-anthropological. The inherent moral certainty such moments of disdain make visible departs from our discipline's commitment to remaining open to social realities and understanding their complexities, as well as the growing need for anthropology to extend the scope of its engagement from the local to the broader domains of the regional, national and global. That is not to say that anthropology should not be critical of government and its projects. But such critiques must draw on a nuanced understanding of why particular governmental projects exist, and the (social) fact that they arise from governmental actors' efforts to respond to real or perceived public needs. Without such a nuanced and balanced approach, anthropological critiques of government risk becoming merely ideologically based performances of 'the good', undertaken at a safe distance.[27] Such performances not only fail to attend to what others actually do and say; they also fail to turn anthropological awareness back onto anthropology's own concepts, actions and lacunae.

Conclusion

My experience of applied anthropology and my move from anthropology to the Civil Service have both touched on the uneasy relationship between anthropology's underlying ethos and the work of government. I believe that this unease can draw our attention to the ways in which our applied work may exceed what might be properly considered to be anthropology, where that term implies a profoundly dialogic engagement with our respondents.[28] When we move from the margins to intervene in and reshape a particular social field, we may exceed our disciplinary ethos even as our actions draw from the insights anthropological practice offers us. Moreover, unless we attend carefully to the trajectories of our practice, this shift may not be noticed, and may even be masked by our self-identity as 'applied' or 'activist' anthropologists.

Conversely, I have also suggested that while we may stray even further from our previous anthropological 'home' (the academy, the field) into new forms of professional work (the Civil Service for example), our anthropological ethos tends to persist, often sitting uneasily alongside our new roles and practice.

Our affective responses to these moments of disjuncture seem to mark the limits of anthropology as they are encountered in our professional practice. In my land claim work, for example, there were definite moments of affective strain, particularly at those moments where reified category and legal process overrode my engagement with respondents, marking key points where the state (manifested partly through my work) and the local Aboriginal lifeworld (and my empathetic orientation towards it) were at odds with one another. More recently, I think some of my affective experiences in the Home Office mark those points where – as a professional who remains an anthropologist 'at heart' – my subjective or ethical inclinations and the needs of my role are not well aligned.

But it is not only moments of concern that are flagged by their affective dimension. Forms of moral certitude may also mark the points at which we exceed our disciplinary ethos. In and of itself, I regard anthropology (as opposed to anthropologists) as essentially amoral and apolitical – qualities that are both essential yet unreachable in practice, and which are closely tied to the necessary but sometimes unbearable displacement that lies at the heart of our work as participant-observers. Where we feel strongly that we are 'doing the right thing' – or that others, including 'the state', are not – we may well have shifted from the practice of anthropology to something else.

Benjamin R. Smith is a civil servant, and currently works on EU policy in the Home Office. He has also conducted long-term field research with Aboriginal Australians in Northern Queensland. His anthropological interests include the state and government, indigenous land claims, and personhood and social change.

Notes

1. This chapter has been written in a personal capacity. I am grateful to Jeremy MacClancy both for his editorial comments and his patience with the delays that resulted from balancing my production of this chapter with my full-time role in the Civil Service. I should also acknowledge my Aboriginal respondents in Far North Queensland and my erstwhile colleagues in various Aboriginal organisations and Australian academia. Without their generosity and collegiality, I would have been unable to undertake the anthropological work that I reflect on here.
2. I use this phrase throughout this chapter not only to mark work within formal government settings of one kind or another, but also to flag the ways in which a wider set of practices is integral to various modes of government.
3. Many anthropologists seem to distance themselves from or studiously ignore the affective aspects of our work. There are exceptions of course, although anthropological accounts tend to focus on others' affective states or emotions, rather than those of the anthropologist her/himself.
4. http://www.merriam-webster.com/dictionary/ethos.
5. Following Ortner (2005: 31), I understand subjectivity to consist of 'the ensemble of modes of perception, affect, thought, desire, fear, and so forth that animate social subjects … as well as the cultural and social formations that shape, organise, and provoke those modes of affect, thought and so on'.
6. The fact that anthropologists' social relations are themselves the principal means through which our discipline is practised is an integral part of this ethos. It is this that Weiner (2001: 151) calls 'the isomorphy of our methodology and subject matter'. A number of considerations follow on from this substantive identity between what we study and how we study it, not least

the question of how we manage our own subjective bias. Further questions arise when anthropologists are engaged in applied work, which sees anthropology move from observation from within a social field (with all the attendant 'ripple effects' associated with our local emplacement) to an active reshaping of the local (and possibly wider regional or national) social fabric. Here Taussig's (1992: 10) comment that taking social determination seriously 'means that one has to see oneself and one's shared modes of understanding and communication included in that determining' takes on a particular importance.

7. In many cases there is a third dimension to this displacement, i.e. our work's implicit or explicit challenge to our respondents' own worldviews. This dimension has increasingly come to the fore as those respondents have come to read our work. It is particularly important (and potentially problematic) where anthropology engages in social fields marked by political struggles – especially those between indigenous groups and other minorities and the nation states within which they are encompassed. However, the difficulties associated with this third dimension do not, in my view, mean that anthropology should (necessarily) avoid critical engagement with the claims and understandings of respondents in such milieus.

8. In case this sounds overly critical, I should add that I understood my supervisor's position, which was primarily based on ethical rather than practical concerns. I continue to regard his viewpoint as defensible, even though my own position remains substantially different.

9. http://caepr.anu.edu.au/.

10. An Aboriginal Board of Directors oversaw the organisation. However, this Board was removed from the day-to-day running of land claim work, and was itself strongly marked by indigenous and intercultural political agendas.

11. Despite the discomfort and strained professional relationships that marked this period, I was able to work effectively with my colleagues on a number of land claims to the benefit of our indigenous clients and the organisation itself.

12. Aboriginal land claims in Australia – particularly those undertaken under the Federal Native Title Act (1993) – tend to depend on some form of legal determination of the continuity of indigenous law and custom (i.e. a determination that these have not been fundamentally transformed or eroded through exposure to the encapsulating 'mainstream' society, and that they therefore continue to underpin a specific and distinct body of indigenous property rights).

13. But specificity may, simultaneously, be required at other points in land claim processes, for example in the biographic details of Aboriginal claimants' connections to land. However, in the eyes of those who oversee land claims processes, such specificity tends to be best provided directly through applicants' own testimony. This creates a split between the desired specificity of claimants' evidence and the generalised analysis expected from expert anthropological reports. The latter, it is supposed, should supersede such specificities, providing a single model or account of the local system of

Aboriginal land tenure or customary connections to land. Of course, such a simplified account masks the dynamic character of markedly acephalous (stateless) social fields, however small in scale; in such fields, differences of perspective are part and parcel of local politics and social life. Here the 'resolution' of the ongoing interplay of different positions into a single, static picture involves a significant act of (mis)translation. There is an interesting comparison here with the tensions between anthropologists and other social scientists I have observed both in Australia and the UK. This tension is evident in the dismissive comment of a senior non-anthropological colleague regarding the particularising (and hence anti-theoretical) tendency they perceived in anthropological interventions: 'Why does it always have to be "my village is different"?'

14. On Government Social Research (GSR), see http://www.civilservice.gov.uk/networks/gsr.
15. The European Migration Network (EMN) is a European Union initiative that develops policy-relevant analysis of migration and asylum issues across the EU and its member states. See http://ec.europa.eu/dgs/home-affairs/what-we-do/networks/european_migration_network/index_en.htm.
16. This is well illustrated by publicly available work produced or commissioned by ARK, for example a longitudinal study of refugee integration in the UK (see Cebulla, Daniel and Zurawan 2010).
17. The official GSR website notes that the backgrounds of Government Social Researchers include 'psychology, social policy, geography, sociology, political science, criminology and social statistics'; anthropology is notably absent. Across government, anthropologists are most commonly employed in the Department for International Development (DfID). More recently, anthropological skills and methods have also been recognised and drawn upon in social research supporting work in the areas of security, defence and counterterrorism.
18. In my experience, policymakers want the facts and figures from others but tend to want to do the analysis themselves.
19. European migration policy has begun to attract considerable anthropological attention, with numerous recent and forthcoming publications and conference sessions dealing with the current situation within the EU.
20. While managerial and administrative skills are also required in university work, my stint in the Civil Service has highlighted how underdeveloped and undervalued such skills tend to be in the academy.
21. A former manager referred to this as 'developing a political antenna'.
22. See Barber (2008) for one account of how policymakers grapple with this issue.
23. David Martin, personal communication (although the gloss is mine). This statement is polemical rather than analytic of course – although as with all good polemic there is a fair degree of truth in it.
24. Years in which they have undertaken their own form of apprenticeship, most commonly through the Civil Service 'fast-track' (an internal scheme

where outstanding recruits are supported through a series of high-profile positions and accelerated promotions).
25. Andrew Garner, personal communication.
26. At the same time, I found myself equally frustrated with some of the more instrumentalist views of my fellow Government Social Researchers and their often uncritical rejection of qualitative approaches.
27. As distinct from the uncomfortable distance generated by anthropology as a *technique du dépaysement*.
28. As such, one might add applied anthropology to Freud's list of impossible professions ([1937] 1961: 248), joining government, education and psychoanalysis. Freud identifies the impossible professions as those 'in which one can be sure beforehand of achieving unsatisfying results'. Of course, it is all too possible to 'exceed' anthropology in its academic practice as well as in applied work. For example, anthropology is exceeded at those points where our theoretical approaches overwhelm our ethnographic understanding.

References

Aretxaga, B. 2003. 'Maddening States', *Annual Review of Anthropology* 32: 393–410.
Barber, M. 2008. *Instruction to Deliver: Fighting to Deliver Britain's Public Services*. London: Methuen.
Cebulla, A., M. Daniel and A. Zurawan. 2010. 'Spotlight on Refugee Integration: Findings from the Survey of New Refugees in the United Kingdom'. HMG Migration Research and Analysis Research Report 37. Retrieved 17 April 2015 from https://www.gov.uk/government/uploads/system/uploads/attachment_data/file/116062/horr37-report.pdf.
Foucault, M. [1982] 1983. 'The Subject and Power', in H.L. Dreyfus and P. Rabinow (eds), *Michel Foucault: Beyond Structuralism and Hermeneutics*. Chicago, IL: University of Chicago Press, pp. 208–26.
Freud, S. [1937] 1961. 'Analysis Terminable and Interminable', in J. Strachey (ed.), *The Standard Edition of the Complete Psychological Works of Sigmund Freud*, Vol. 23. London: Hogarth Press, pp. 209–54.
Lévi-Strauss, C. [1963] 1977. *Structural Anthropology*. Harmondsworth: Penguin.
Ortner, S. 2005. 'Subjectivity and Cultural Critique', *Anthropological Theory* 5(1): 31–52.
Parr, S., N. Bashir and D. Robinson. 2010. 'An Evaluation of the Deaf Third-Country Nationals Integration Project: A Report to the United Kingdom Border Agency'. Centre for Regional Economic and Social Research, Sheffield Hallam University. Retrieved 17 April 2015 from http://www.shu.ac.uk/research/cresr/sites/shu.ac.uk/files/eval-deaf-third-nationals-project.pdf.
Povinelli, E. 2002. *The Cunning of Recognition: Indigenous Alterity and the Making of Australian Multiculturalism*. Durham, NC: Duke University Press.

Scott, J.C. 1998. *Seeing Like a State: How Certain Schemes to Improve the Human Condition Have Failed*. New Haven, CT: Yale University Press.

Shore, C., and S. Wright. 1997. 'Policy: A New Field of Anthropology', in C. Shore and S. Wright (eds), *Anthropology of Policy: Critical Perspectives on Government and Power*. London: Routledge, pp. 3–39.

Smith, B.R. 2002. 'Decentralisation, Population Mobility and the CDEP Scheme in Central Cape York Peninsula', CAEPR Discussion Paper No. 238. Canberra: Centre for Aboriginal Economic Policy Research, Australian National University.

Smith, B.R. 2004. 'The Social Underpinnings of an "Outstation Movement" in Cape York Peninsula, Australia', in J. Taylor and M. Bell (eds), *Population Mobility and Indigenous Peoples in Australasia and North America*. London: Routledge, pp. 239–61.

Smith, B.R. 2008a. 'Regenerating Governance on Kaanju Homelands', in J. Hunt, D. Smith, S. Garling and W. Sanders (eds), *Contested Governance: Culture, Power and Institutions in Indigenous Australia*. Canberra: ANU e-Press, 153–73.

Smith, B.R. 2008b. 'Still Under the Act? Subjectivity and the State in Postcolonial North Queensland', *Oceania* 78(2): 199–216.

Smith, B.R., and F. Morphy. 2007. *The Social Effects of Native Title: Recognition, Translation, Coexistence*. Canberra: ANU e-Press.

Taussig, M. 1992. *The Nervous System*. London: Routledge.

Trouillot, M.-R. 2001. 'The Anthropology of the State: Close Encounters of a Deceptive Kind', *Current Anthropology* 42(1): 125–38.

van Gennep, A. 1961. *The Rites of Passage*. Chicago, IL: University of Chicago Press.

Wafer, J. 1996. 'After the Field', in M. Jackson (ed.), *Things As They Are: New Directions in Phenomenological Anthropology*. Bloomington: Indiana University Press, pp. 259–72.

Weiner, J. 2001. *Tree Leaf Talk: A Heideggerian Anthropology*. Oxford: Berg.

Weiner, J. 2003. 'The Law of the Land: A Review Article', *The Australian Journal of Anthropology* 14(1): 97–110.

Wolfe, T. [1940] 1998. *You Can't Go Home Again*. New York: Harper & Row.

Chapter 4

ANTHROPOLOGY IN THE CLOSET
Contributions to Community Development and Local Government

Robert Gregory

Setting the scene: community as local government discourse

> Whether we see it as the nostalgic desire for a lost past or the creative reformulation of a postmodern society, the focus of community has become ubiquitous in the way we talk and think about life in the twenty-first century. (Creed 2006: 3)

'Community' remains one of anthropology's most contested and debated terms. Often overused and misunderstood, the word evokes notions of a bounded, homogenous group, connected through shared social and symbolic bonds. Such descriptions have long been attributed to tribal and semi-nomadic groups in sub-Saharan Africa, but have increasingly been used to define urban minorities and displaced peoples across the globe. So too do we find the term used in far broader frames of reference. The notion of nation-state as an 'imagined community' was first described by Benedict Anderson (1983) when he ascribed the emergence of print capitalism as being responsible for the creation of national consciousness, creating concepts such as nationhood and community. Such meta-narratives permeate much literature and thought in today's globalised world. Even more pertinent is the growth of electronic and virtual communications, creating 'cyber communities' between groups permeating a virtual global space (Wilson and Peterson 2002). In their seminal book *The Trouble with Community* (2002), anthropologists Amit and Rapport explain the discipline's preoccupation with the term. They state that the foundation of participant observation as anthropology's defining feature in the twentieth century as a study of human behaviour posited the discipline's focus on community, which 'read as a convergence of place, people, identity and culture [and] was construed as the proper subject matter of anthropology' (2002: 15). They state that 'key lexical terms like community persist in usage because they evoke a thick assortment of meanings, presumptions and images' (2002: 13). While debates continue inside academe, outside and across other disciplines the term continues to be used even more obscurely in fields such as media, law and politics to the point that it has saturated current public policy discourse. For local government in Britain, namely municipal councils via local town or city halls, this becomes immediately apparent. Recent key legislation to pass through British parliament, such as the Localism Act (2011), the Anti-Social Behaviour, Crime and Policing Act (2014) and the Care Act (2015), repetitively overuse terms such as 'community rights', 'community remedies' and 'community care' to embody an ideology of freeing the market and reducing the role of the state. Community therefore remains the lynchpin of local government and its necessary preoccupation.

It is on this arena of public policy that I intend to focus. This chapter offers an experiential perspective of the application of anthropology in a local government setting, in a district council on the east coast of England. It considers the limited appreciation of anthropology in local government discourse when considering 'community' and more specifically community development 'at home'. It highlights the necessity to repackage and present anthropological training as a highly relevant tool in shaping policy and better appreciating the interplay between citizens and the state via local government. The chapter ends by considering the value of anthropology beyond its application in the more obvious 'development' agendas of government institutions and proposes its usefulness across a range of local council functions.

Anthropology and development 'at home'

I remain somewhat of a 'closet' anthropologist. Even with every confidence in the integrity of the discipline and the contribution it makes to my work in local government, I still maintain my discretion on a 'need to know' basis. Some like-minded colleagues and friends are aware of my academic background, but not many. This is, no doubt, a direct consequence of my naive entrance to life outside of academe as a fresh-faced graduate embarking on a career in community development attached to a small district council in 2003. Much of my final year dissertation thesis had focused upon anthropological debates around 'community' and 'consciousness'; I was particularly interested in 'anthropology at home' (Rapport 2002) and had asserted a geographical focus on my home town of Great Yarmouth. It was hardly surprising, therefore, that when a job as a community development worker was advertised in the local press, just prior to my graduation, I was keen to apply. Faced with spiralling student debt and the anxiety faced by many of my graduate peers pondering 'what next?' it seemed a swift solution. With my local knowledge of the town, my academic appreciation of 'community' and an eagerness to share anthropological insight with the place that had nurtured and raised me, I was confident and somewhat arrogant in the belief that I would be eagerly recruited for the role. In my interview presentation I threw in the concept of 'symbolic communities' (Cohen 1985), 'diverse world-views' (Rapport 1993) and a bit of Bourdieu's 'Theory of Practice' for good measure (1977), and I eagerly awaited the reaction from the interview panel. 'But what would you actually do in your first six months in post?' the chairperson of the interview panel barked rather abruptly. The chairperson later became my manager and teacher in all things community development, but that first interview cemented my feet firmly on the ground and awakened me to life outside of academe. It was not that the panel did not recognise my academic credentials; rather it was that they wanted to be confident that I could apply these outside of academia. It was also clear that the panel were not overly familiar with anthropology as a discipline. This became a reoccurrence as I embarked on my graduate career in community development, which I believed was closely aligned to an applied form of anthropology. It became increasingly clear that as a consequence of being outside of a major city and with no large government departments, non-governmental organisations (NGOs), universities or major companies in the vicinity, the local awareness of anthropology was limited and at best weak. The closest reference colleagues were able to make was to the generalist association with tribal cultures and archaeology. There was not an immediate recognition of the link between my academic training and the contribution it could make to my new role.

My first months in post as a community development worker, working for a small NGO contracted by the local council to provide support to 'communities' living across the borough's deprived neighbourhoods, provided a very steep learning curve. My role was not about research. I was employed to facilitate the development of projects and initiatives led by groups of local residents to address the collective issues they faced. The focus was on participatory democracy and building social capital through developing the skills of activists and collective capacity. Part of my role was about facilitating a community partnership, led by local residents, which shaped issues for action and called upon service providers and elected representatives to be held to account. I would also spend time supporting a range of resident groupings, like a collective of lone parents who had come together to provide a support group for others in the neighbourhood experiencing the trauma and challenge of single parenthood. I also helped groups to develop skills and training projects to boost local employment opportunities. I was in effect a development practitioner practising 'development at home'. It was surprising, however, that the relationship between development overseas and such domestic practice was not explicitly recognised.

The 'anthropology of development' has grown as a subfield of the discipline in its own right. There exists rich and wide-ranging literature dating back to the 1970s, though its legacy dates back even further (Little 2005: 33). Like anthropology, 'development' emerged out of the colonial administration (Willis 2005: 18), its main purpose being to aid 'the integration of colonial territories into the capitalist system' (Popple 1995: 8). Anthropology's interest in development has been largely focused on such processes and has concentrated almost exclusively on the relationships between the rich north and the poor south. Accounts on issues such as participatory development, rural appraisal, microeconomics and the politics of aid have featured significantly in anthropological literature, as have the critiques of 'development' itself (see Ferguson 2002 and Escobar 1995). Consequently, 'anthropology is now an acknowledged partner in development practice' (de Waal 2002: 254), with many anthropology graduates embarking on careers in international aid agencies and overseas consultancies. The concept of considering such a career 'at home', however, has been somewhat understated. It is true that 'development' emerged at a slightly later date in Britain, mainly as a consequence of growing an increasing 'class consciousness' among the poor in the later nineteenth century. Social work emerged out of government reforms at the turn of the twentieth century to address endemic poverty in the industrialised inner cities, with community-based intervention evolving soon after. Such intervention also embodied the principle of economic development and integration of the poor into the capitalist system, although the agents were more commonly the church and universities rather than the colonial office (Popple 1995: 8). Today, while the term 'community development' is favoured in domestic usage, the practice and underlying principles, such as participation, capacity building and empowerment, remain akin to the development endeavour in the global south. The relationship between the two is not, however, widely acknowledged.

As I started to read academic texts relating to community development in Britain, I was surprised that there was often limited reference to development overseas and vice versa. Perhaps more frustrating, however, was that anthropology was almost entirely disregarded in such texts. This suggests not only a limited recognition of the contribution anthropology has made to development practice in the West, but more importantly a missed opportunity for the discipline itself. Kedia and van Willigen (2005: 342)have emphasised the need for us to embrace 'backyard anthropology' to maintain the discipline's relevance in the twenty-first century. If we accept that there is a role for anthropology at home, then we also ought to further stress the opportunities for applying anthropology at home in subfields such as development.

Applying anthropology to community development practice

My immersion into the world of community development was heavily influenced by central government policy. Hoggett, Mayo and Miller (2009: 38) describe how over the past forty years the state has been the major employer of community development practitioners in Britain. In an earlier work, Smith, Lepin and Taylor (2007: 3) state how successive postwar governments have focused on neighbourhood-based policy to target resources to alleviate poverty. This remained central to New Labour policies in the early 2000s. Wrapped up in this policy discourse was 'community' as something the poor needed to foster development. I was employed through funds awarded by central government to address issues of deprivation. The cross-cutting principle of the government's neighbourhood renewal agenda was empowerment – putting communities in control, further endorsed through the publication of its Stronger Communities White Paper in 2006 (Department for Communities and Local Government 2006). The underlying tenet of this policy remained that community development was a vital ingredient in addressing poverty and disadvantage in Britain.

The council, health, police and other public and civil society organisations therefore eagerly embraced service delivery models that focused on engaging 'communities', pumping resources and energy into delivering new and innovative services to engage people they often failed to serve effectively. What appeared commonplace, and was not isolated to Great Yarmouth, was the failure to actually engage with those local residents most in need, in a way that was meaningful to them. Participation was fragmented and somewhat tokenistic and there was limited scope to fully appreciate a range of local voices and views. Questionnaires and piecemeal consultation had helped to validate claims of community involvement but failed to capture the authentic voice of residents living in the neighbourhood. As I began to understand these challenges, I really started to see value in my training as an anthropologist. I was able to highlight the limited appreciation of local people's lives in different forums. Through a range of participatory approaches with residents, I sought to build up a greater base and cross-section of local voices, the voices at odds with one another as much as at odds with those of the state. I was able to facilitate rather than advocate and I was able to challenge colleagues and partner agencies more constructively. I also made a conscious decision to live in the area I was working in. Perhaps this was because I believed I was doing some form of applied anthropology, but it was also driven by an ethical desire. It felt mildly hypocritical to champion a neighbourhood I myself had not made any personal commitment to. I gained credibility and acceptance from those I was working with for this.

Operating as a practitioner in development required new and more pragmatic skill-sets. These included managing meetings and resolving conflict, writing proposals and bids for funding, planning and delivering participatory workshops and, importantly, facilitating actions for change. It was fortunate that my organisation invested in practice-based training and I soon grew in confidence to utilise my anthropological insight in an applied way. I purposefully avoided presenting the social context through an academic lens. When discussing high levels of intergenerational unemployment with colleagues, I chose not to refer to Oscar Lewis's 'culture of poverty' theory (1959); instead I opted to offer insight and challenge to our thinking by projecting the voices and experiences of local residents directly. This seemed to gain more traction than referring to abstract theoretical concepts and helped policymakers to still arrive at similar conclusions. I continued to facilitate opportunities for decision-makers to hear these experiences directly from local residents. The subtlety of my approach started to gain credit, enhanced further as I supported new residents to engage in local structures, and particularly those who were not likely to attend town hall meetings. The voices captured during this process, including those with drug and alcohol problems, young people and people with disabilities, provided far greater authenticity than consultations had done to date. I was eagerly courted by colleagues in the police wishing to get 'community representatives' to help inform policing priorities. This was clearly not part of my role, but I was seen as a gateway and conduit to engage local residents.

One of my first major undertakings in community development was working with Portuguese migrants newly arrived to the town. Great Yarmouth is an urban conurbation and seaside resort on the edge of rural Norfolk, where agricultural and food-processing industries dominate the low-skilled employment scene. In recent years, many such businesses have directly recruited contract workers throughout Europe, as local labour has become more difficult to source and demands for production have increased. Some businesses actively set up recruitment agencies in Portugal in the early 2000s. Upon recruitment, workers were provided with flights, accommodation and contracted hours at a designated site. Much of the workers' accommodation was sourced in Great Yarmouth, utilising the pool of redundant and run down guesthouses often used as housing for those on low incomes. This was the neighbourhood that I was based in, where up to five thousand migrant workers were thought to be living (Gregory 2012).

I considered my role. A major focus was on promoting issues of social justice and community empowerment. I spoke at length with my manager about the possibility of attempting to undertake some fieldwork with the Portuguese migrants. I suggested that the most empowering stance for our organisation was to understand the ways in which Portuguese migrant workers made sense of their experience in Great Yarmouth, by listening to their authentic voice. Fortunately, my request was endorsed and supported. I purposefully did not suggest 'doing anthropology' in fear that intensive ethnographic fieldwork would be deemed detrimental to the short-term outcome-driven environment we were operating in. What I wanted to establish, however, was that the 'approach' was of relevance and value. The opening of the first Portuguese-run café in the town provided me with an obvious gateway. Upon explaining my role and intentions, the owner was remarkably enthusiastic. She eagerly invited me back the following Sunday to talk to some of her friends. These friends had been discussing the idea of doing something to help new arrivals in the town and were not quite sure how to progress. We agreed to establish a range of informal meetings on Sunday afternoons to work through ideas. This provided my initial group of informants, which soon expanded. I was able to further substantiate this initial fieldwork by capturing a number of life histories and conducting a range of informal interviews as part of a research paper for my Masters degree, which I subsequently undertook the following year.

The ability to do short-term ethnography within my role provided a real opportunity to contribute to a greater appreciation of the migrant experience in Great Yarmouth, but equally it found me questioning the system in which I was operating. An assumption that continued to resonate throughout the discourse of local agencies and institutions was that a 'well-established Portuguese community' existed (Great Yarmouth Local Strategic Partnership 2007: 2). There was a certain naivety in this assumption. In 2001, the ethnic make-up of the borough was 97% white British.[1] With relatively limited ethnic diversity, the arrival of Portuguese-speaking migrants, mainly from Portugal but also from East Timor, Mozambique and Brazil, provided an 'ethnic other', neatly banded as a 'community'. My fieldwork found this concept problematic, as frames of belonging, association and identity did not lend themselves to a fixed notion of community. Such labelling ignored the complexity of the migrant worker experience (Gregory 2012).

As a practitioner I was under significant pressure to quantify the community work I was doing. I had to monitor the number of groups I was working with and the individuals representing certain population demographics on particular decision-making bodies. This felt somewhat cumbersome and tokenistic, but was a requirement of the funding regime I was reporting to. There was also a very conscious desire to establish a group representing the 'Portuguese community' to act as a sounding board and conduit for public agencies. It was not by coincidence that the group I met on Sunday afternoons went on to form the Portuguese community association Herois do Mar – Heroes of the Sea, the first line of the national anthem. I was a major influence in facilitating this and while it chimed with the desires of the group, it also challenged my role as effectively an agent of the state, as opposed to the impartial and detached anthropologist.

Herois do Mar went on to hold a hugely successful launch event, with over a thousand people in attendance. Unfortunately, the follow-up inaugural meeting of the association scheduled several weeks later saw few volunteers come forward. The association launched a newspaper and an employment and training project, but struggled to sustain either. There were a number of reasons for this. Margolis noted a similar lack of 'community ethos and community associations amongst Brazilian migrant workers in New York in the 1990s, attributing both a lack of permanence and the pursuit of individual economic gain' (1994: 195). I was approached numerous times by migrants with business ideas or proposed ventures that were not necessarily about collective self-help and mutual support. There was also significant mistrust between migrants, and competitive tensions around status and establishing hierarchy. I became acutely aware of the cultural construction of 'community' as interpreted by those working in public agencies and NGOs. The success measures for a community to be fully integrated into the social life of the borough were about having a bone fide association, with a well-functioning committee, with robust governance, overseeing a number of successful projects to aid integration and cohesion. This was at odds with the transient lives many migrant workers led, moving frequently within and beyond the neighbourhood, working unsociable hours and negotiating a migrant identity in an often less than welcoming environment.

As a consequence of my time spent with Herois do Mar and other Portuguese migrant workers, I urged my organisation to take a far more flexible approach to community development. Understanding networks and permeating friendship and peer groups was more effective than navigating formal structures alone. The subtleties of the migrant worker experience would not have been so appreciated had an anthropological lens not been applied. My challenge was about maintaining my commitment to community development while teasing out the anthropological tools I thought to be of relevance, i.e. ethnography, discourse analysis and the communication of worldviews. This was not anthropology by any traditional sense; rather it was practice-based anthropology, although admittedly understated, but particularly powerful in this context.

The Portuguese migrant worker case is perhaps a more tangible concept for an anthropology graduate emerging from university to grapple with. An appreciation of 'ethnic groups' (Eriksen 1993: 10) remains familiar territory for academics. This is about appreciating a group of people, culturally and linguistically bounded, sharing a social space and cultural norms that are markedly distinct from the wider population. The real challenge for an anthropologist in such a role is translating their skills when working with a broader population and through different manifestations of identity and belonging. This is particularly true where cultural boundaries are less demarcated between groups, and social groupings mean different things at different times. As I grew in my role, I learnt to apply the same principles to work with young people, older people, collectives of angry and agitated residents on a particular street and even through building partnerships across and between civil society and government organisations. All of these drew on participatory problem solving, articulating the voice of often under-represented groups and informing policy based on empirical evidence. This presents a more subtle challenge for an anthropologist, often studying up and within, rather than the traditional view of studying down (MacClancy 2002: 12). A more intuitive skill-set is necessary, along with a far more perceptive sense of the 'social group' and the power and relationship dynamics that accompany it.

Finding a role in local government

It is with this appreciation that I entered local government proper. I joined Great Yarmouth Borough Council in 2006 as part of a new dedicated neighbourhood management programme. Moving from a contracted NGO into the folds of local government further tested my ability to translate anthropological training into a relevant set of skills for local government. I was recruited as a research and evaluation officer to help design a performance framework for the programme, which would invest £1.6 million into the same neighbourhood I had been working in as a community worker. This programme was the latest in a number of regeneration efforts in Great Yarmouth. Its overarching aim was 'to improve the quality of life for local people in deprived neighbourhoods and ensure services improve to better meet their needs' (Office of the Deputy Prime Minister 2005: 11). 'Simple', so I thought. This would provide a real opportunity to influence from within the machinery of local government rather than from an NGO at arm's length. As a research officer I also hoped there would be ample opportunity to conduct similar ethnographic endeavours to my work with Portuguese migrants. Following the issuing of more detailed implementation guidance from central government and my induction into the council, it was clear that this was not going to be quite so straightforward.

Entering the fold of local government required taking a deep breath and an approach similar to an ethnographer entering the field for the first time. I was about to learn a range of new customs and traditions that had no immediate explanation but were routinised in the lives of their members. My job was to observe, learn and participate in this new culture. As with all government programmes, there comes a degree of national guidance and associated bureaucracy. Great Yarmouth's neighbourhood management programme was no different. A weighty volume of implementation guidance was issued, providing a somewhat prescriptive and formulaic approach to planning, delivering and evaluating the programme. We were urged to join a national network and digest the learning from early pathfinders. Many of the evaluations were based on quantitative indicators and quality of life surveys rather than any major qualitative research and made recommendations such as improving street lighting and litter patrols. What much of this research failed to capture, however, was an in-depth appreciation of some of the enduring challenges for people living within such neighbourhoods and how these were manifest and understood. It was clear that the Great Yarmouth approach would need to be tailored to particular circumstances and therefore the gathering of local knowledge would be essential.

In early 2007 I was asked to act as the Neighbourhood Manager. The commissioning of consultants to undertake the initial consultation and action planning for the programme had already been decided. There was a certain reticence from colleagues that we did not have the skills or capacity to prepare for such an ambitious programme (Gregory 2010: 33). In retrospect this was a fundamental flaw to the approach adopted by the project board. Several weeks of intensive meetings with stakeholders and a poorly attended community consultation workshop saw a baseline report and action plan, capturing local statistics and agency aspirations, assumedly ratified by a community consultation event. The presentation of this plan back to the resident activists, who would later form part of the Neighbourhood Board, was less than positive. I undertook to spend a further month reworking the action plan with residents through a series of participatory workshops. The time taken to do this was frustrating for many colleagues and partner agencies desperate to get hold of the cash and deliver things. Investing in the process was, however, fundamental to ensuring that the actions identified were meaningful and relevant, but most importantly owned by local people.

It is perhaps recognition of this process of interaction and power dynamics between communities and the state that is of value anthropologically. Gledhill (1994: 20) argued that Western political analysis is often too preoccupied with the role of the state and that we must consider the politics of everyday life at the level in which we see it manifest in social practices. Investing time in process rather than immediate capital projects, such as dog litter bins or renewed street signs, helped to further make sense of power struggles within the neighbourhood and enabled dialogues between and across groups that had never happened before. There was a growing collective consciousness around the root causes of particular issues and a sense of how to address them for the longer term. This created a new power dynamic for the council. They were no longer 'doing to' they were 'doing with'. Collectives of residents undertaking landscape projects, setting up drop-in centres and establishing training programmes presented a number of not insurmountable challenges around procurement and financial audit for the council, but the social return on investment was significant, i.e. local ownership of public places, increased community cohesion and greater social capital. These were far more enduring outcomes as a whole. It was hardly surprising that by the end of the first year, the programme was significantly underspent against its anticipated budget. In effect, the process of capacity building had been more effective than the physical delivery of a regeneration project in facilitating community empowerment. The appreciation of process and interaction as an analytical tool was clearly consequential of an anthropological approach.

As an anthropologist there was, however, an ongoing dilemma with my role, namely navigating and being part of the discourse of the state. Inevitably, with so much public money invested, there was an expectation that tangible outcomes would be seen. How might we measure 'quality of life'? Whose definition were we using? It was clear that such measures were ultimately going to be determined by the state and while the neighbourhood management programme provided real opportunity for local decision-making, it was undoubtedly being assessed by its impact on a set of predetermined indicators of social change. Indeed, as time progressed and the recession of 2008 started to take hold, the future of the programme was based upon its ability to meet national indicators of wellbeing as identified by central government. These indicators were ones selected by state interfaces, not local residents, and therefore the programme needed to find a careful balance between demonstrating outcomes to the funders but also delivering meaningful outcomes with local residents. For example, an arbitrarily structured survey was delivered to a selection of households in the neighbourhood in order to quantify empowerment. The questions asked were prescriptive and probed very little about the everyday power relations Gledhill argues would otherwise 'remain somewhat obscure' (1994: 127). We decided to supplement the survey with a set of case studies and life histories that helped to demonstrate the nuances of community empowerment, but most importantly, distance travelled as a consequence of the programme. This kind of adaptation and subtle challenge requires a more sensitive and fluid approach. While the ideal would have been an evaluation framework agreed consensually between residents and the state, this was not possible. It would have been maverick and potentially detrimental to outright refuse to cooperate with central government's requests. The outcome could have been the withdrawal of funding to continue the work because it was deemed non-essential. Instead the solution was to present success to different audiences in different ways, using a style that was not mired in anthropological jargon. Central government wanted figures, local residents wanted to see 'action' that they had some influence over.

By 2009 a range of more tangible outcomes had been achieved; more people were entering employment, there was a marked improvement in open and communal spaces and there was evidently more civic involvement through community action. The council also received national recognition, being awarded 'programme of the year for greatest local impact' by an international journal. This created a platform to engage others in discussions about developing the approach as a model for improving other neighbourhoods. I led the formation of a business case. This was a standard requirement given the investment needed by the council at a time of austerity in the public sector. What strengthened this business case was the ongoing involvement of local residents in its shaping. While the business case was not anthropological in its construction, it had a particular strength in depicting local circumstances and the cultural constructions of the borough's communities. It further demonstrated that such an approach was vital in working with people where they lived. As a consequence, further funding was secured and staff recruited. Among the most important attributes we sought when recruiting for the roles were those of empathy, careful reasoning, analysis and the ability to capture the authenticity of local people's lives. My post changed and I was fully internalised into the machinery of local government as a service manager, subsequently assuming responsibility for the council's corporate strategy and partnerships agenda, with an intention to institutionally embed the community development approach we had pioneered.

Permeating policy

Embracing the machinery of local government requires an immediate departure from the reflective, theoretical debates of academia. The environment is policy driven and focused on delivery and service improvement. Given the nature of life in a district council, the work can be fast-paced and the digestion of new government strategies spanning public health, unemployment, planning, environment and social housing requires an ability to translate technical and often lengthy jargon into a practical synopsis for action. These are skills an anthropologist should be comfortable with, summarising often complex and competing data into something meaningful for the reader with a clear narrative and argument. There is also a significant interrelatedness with other public sector bodies: the police, the Job Centre, the health service, neighbouring councils and, increasingly, civil society organisations and the private sector. This requires a broad appreciation of often conflicting agendas and viewpoints. Once again, this is likely to draw upon anthropological ability to reason and interpret differing worldviews. This does, however, require a different report-writing style, free of academic jargon, succinct and action focused. Raising further questions is fine, but these need to be grounded and indicate where the answer may lie. In other words, anthropology in this context needs to remain action focused. Working for a district council requires flexibility, given that there is limited back office expertise and capacity to draw upon, unlike larger upper tier and unitary authorities or government departments. I immediately needed to grapple with multi-million pound budgets, managing property, human resources, communications and staff training and development. There are benefits to working in a smaller state institution, however. Prescriptive procedures or large teams resistant to change did not hinder me. Some departmental silos existed but these were not entrenched. The daily variety kept me fresh and enthused and there was a very real sense of being able to change things for the better.

Writing culture remains at the forefront of the anthropological enterprise. In local government, writing requires the author to consider a number of different audiences, different sections of the population, fellow council officers and colleagues from other organisations and, very often, elected representatives. The relationship with the party political dimension of life in a district council may be one of the biggest challenges for an anthropologist. While deemed apolitical, a council officer is charged with delivering the policy of the ruling administration. This political charge is certainly present in any publicly funded institution, even universities, where policies on student welfare, loans and departmental budgets are influenced by the political dimension of the state. But in local government the link between politics and policy is often more direct and more immediate. For example, the change of administration in the local elections in Great Yarmouth in recent years has seen an immediate U-turn on several major projects, which has meant some work programmes have been abandoned indefinitely. The political dimension of life in local government requires swift and substantive outcomes that can be communicated back to the electorate in time for the next local elections. This often denies the opportunity for real 'ethnography' or longitudinal work. It also challenges the ability to find space for reflection and meaningful analysis. The added frustration of the changing priorities of central government means that work can often be abandoned or superseded by the next policy directive, often informed by short-term, quantitative, broad-based national research, much to an anthropologist's disdain.

The direct relationship with politicians is also an arena in which a practising anthropologist may struggle. By their virtue of being democratically elected, there is a position of power assumed by politician over council officer. This requires respect, diplomacy and a good professional working relationship. This is not to say that a council officer should remain subordinate, but it rather suggests there is a line of accountability that needs to be respected. In my experience in Great Yarmouth, elected members of differing political persuasions have been open to democratic debates with officers around a range of issues provided the points are rooted in a sound evidence base and presented clearly as advice, rather than direct challenges to their decision-making. As I noted previously, the rollout of neighbourhood management was borne out of New Labour government policy, but it was agreed and overseen by a Conservative council administration. This was not driven by their political manifesto; it was realised because the business case was presented in the right way, with a sound, empirical evidence base. There are, however, a whole range of political tensions, which can slow and derail contentious programmes. This is often an added frustration with the complexity of democratic and governance procedures one has to deal with. Forward planning is essential to ensure that the myriad of political processes are navigated in time for any new initiative or piece of work to be ratified, but there is also scope to permeate and influence such political systems.

In 2005 the USA's National Association for Practicing Anthropologists found that 22% of their respondents were in managerial positions outside of academia (Kedia and van Willigen 2005: 13). Today that figure is likely to be even higher. Applied anthropologists are increasingly in positions of power and influence, particularly in terms of policy. In local government in Britain, the policy framework enables us to start thinking about social issues within society and facilitate change. If, as Chambers states, applied anthropologists use 'knowledge, skills and perspectives of their discipline to help solve human problems and facilitate change' (1985: 8), then there is clearly a role for anthropologists in local government.

After a sabbatical and short period of research in Brazil in 2011, I was able to bring back to the council a more insightful appreciation of budget-setting processes. By looking at *orcamento participativo* (participatory budgeting), I was able to evidence an effective way of involving local communities in the wider arena of local government fiscal policy. This was based on my acquired knowledge and ability to translate learning into practical application. It also helped to demonstrate a role for ethnography in the financial processes of the council. Chambers (1985: 64) suggested that from an anthropological point of view one must view the apparatus of the state within a 'culture of policy'. Applied anthropologists must appreciate this culture and navigate it to demonstrate the discipline's relevance. This has certainly been my experience since assuming a senior management role. My job is to ensure the council's services are fit for purpose in responding to new and emerging agendas and shaped by the borough's citizens. My role oversees a number of service functions, from crime to health, leisure, heritage and the arts. In spite of these areas being distinct disciplines in their own right, anthropology continues to offer an invaluable contribution, but rightly does not exist in isolation. As Kedia and van Willigen (2005: 351) argue, successful applied anthropology relies on integration of technologies and vocabulary from other fields, and in spite of changes to my role over the years, I still see my vocation as a practising anthropologist working in local government, my particular interest being the relationship between communities and the state. Directives and policies come and go. My day job is both reactive and proactive, and often consumes my working life with procedure and service delivery. My motivation and anthropological interest, however, remain the same.

I would like to conclude with a current example of anthropology's application in a local government setting. In 2011 the launch of the Troubled Families Unit placed a requirement on every local council in England to 'turn the lives of troubled families around', i.e. those families with the most complex needs costing 'communities' the most, in social security benefits, healthcare, crime and unemployment. This would require significant intervention from councils to reduce the burden on the public purse.[2] The kneejerk reaction for many councils was to enhance existing 'intervention' models or commission consultants to facilitate stakeholder workshops and action plans to achieve mandatory government targets. The Great Yarmouth approach was different. We sought to help influence the approach to 'troubled families' in Great Yarmouth through what I would refer to as practice-based anthropology.

The issues faced by such families in Great Yarmouth had long been at the forefront of our work in neighbourhoods across the borough. Residents' concerns about youth drinking, antisocial behaviour and run-down and neglected areas were all symptomatic of more deep-rooted issues of unemployment, poor living standards and complex mental health issues experienced often by several generations of the same family living in the same household. The approach we had adopted built on the experience of neighbourhood management I noted earlier. We were creating spaces for residents to express concerns, assess options and propose solutions collectively, with local agencies and services responding and supporting where necessary. A group of mothers had started to voice concerns about young people getting into drugs and alcohol and causing a neighbourhood nuisance. The council provided support and space to enable these residents to look towards a solution. They proposed a youth club and were successful in recruiting friends and neighbours to volunteer to run the group. As the group became established and numbers started to grow, the mothers started to build up trust with some of the young people, who confided in them and shared concerns and issues. Some of these issues were about dealing with adulthood and learning life-skills. The mothers maintained an action focus and wanted to address some of the anxieties they were noticing. Many of these anxieties stemmed from problems at home in the family. The mothers decided they wanted to set up an informal drop-in centre, which they entitled 'The Den'. The Den launched from an empty house in the neighbourhood. Instead of using problem-solving funds available to commission consultants, the council decided to pass the money directly to these local residents as a grant to develop the initiative. This was in firm recognition that these issues could only be understood from the perspective of those experiencing them, and that direct resources should be made available at the lowest possible level. This policy had been informed by the council's greater regard for community development I plotted earlier, an approach borrowing heavily from applied anthropology.

The Den went on to achieve outstanding success in terms of helping families, individuals and communities at large through a range of support and advice. This ranged from coffee mornings to cooking demonstrations, to support with housing, employment and legal advice. The volunteers used their own experience as residents within the neighbourhood to relate to others. Other friends and neighbours would donate clothes and food to help those families in need. The Den received a number of awards and accolades over the following months. The work of The Den gave far greater insight into 'troubled families' in Great Yarmouth than any consultant or room of blue-sky thinkers could have done. The greatest challenge this approach presented to service providers across the public sector was a greater appreciation of how best to understand an issue through lived, everyday experience. There was indeed a prescriptive definition of a 'troubled family', but this was not the definition assigned by residents living in that particular neighbourhood. The definition was a formulaic prescription by government, which disregarded the way people lived their lives and interacted with others. Indeed, a 'troubled family' is not likely to live next door to another 'troubled family'. Their terms of association will be entirely different. From a local council, or indeed many NGOs, the assumed approach would be to 'deal with' a cohort of troubled families, potentially do some 'user involvement' and then shape a service around the original definition and deliver an intervention. By its virtue of being entirely responsive to a range of neighbourhood issues experienced by local residents, The Den provided support to older people who were struggling in their own homes, debt advice to those on low incomes and befriending support to those suffering domestic violence. The initiative was shaped by the people it was serving, building and strengthening community capacity in the process. It was informed by an altogether different approach to the mechanics and predeterminants of local government. The philosophy continues to be embodied as part of Great Yarmouth's 'Early Help' approach to this day. Through facilitating such processes and influencing policy, there is a pertinent role for a form of applied anthropology in local government.

Conclusion: an anthropology of reinvention and relevance

It is certainly true that being an anthropologist in local government can be lonely. There is rarely an opportunity to have broader, theoretical discussions and test deeper ontological ideas. As I have built relationships and alliances with colleagues, however, I have found a far greater opportunity to test concepts, not packaged as anthropological reasoning but rather a range of social dilemmas facing all who work in local government regardless of academic persuasion. I have also been in a fortunate position to recruit and build a small team around me, who are able to grapple with more probing social issues through a number of media, an anthropological lens being one of them. I have indeed found merit in maintaining a foot in academe since leaving higher education proper, initially through a part-time Masters course but also through maintaining active links with more 'applied' publications and events. The emerging issues for the discipline to grapple with are both exciting and fast-moving, and it is critical to keep an eye on both camps to really relate the synthesis between theory and practice.

As I have outlined, anthropological training has been of huge value throughout my career in local government. It has enabled me to better appreciate diverging worldviews through media such as ethnography and life histories. Also, it has provided me with a critical approach to dominant discourse and the meta-narratives of the state; this enables me to be self-reflexive in my work and more balanced in my approach. Furthermore, training in anthropology has provided me with some practical tools in subfields such as community development, where methods such as participatory appraisal and emancipatory research are central to working with people and their communities. These diverse resources from the anthropological toolkit are often lacking in other disciplines.

Anthropology has also steered the path my career has taken in local government. As a consequence, I have overseen a number of change management programmes which have altered the way the council works with the populations we serve, helping it to better appreciate complexities, understand different perspectives and respond appropriately. This has not only changed the interface between the council and 'communities'; it has also influenced other organisations such as the health service, and funders such as the lottery, to think differently when targeting their services at communities 'in need'. As a consequence, Great Yarmouth was awarded funding from the Big Lottery Fund to develop a five-year community economic development programme, 'Neighbourhoods that Work', with an associated longitudinal academic study drawing heavily on qualitative research methods and case studies. In these cases, we can see clear pragmatic benefits to the deployment of anthropological approaches to social issues in the UK today.

Applying these various skills in UK public services is especially pertinent for those in leadership positions. Many of the systems my colleagues and I have to deal with are messy, intricate, and involve a variety of factors: an ageing population, shortages of skills in key sectors, a national housing crisis. And all this against the backdrop of unprecedented cuts in welfare spending. This messiness forces public servants to think across the complexities of social life for local populations, and to be 'comfortable with the chaos' as a result (Timmins 2015: 4). As far as I can judge, anthropological training is highly pertinent for those who have to work with such notions of 'systems leadership'.

It is highly unlikely that an 'anthropologist' position will ever become available in a district council setting. Substantive research posts may favour those with anthropological training, but with the continued downward projection in local government finance it is likely that council officers will carry a far greater variety of roles and tasks, no longer confined to one area of expertise. Specific expertise is likely to be contracted in on an 'as and when' basis. This is not to say that there is no hope for methods such as ethnography in a local government context, but it is to say that applied ethnography may need to evolve even further from academic undertakings. Building the knowledge and skills of other council officers should be part of this. I would argue that this is not about diluting ethnography, but rather about relying on a more resourceful and skilled facilitator to co-opt others, summarise the findings and articulate the key messages in a timely and considered way.

Anthropologists reading this chapter may question whether what I am doing is anthropology at all. I am happy to be challenged. However, I am certain that I would not approach my work in local government with quite the same critical thought and empathetic approach if I did not have a background in anthropology. Some may say that I lack a backbone and if I am that confident in the disciple I should come out and be 'loud and proud'. If I am not, then how does anthropology make its mark in the wider world in the twenty-first century? My fear is of the popular perceptions that continue to exist of academic arrogance. There remains, in places, a demarcation between academe and real world application, particularly with those issues that are most pressing and relevant in today's society. Anthropologists such as Robert Borofsky have suggested renaming the applied subfield 'public anthropology' to ensure that the focus remains on the world's problems rather than the discipline's traditional formations (cited in Kedia and van Willigen 2005: 474). I would argue that we all have a responsibility to change dismissive perceptions, but to do so in a considered and subtle yet compelling way. This must be in a way that sacrifices unnecessary jargon and terms only familiar to anthropologists for the sake of terms that enthuse and inspire others to probe deeper. The embodiment of anthropology through applied practice should be more important than its articulation within the confines of academic journals and publications.

It is in public institutions like local government and the broader public sector that anthropology can find a home outside of academe. Local government's preoccupation with 'community' provides fertile soil for someone with anthropological training. I have outlined that the pathway for me was using community development as a platform, but I hope to have described how anthropology is of relevance across a range of functions of a local council – a setting that is often the most overt interface between citizens and the state. Joining local government requires the same sacrifices made by all who pursue a career outside of academe, and will inevitably require not only a skill-set related to the discipline but an ability to adapt, reinvent and repackage anthropology in an often fast-changing and deeply political environment. This also presents an opportunity for anthropologists to assume positions of relevance and exert influence, build alliances, grow capacity and more importantly instigate social change through policy. Although clichéd and long disputed, the words of Margaret Mead gain new meaning in this context, as one learns the subtle power of practising anthropology where 'a small group of thoughtful, committed citizens can [indeed] change the world' (Sommers and Dineen 1984: 158).

Robert Gregory was Group Manager for Neighbourhoods and Communities at Great Yarmouth Borough Council. He is co-founder of the Centre of Excellence in Community and Social Development: CoSocial and sits on the Board of the International Association for Community Development.

Notes

1. Great Yarmouth 2001 census area statistics, retrieved 20 August 2012 from www.neighbourhood.statistics.gov.uk.
2. 'Trouble Families' press release, retrieved 24 September 2012 from https://www.gov.uk/government/publications/the-cost-of-troubled-families.

References

Amit, V., and N. Rapport (eds). 2002. *The Trouble with Community: Anthropological Reflections on Movement, Identity and Collectivity*. London: Pluto Press.

Anderson, B. 1983. *Imagined Communities: Reflections on the Origins and Spread of Nationalism*. London: Verso.

Bourdieu, P. 1977. *Outline of a Theory of Practice*. Cambridge: Cambridge University Press.

Cohen, A. 1985. *The Symbolic Construction of Community*. London: Tavistock.

Chambers, E. 1985. *Applied Anthropology: A Practical Guide*. New Jersey: Prentice-Hall.

Creed, G. 2006. *The Seductions of Community: Emancipations, Oppressions, Quandaries*. Oxford: James Currey.

De Waal, A. 2002. 'Anthropology and the Aid Encounter', in J. MacClancy (ed.), *Exotic No More: Anthropology on the Front Lines*. London: University of Chicago Press, pp. 251–269.

Department for Communities and Local Government. 2006. *Strong and Prosperous: The Local Government White Paper*. London: Department for Communities and Local Government.

Eriksen, T. 1993. *Ethnicity and Nationalism: Anthropological Perspectives*. London: Pluto Press.

Escobar, A. 1995. *Encountering Development: The Making and Unmaking of the Third World*. Princeton, NJ: Princeton University Press.

Ferguson, J. 2002. 'The Anti-Politics Machine', in J. Vincent (ed.), *The Anthropology of Politics: Ethnography, Theory and Critique*. Oxford: Blackwell, pp. 399–408.

Gledhill, J. 1994. *Power and its Disguises: Anthropological Perspectives on Politics*. London: Pluto Press.

Great Yarmouth Local Strategic Partnership. 2007. 'Community Cohesion Report'. Great Yarmouth: Great Yarmouth Borough Council.

Gregory, R. 2010. 'Developing Communities – Developing Practice: Reflections on the Evolving Role of Community Development in Neighbourhood Renewal in Great Yarmouth', *International Journal of Neighbourhood Renewal* 2(2): 32–38.

Gregory, R. 2012. 'How Have Community Development Approaches Aided Our Understanding of "Community" for Newly Arrived Portuguese Migrant Workers in Great Yarmouth, UK?', Paper presented at the RAI Conference, London, 8 June.

Hoggett, P., M. Mayo and C. Miller. 2009. *The Dilemmas of Development Work: Ethical Challenges in Regeneration*. Bristol: The Policy Press.

Kedia, S., and J. van Willigen (eds). 2005. *Applied Anthropology: Domains of Application*. Westpoint, CT: Praeger Publishers.

Lewis, O. 1959. *Five Families: Mexican Case Studies in the Culture of Poverty*. New York: Basic Books.

Little, P. 2005. 'Anthropology and Development', in S. Kedia and J. van Willigen (eds), *Applied Anthropology: Domains of Application*. Westpoint, CT: Praeger Publishers, pp. 33–60.

MacClancy, J. (ed.). 2002. *Exotic No More: Anthropology on the Front Lines*. London: University of Chicago Press.

Margolis, M. 1994. *Little Brazil: An Ethnography of Brazilian Immigrants in New York City*. Chichester: Princetown University Press.

Office of the Deputy Prime Minister. 2005. *The Safer and Stronger Communities Fund: The Neighbourhood Element: Implementation Guidance*. London: Neighbourhood Renewal Unit.

Popple, K. 1995. *Analysing Community Work. Its Theory and Practice*. Buckingham: Open University Press.

Rapport, N. 1993. *Diverse Worldviews in an English Village*. Edinburgh: Edinburgh University Press.

Rapport, N. (ed.). 2002. *British Subjects: An Anthropology of Britain*. Oxford: Berg.

Smith, A., E. Lepin and M. Taylor. 2007. *Disadvantaged by Where You Live: Neighbourhood Governance in Contemporary Urban Policy*. Bristol: Policy Press.

Sommers, F.G., and Tana Dineen. 1984. *Curing Nuclear Madness*. York: Methuen.

Timmins, N. 2015. *The Practice of Systems Leadership: Being Comfortable with Chaos*. London: The Kings Fund.

Willis, K. 2005. *Theories and Practices of Development*. London: Routledge.

Wilson, S., and L. Peterson. 2002. 'The Anthropology of Online Communities', *Annual Review of Anthropology* 31: 449–67.

Chapter 5

PARADING THROUGH THE PEACE PROCESS
Anthropology, Governance and Crisis in Northern Ireland
Dominic Bryan and Neil Jarman

There used to be a small terraced Quaker Peace and Service house on University Avenue close to Queen's University in South Belfast. It was an unassuming terraced house which, in the mid 1990s, was home to Janet and Alan Quilley. Unbeknown to many local residents, this house was playing an important role in the peace process. The Quilleys routinely hosted visits and meetings involving a range of different political actors: senior members of British, Irish and American governments; members of both local and national political parties; senior police officers; and members of loyalist and republican paramilitary groups. People were invited to meet in the privacy of their home for off-the-record discussions. The aim was to explore contentious issues related to the political transition and to begin to build relationships among people otherwise connected by enmity and violence.

In June 1996 the Quilleys arranged for three anthropologists to meet to discuss an issue which over the two previous summers had threatened to undermine the still fragile Northern Ireland peace process: protests against Orange Order parades. Disputes over parades had rumbled on the edge of media interest through the spring of 1995, but they emerged as a major issue in July, when the Royal Ulster Constabulary (RUC) responded to protests by the Garvaghy Road Residents' Coalition and blocked the annual Orange Order church parade from Drumcree Church through the mainly Catholic Garvaghy Road estate into Portadown. The decision led to widespread protests by members of the Protestant community. The immediate crisis was only resolved some forty hours later, following intensive mediation, when the residents' group agreed to allow the Orangemen to complete their route on the morning of Tuesday 11 July pending further dialogue. The dispute polarised opinion and led to the mobilisation of people in both main communities; the increase in sectarian tensions threatened to undermine the slowly developing peace process; and the annual nature of the Orange parades meant that protests would reoccur the following year, unless an acceptable means of responding to disputes was found.

The authors of this chapter were two of those at the meeting. Neil Jarman had completed a PhD at University College London the previous year. Dominic Bryan was a year away from finishing his doctoral studies at the University of Ulster at Coleraine. The third anthropologist was Marjorie 'Mo' Mowlam, who had studied anthropology and sociology at Durham University before receiving a PhD in political science at the University of Iowa. In 1996 Mo, Labour MP, was the Shadow Secretary of State for Northern Ireland.

Bryan and Jarman had met in 1992 when individually carrying out research on parades in Northern Ireland, and increasingly worked together over the following years. When nationalist residents' groups began to organise protests against Orange parades in the spring and early summer of 1995, we began to monitor developments. We attended contentious events, observed the activities and made contacts with some of the key protagonists. As chance would have it, Bryan had recently co-authored a report on loyalist parades in Portadown (Bryan, Fraser and Dunn 1995). While the report focused on the events as rituals, it also documented the contentious nature of parades in the town since the mid 1980s. On the back of that report and the fieldwork we had conducted through 1995, the Centre for the Study of Conflict secured a small grant from the Northern Ireland Office's Central Community Relations Unit to enable us to produce what became our first policy-orientated report. Entitled *Parade and Protest: A Discussion of Parading Disputes in Northern Ireland* (Jarman and Bryan 1996), it provided a detailed chronology of the events of 1995, outlined the arguments of the various parties to the disputes and offered a series of suggestions for how the disputes might be addressed. It was hurriedly published as tensions began to rise in the early weeks of the 1996 'marching season', and received widespread publicity in the local media, with both the Deputy Chief Constable of the RUC and the President of Sinn Féin welcoming the report's publication, on BBC Radio Ulster.

The Quilleys arranged for us to meet with Mo so we could give her an overview of the developing parades disputes, and discuss possible policy options. Our meetings with Mowlam, and her special advisor Nigel Warner, continued on an occasional basis through 1996 and into 1997. On 1 May 1997, the Labour Party under Tony Blair won a landslide election and Mowlam was made Secretary of State for Northern Ireland. The peace process and the parading disputes were now her political responsibility. We therefore found ourselves with a direct link to the most senior politician in Northern Ireland at one of the most important moments in recent Irish history.

This chapter outlines our involvement in a key policy area in Northern Ireland during the formative years of the peace process, 1995 to 2001. During this period our work was focused on one particular issue – the disputes over parades – but as they developed, our orientation shifted from initial engagement at the political level, through the development of law and the application of policy, to working with those practically involved with the issues on the ground. We thus engaged with a diverse range of individuals, groups and organisations in trying to understand and review the issues and arguments, monitor events and activities, and help to influence new approaches in policy, law and practice. Coming from an academic background, we always strove to remain independent; we sought to work both with and between government and civil society, and between paraders, protesters and the police. The challenges were to remain informed but impartial, and to reflect the diversity of voices, opinions and concerns of those actively involved in the various locations and disputes. The fact that we came from an academic background seemed to help us maintain a neutral position, but so did the fact that we were 'blow-ins', that is, neither of us was from Northern Ireland. We were thus from one perspective the stereotypical outsider anthropologist, but we were also informed outsiders living and working in the society we had studied; we sought to use that knowledge to influence events in real time.

While we took active steps in positioning ourselves to be able to have an impact on the process, we were also fortunate because the specific context at that time created an unusual opportunity for engagement. First, for most of this period there was no local form of government, rather 'direct rule' from London. One consequence of this 'democratic deficit' was that Westminster politicians, under both the Conservative government up to 1997 and the Labour government after May 1997, actively sought to engage with local civil society: churches, trade unions, non-governmental organisations (NGOs) and academics were all invited to offer their insights on the situation. Second, this was a period when Northern Ireland and its key institutions were undergoing significant change. This was most obvious, from our work, in relation to the RUC. Following the Patten Report of 1999, the force was reformed as the Police Service of Northern Ireland (PSNI). However, prior to the Patten Report, the RUC had undertaken an internal 'fundamental review of policing' to propose areas of change. This led to a number of senior officers entering into dialogue with civil society about less security-led approaches to policing, including alternative ways of dealing with parades. Third, and crucially at the time, there appeared no obvious response to the disputes over parades, other than a massive policing operation. But such a response in 1995 had only served to increase tensions and polarise opinions.

Anthropology and parades in Northern Ireland

Our original research projects were very much within the formal boundaries of academic anthropology. We were both interested in ritual practice, with Jarman concentrating on material culture, examining the use of visual display of banners and flags and the performative elements of parading (Jarman 1997), and Bryan concentrating on the politics of ritual, the control of the Twelfth of July Orange parade in Belfast, and the conceptualisation of the parade as 'traditional' (Bryan 2000). We had both largely ignored the elements of contestation that we witnessed through our early research. Instead we had concentrated on the internal narratives and dynamics involved in the production of rituals and symbolic displays.

Anthropology as a discipline, and ethnography as a method, is particularly good at looking at certain sorts of problems. It is good at examining the worldviews or narratives of groups of people. It is good at exploring the relationships between the formal and the informal in social and political situations. Participant observation offers the possibility of engaging with events, observing behaviour and talking to participants about what they are doing and why. This can reveal the diverse motivations of participants, and a variety of understandings for a diversity of spectators. Anthropology also had a long history in Ireland, initially focusing on rural environments (Wilson and Donnan 2006). Increasingly, however, anthropologists had developed a strong track record of looking at wider issues and urban locations (Curtin and Wilson 1989; Curtin, Donnan and Wilson 1993); they were also exploring ways to apply field research and ethnography to the policy arena (Donnan and McFarlane 1997a, 1997b).

Although parades had long been recognised as a significant feature of social, cultural and political life in Northern Ireland, and disputes over parades have a long history (Boyd 1987; Bryan 2000; Jarman 1997; Farrell 2000), it was not a subject that had attracted much academic attention prior to our work. There was very little written about them as events and practices or their meaning to those involved. Observing the events of 1995 had led us to apply our academic understanding of the issues to inform and influence the emerging debate. We were influenced and encouraged at the outset by Janet and Alan Quilley, and by Robin Wilson, who ran Democratic Dialogue, a local think tank. We were provided with financial and institutional support by Seamus Dunn and Tom Fraser at the Centre for the Study of Conflict at the University of Ulster, Coleraine.

Above all, our ethnographic observation-based approach meant we had established a unique set of relationships with individuals and groups who were involved in both parading and protesting the parades, and in many of the key locations where disputes were being acted out across Northern Ireland.

Parade and protest

There are between two and three thousand parades each year across Northern Ireland organised by the various loyal orders, the Orange Order, Royal Black Institution, Apprentice Boys and by the many loyalist marching bands. Such is their prominence that the period from June to September has come to be known as the 'marching season'. However, no one had mapped the overall marching season, provided a general categorisation of different types of parades or offered an outline of why the different parades took place. *Parade and Protest* (Jarman and Bryan 1996) was a first attempt to provide a broad overview of the parading organisations, a typology of parades and the social and historical reasons for the various events. While we provided a background context, the report also set out a chronology of the disputes, offered an outline of the history and context in each of the contested locations, and analysed the arguments for and against of the main protagonists.

Perhaps most importantly we also set out a range of policy options for dealing with the issues that were raised, some of which emerged directly from our engagement with the protagonists or the police, and some from our own thinking. We highlighted the importance of organisational responsibilities and the need to try to secure consensus; emphasised the value of dialogue between the disputing parties at a local level; underlined the role that mediation might also play in addressing the conflicts; and stressed the potential of stewarding or marshalling to manage behaviour. Significantly, we discussed the benefits of an independent commission or a judicial tribunal to deal with unresolved disputes, and which would remove responsibility from the police for deciding whether a parade should be allowed to continue or should be rerouted. We contextualised this suggestion within a framework of the need to balance the 'civil rights' of different communities with the responsibility of the police to maintain public order.

We had discussed some of our thinking with Mowlem at an early stage, and she had floated the idea of an independent body in February 1996. While this received some support from Archbishop Robert Eames and others, it was not taken up by the Conservative government. We met with Mowlem again on 24 June 1996 to discuss the suggestions in more detail, and the following day she wrote to Patrick Mayhew, the Secretary of State, formally asking him to consider setting up an independent commission to make judgements on parades. He did not respond immediately, although we were informed that he had seen our report. Following major rioting associated with the Drumcree parade in July 1996, Mayhew announced that he was setting up an independent enquiry into the disputes over parades.

Broadening engagement

At the same time as we were discussing future options with the Shadow Secretary of State, we tried to maintain our contacts and relationships with those involved in the disputes at other levels. In particular, this included making contacts with the police and with local human rights groups: both were involved in aspects on the ground, and in suggesting ways to respond to the disputes.

Looking back at the paperwork for this project, it is obvious that funding from the Central Community Relations Unit and working with Seamus Dunn at the Centre for the Study of Conflict assisted in establishing a relationship with the RUC. Dunn put considerable effort into getting data from the RUC Central Statistics Unit. But it is clear, from a letter sent at a later date by Ronnie Flanagan, by then Chief Constable, that until 1996 the RUC did not centrally collate any detailed figures on parades, and that our enquiries, as well as the announcement of a review of parades, were factors that led to the police publishing more comprehensive figures on the number of parades each year. As part of the research for *Parade and Protest*, we also met with a number of senior officers, and we followed this up by sending the Deputy Chief Constable a pre-publication draft, for which he provided comprehensive and largely positive feedback, including comments on the possibility of an independent tribunal for taking over responsibility for decisions on contentious parades. By this point our research seems to have been taken seriously by the police and Bryan has a note of taking a call from Flanagan on the day the report was published.

Engaging with local independent human rights organisations in Northern Ireland, such as the Committee on the Administration of Justice (CAJ) and the Pat Finucane Centre (PFC), was formative in our work. Both organisations were critical of the policing of the events, and in particular of the use of baton rounds (known locally as plastic bullets), especially in the riots of July 1996 (CAJ 1996; PFC 1996). Some members of CAJ expressed concern at the engagement we were developing with the police, and the impact that might have on perceptions of our independence. At that time the RUC was viewed with considerable mistrust by many academics and those working within civil society, and was seen as part of the problem rather than a part of any solution. While we acknowledged these sentiments, we also believed that it was important to engage with all parties to the disputes in order to understand their perspectives and concerns. In retrospect, we consider it was the right thing to have done.

It is also worth noting that having approached the issues we were analysing from an anthropological and academic approach, we were both on a steep learning curve in relation to working in a more applied way and in trying to engage with policy and practice. At this time, we were working things out as we went along. For example, although we discussed the importance of 'civil rights' in *Parade and Protest*, we did not formally contextualise our ideas within a human rights framework, which with hindsight could seem naive. Our discussions with CAJ and PFC were important in helping us to develop our subsequent ideas; we also later worked closely with Prof. Tom Hadden and Anne Donnelly at the Centre for International Comparative Rights Law, Queen's University, in the preparation of their contribution to the ongoing discussion, *Legal Control of Marches in Northern Ireland* (Hadden and Donnelly 1997). This in turn helped broaden our thinking on the role of law and human rights in comparative and historical perspectives and informed the direction of our subsequent research on the parades issues. For example, in 1997 we carried out comparative research, published as *Politics in Public* (Jarman et al. 1998) (see below), and we later undertook a more extensive human rights-orientated review of the issue for the newly constituted Northern Ireland Human Rights Commission (Hamilton, Jarman and Bryan 2001).

From Drumcree to the North Review

The civil disorder of July 1996 was, even by Northern Ireland's standards, substantial. As is perhaps often true of social science research, traumatic social events can create rich opportunities for research.

By early July, the Garvaghy Road Residents' Coalition and local members of the Orange Order, who refused to meet directly with the residents' group leaders, had come to no agreement. On 7 July 1996, the Chief Constable, Hugh Annesely, decided the parade would not be allowed to walk the return route along the Garvaghy Road. An estimated four thousand people gathered to support the Orangemen outside the church and clashed with the RUC. Late that night, Michael McGoldrick, a Catholic taxi driver in nearby Lurgan, was shot dead by a breakaway faction of the Ulster Volunteer Force, which was nominally on ceasefire. Over the nights that followed, Orangemen organised protest parades and blocked roads in locations across Northern Ireland. The security forces struggled to control the situation and on 11 July, with the main Twelfth of July parades only a day away, the Chief Constable reversed his decision and the parade proceeded down the Garvaghy Road. This was followed by three days of rioting in Catholic nationalist areas. By the time it had finished, it was estimated that some twenty-four thousand petrol bombs had been thrown, the police had fired six thousand baton rounds, and another young man, Dermot McShane, was killed by an army vehicle in Derry. At the end of the year, the Secretary of State estimated the cost of the disturbances to be around £40 million (Ryder and Kearney 2001: 174). Support for, and trust in, the police appeared low and community relations seemed worse than ever.

Through the protests in July 1996, we tried to monitor the situation as best we could. But it was a difficult time to do fieldwork, although the work we had undertaken for the report meant we often knew the protagonists, which provided us with some degree of safety when observing events. In Belfast we watched as groups of teenagers burnt cars with apparent impunity. In Bellaghy we discreetly hid in a local shop as loyalist paramilitaries marched a television camera crew, whom we had been talking to earlier, out of the village. In Newtownbutler we were forced to move as the police used dogs to clear protesters. In Portadown we had to negotiate our way around barricades. But our presence at events and the conversations we had with those involved (which served to enable us to be seen as much as to gather information) served us well in subsequent interviews. We watched the policing of events, the role of mediators, observers, politicians and the media as well as the interactions between them all. We recorded hours of news video, occasionally appearing ourselves. We even noted how our own report became part of events as the media picked up on one of our categories – 'feeder parades' – and used it to describe what was taking place.

On 24 July 1996, with more confrontations likely over the Apprentice Boys parade in Derry in August, Mayhew announced that he was setting up an independent review of the legal environment for parades and marches in Northern Ireland. The agencies of the state were in a weak position, and politicians and civil servants were short of ideas, while we, encouraged by influential people in civil society, were full of ideas and keen to make a difference. Our report had proved to be extremely timely. Over the next few months we had numerous meetings with members and the secretariat of the Independent Review on Parades and Marches in Northern Ireland, Peter North, Father Oliver Crilly and Rev. John Dunlop. The North Report was published on 29 January 1997. It quoted the anthropological analysis of the importance of 'ritual' and 'tradition' that Bryan had written in the 1995 report on Portadown (North Report 1997: 43), it drew explicitly on our categorisation of parades (1997: 26-28) and commended our overview of the previous year's events (1997: 33). It also recommended that the government set up an independent body, to be known as the Parades Commission, which would make decisions, termed 'determinations', on contentious parades.

The government broadly accepted the recommendations set out in the North Report. The Parades Commission was set up in March 1997, but until new legislation was enacted, which occurred in February 1998, it had only a watching brief (Jarman 1999: 1433-34). This meant that decisions over the 1997 marching season would continue to be made under the existing legal regime, albeit with one significant change. In May 1997, the Labour Party won a massive victory in the general election; Mowlem became the new Secretary of State for Northern Ireland and would ultimately be responsible for the key decisions over contentious parades.

The Drumcree decision in July 1997 introduced us to some of the challenges and limitations facing independent academics in this type of engagement. Like a number of people working around the issue, we were given the impression by Mowlem and others that the Drumcree parade was likely to be blocked. In the event, however, the security forces entered the Garvaghy area early in the morning of 6 July to secure the route for the Orangemen to march home from the church a few hours later. We were not alone in thinking that we might have been used as a conduit for misinformation, and indeed Mowlem recognised in her autobiography the disappointment that we and others were likely to have felt in the outcome (Mowlem 2002: 99). Over the four days that followed, there was rioting in nationalist areas, with sixty police officers and fifty-six civilians injured, 2,500 baton rounds fired, 402 hijackings and 1,506 petrol bombs thrown (Ryder and Kearney 2001: 222).

It was not the decision that worried us, although it was horrible to watch the operation on the Garvaghy Road, so much as possibly being part of a deception. Along with others, we wondered whether we had been fed the idea that the parade was likely to be blocked in order to provide the police with an element of surprise when they eventually came to clear the Garvaghy Road of protestors. We have no evidence for this, but we know of others who felt the same.

Working with the Parades Commission

From the time when the North Review team was established, we were fully engaged with developments in policy and practice. Among other things, we tried to inform and influence decisions by the key bodies responsible for developing a new approach to the regulation of parades. Between September 1996 and March 1997, we had produced six working papers that we sent to the Parades Review team. These included potential guidelines for the managing of parades in contentious areas, some ideas on dealing with the forthcoming parades in 1997, and, after the publishing of the North Report, a critical analysis of its recommendations. In March 1997, we began working with the secretariat of the newly established Parades Commission, and with colleagues such as Robin Wilson at Democratic Dialogue. We also met with civil servants responsible for drafting the Public Processions (Northern Ireland) Bill, who were keen to discuss the potential contents. However, it was clear that the legislation would be broadly focused on the concept of public order rather than on the right to freedom of assembly, which we were keen on and which had been explicitly emphasised in the North Report.

Engagement with the Parades Commission was relatively easy. Since it had no institutional history, the new body of commissioners and their secretariat were very keen on looking at a range of ideas to enable them to have a positive impact on the disputes. We worked with them on a consultancy basis to produce background materials on parading in a number of the contentious areas. Neither of us had a permanent job at this time and we were dependent on securing funding from a variety of sources to enable us to continue our work. But our ongoing ethnographic fieldwork allowed us to contribute to a number of key discussions, most notably in relation to issues associated with some of the hundreds of marching bands. The bands were hired by Orange lodges for the main commemorative parades, but they also organised their own circuit of competition parades across Northern Ireland and, as we pointed out in *Parade and Protest,* bandsmen are likely to take part in many more parades than members of Orange lodges. And because many of the bands marched behind paramilitary regalia, they were often cited as the main cause of many of the problems associated with parades. The difficulty for the state and for the Parades Commission was that the bands were independent of other organisations, and at that time they had almost no broader organisational structures. Engaging with this constituency was thus difficult for the Parades Commission. To complicate matters further, there was an unused section of public order legislation that provided for the registration of bands, and some in the police and civil service were keen to utilise this. However, we argued that registration was both unworkable and an unreasonable imposition on small local organisations (Jarman and Bryan 1997). We drew on our networks to facilitate meetings between some of those involved in the bands and the Parades Commission. These discussions aimed to inform the Commission about band culture, and in particular the history and meaning of the flags carried by some of the bands in parades. The discussions between the bandsmen and the Parades Commission, plus a subsequent working paper that we produced, provided the basis for the Commission to adjudge which flags would be recognised as legitimate historical symbols, and which would be deemed unlawful to be carried at a parade.

In 1998 the Public Processions Act was passed by Parliament. It empowered the Parades Commission to make determinations on contentious parades. In preparation for this, one idea that was widely discussed with the Parades Commission proved to be deeply problematic. We were aware that, to gain legitimacy, the Parades Commission needed to be seen as balanced and fair. We also knew that there may be a number of parades each year where there were likely to be determinations against those organising the parades. An idea we developed with the Commission was that they would issue what was termed a 'preliminary view', which would provide an overview on how the summer was likely to proceed, with their thinking on which parades should be allowed to proceed along their desired route and which would be rerouted. Looking back, we are not sure this was ever a good idea. But in late April 1998, the Parades Commission planned to make an announcement giving its 'preliminary view' of the forthcoming marching season. However, just a couple of weeks earlier, on 10 April, the Belfast/Good Friday Agreement had been reached by the political parties and the two governments, and a referendum to attempt to secure popular support for it was set for 22 May. It was important for the consolidation of the peace process that a majority of both unionists and nationalists in Northern Ireland gave their support to the Agreement. It was understood that the preliminary view would probably suggest that the Drumcree parade should be rerouted away from the Garvaghy Road. When Unionist leader David Trimble and Prime Minister Tony Blair learnt of this, they persuaded the Parades Commission not to go ahead with their plans for a 'preliminary view'. On 24 April, after this political interference, two of the commissioners who were from a loyalist background, Glenn Barr and Tommy Cheevers, resigned (Ryder and Kearney 2001: 236). In the end, the Parades Commission determined that the 1998 Drumcree parade should not return along the Garvaghy Road. Once again there were violent protests. Early in the morning of 12 July, three young boys, Richard, Mark and Jason Quinn (aged nine, ten and eleven respectively) died when their home in Ballymoney, County Antrim, was petrol bombed by members of the Ulster Volunteer Force. The boys were from a mixed family background and lived in a predominately Protestant housing estate. This terrible act was widely condemned, both locally and internationally. It also revealed significant divisions within the Orange community, and with hindsight this proved the high point of protests over the Drumcree parade. The Orangemen were forbidden to walk the Garvaghy Road in 1998, and despite an ongoing weekly notification of intent to complete their 1998 parade, have not been allowed to since.

Comparisons and lessons

Throughout our engagement with government, civil servants and the Parades Commission, we continued our ethnographic approach to events on the ground. We observed frequent protests, and watched riots erupt and dissipate. We spent many hours talking about policing and about what conflict mitigation might look like in these circumstances. We also became interested in trying to learn how similar problems had been addressed in other societies. We utilised our relationship with the think tank Democratic Dialogue to secure funding from the Community Relations Council and the European Union Peace and Reconciliation Programme, to enable us to examine legal and policing approaches to protests in nine countries: England, Scotland, Ireland, the United States, Canada, France, Italy, Israel and South Africa (Jarman et al. 1998). The research was done on a shoestring, with the funding covering just basic travel and publication costs, but the work had a considerable influence on how we subsequently approached the ongoing problems in Northern Ireland. The comparative studies made us more familiar with a human rights approach, which increasingly framed our work from this time on, as we became gradually familiar with a range of legal and institutional structures used to govern and police public assemblies in different parts of the world. In London we observed how the Metropolitan Police had established a team to engage with the organisers of the Notting Hill Carnival on a year-round basis. This had facilitated the development of mutually respectful relationships, which had helped transform the event from one marked by regular confrontations between young black men and the police to a truly diverse celebration of Caribbean culture. In Boston we learnt how the police had dealt with excessive alcohol consumption on St Patrick's Day, and in New York we observed a community police team liaising with protesters, while a team of lawyer activists monitored the police arrest teams.

We profited most from our trip to South Africa. This country was becoming more and more of a touchstone for those working on peacebuilding in Northern Ireland, as people sought to learn from the South African experience in transitioning from apartheid. The South African peace process between 1990 and 1994 produced an invigorated political environment with thousands of demonstrations, many of which resulted in violence. Similar to events in Northern Ireland, an independent body, the Goldstone Commission, had been set up to examine how to reduce violence at demonstrations; its report highlighted the importance of recognising the right to peaceful assembly and the need for radical changes to the way that the police managed protests (Heymann 1992). We met with local activists in Cape Town who explained how some seventy organisations across the country had established a network of independent monitors in 1992 to liaise between police and demonstrators, to reduce tensions and hold the police to account. In addition, in a number of locations we heard about the value of having trained stewards or marshals to help manage crowds at protests and sporting events, and so reduce interventions by the police. We used the findings from this comparative research to outline a number of general principles relating to the facilitation of peaceful assemblies in our next report, *Politics in Public: Freedom of Assembly and the Right to Protest* (Jarman et al. 1998). We also discussed with the secretariat of the Parades Commission how some of these ideas might be developed. In particular we were keen on seeing how a code of conduct and the Commission's legal determinations might be 'monitored' independently of the police, and whether better trained marshals might help large events pass off with fewer incidents. The research and discussions ultimately led to three interlinked projects we developed over the next three years. These focused on improving the 'policing' of events, and led to monitoring of the behaviour of those involved in different aspects of the parade, improving the marshalling of those parading, and changes to ways in which the police approached the events.

The years from 1995 to 1998 had seen an enormous influx of different forms of 'monitors' who attended contentious parades to observe the behaviour and interactions of the different groups. As a result of one of our suggestions, the North Report had recommended a system of monitoring parades, and the Parades Commission subsequently invited us to write a review of the potential for monitoring. In December 1998, we produced a report recommending that the Parades Commission establish its own procedures for observing activities at parades, independently of the RUC (Bryan and Jarman 1998). In February 1999, we invited nine of the independent monitoring groups to a roundtable discussion to discuss the types of work each were doing, their aims and styles of intervention. From this we published *Independent Intervention: Monitoring the Police, Parades and Public Order* (Bryan and Jarman 1999), which documented a range of international and Northern Irish approaches to monitoring and marshalling at public events; it also made a series of recommendations for how these might be developed to contribute to the better management of the disputes. The Parades Commission eventually set up their own teams of monitors in 2002 and we, along with colleagues from other monitoring groups such as INNATE and Mediation Northern Ireland, were involved in delivering their training.

We held discussions with the Parades Commission to encourage them to support a training programme for parade marshals. We had heard about the impact that well-trained marshals could have from our visit to South Africa. The chair of the Parades Commission, Alistair Graham, helped us make contact with Sue Watson, who had developed and delivered a steward training programme at Leeds United Football Club. We also worked with a London-based police consultant, Dianna Yach, who had previously been based in South Africa, to develop a National Vocational Training (NVQ) programme for marshals in Northern Ireland. The Orange Order were resistant to the idea, probably because it had the stamp of the Parades Commission on it. But thanks to the efforts of Tommy Cheevers, one of the Parade Commissioners, and William Hay, a Democratic Unionist Party councillor in Londonderry, the Apprentice Boys of Derry, who hold two large annual parades in the city, showed considerable enthusiasm for the idea. Due, in part, to the leadership of two senior members of the Apprentice Boys, Allister Simpson and Billy Moore, who championed the idea, and with funding from the Parades Commission and the Community Relations Council, a number of Apprentice Boys took an NVQ Level 3 in Spectator Control. The newly trained marshals were deployed on the ground later that year to better manage their members on the parade. The following year, candidates from the Orange Order undertook the training, as did volunteers from the Gaelic Athletic Association. After these initial trainings, the training programme was hosted by the East Tyrone Further Education College and some of those Apprentice Boys who had undertaken the initial course became trainers themselves (see Bryan 2006; Jarman and Bryan 2000). By the end of 2003, more than 1,100 people had been trained as marshals over a four-year period (Jarman 2004).

We also sought to highlight the role that monitors and marshals could play in the wider policing of parades and protests. We achieved this by engaging with the Independent Commission of Policing for Northern Ireland, chaired by Chris Patten, which had been set up as part of the 1998 Agreement to make recommendations for the reform of policing. The latter was a major and controversial issue, and we felt we had some contribution to make, particularly in relation to public order policing and its relationship to community relations and community policing. Community policing and human rights were seen by many as key elements of any future policing model in Northern Ireland, and traditional public order policing was still very militaristic and relied on both a heavy police presence and frequent use of force. This style of policing seemed to be the very antithesis of community policing. Building on the work published in our report *Independent Intervention* (Bryan and Jarman 1999), we argued that independent monitoring and marshals were ways in which community engagement with the broader policing of events could be introduced. The Patten Report subsequently highlighted the marshal training programme and recommended that it be further developed (Patten Report 1999: 53). Although the report did not make any reference to the role of independent monitors, it did recommend that the Police Ombudsman's office should be responsible for monitoring police performance in public order situations (1999: 56).

As well as these efforts, we began to work more closely with the police on how they dealt with contentious parades. We had been invited by South African colleagues to contribute to a workshop as part of a project they were involved in with the South African Police and the Belgian Gendarmerie. The workshop focused on how community policing principles could be used to underpin the policing of public order. We subsequently approached officers in the RUC about the Belgium-South Africa project and suggested that they should become involved, since the project on public order policing would intersect neatly with the recommendations in the Patten Report. In turn, we secured funding from the Police Authority of Northern Ireland to document and support the work of the three police organisations. Over the next two years, the three forces engaged in a series of exchanges and workshops to share experiences, explore ideas and discuss the challenges of adapting community policing principles to a range of public events. In Northern Ireland these ideas and activities fed into a process of ongoing dialogue with event organisers and protesters, which eventually became known as the 'no surprises' approach. This was highlighted as good practice by the UK Parliament's Joint Committee on Human Rights (2009) and still underpins current policing practice. In Belgium the imperative for the work was their hosting of the Euro 2000 football tournament (Adang and Cuvelier 2001); in South Africa the project was part of a wider reform of the public order policing units (Marks 2005).

Finally, we used the comparative work to further develop our thinking about how human rights principles might be applied in the context of contentious parades and protests. The 1998 Agreement had included a commitment to introducing the European Convention of Human Rights into UK law and the establishment of a Human Rights Commission in Northern Ireland. In 2000 we were commissioned by the Northern Ireland Human Rights Commission to review the human rights framework around parades, protests and policing. By this time, we were working closely with Michael Hamilton, who came from a legal background and was finishing a PhD on the early development of the Parades Commission. This review was published in March 2001 (Hamilton, Jarman and Bryan 2001). For Hamilton and Jarman, this marked the start of a new direction, by drawing on their experiences in Northern Ireland to inform principles and practices internationally. Since 2004, Jarman and Hamilton have been members of the Panel of Experts on Freedom of Peaceful Assembly at the Office for Democratic Institutions and Human Rights, which is part of the Organisation for Security and Co-operation in Europe, a state-level body that works across Europe, the countries of the former Soviet Union and North America. This work has involved the preparation of two editions of the *Guidelines on Freedom of Peaceful Assembly* (Organisation for Security and Co-operation in Europe/Office of Democratic Institutions and Human Rights [OSCE/ODIHR] 2010), which has become an authoritative soft law text. Jarman has also delivered training in the monitoring of assembly to human rights groups in a variety of countries across Eastern Europe, the Balkans and Central Asia (Jarman and Hamilton 2009; OSCE/ODIHR 2011).

Anthropology at a moment of crisis

Looking back, there are a number of striking features in the level of engagement we had with government, the police, independent review bodies and civil society organisations in the period between 1995 and 2001. The disputes over parades, particularly between 1995 and 1998, created an annual crisis in Northern Ireland. There were very high levels of public disorder, a number of deaths and, during such cycles, the media speculated that the peace process was on the brink of collapse. However, the sensitivities of the wider political context made the kind of militaristic policing solutions that had been adopted in earlier decades simply not feasible. In addition, it was a period marked by a 'democratic deficit' and an absence of locally accountable political structures. Instead, decisions were made by politicians who were not answerable to the Northern Ireland electorate and who had limited knowledge of the local context. As a result, the British government largely relied on their civil servants, though at times they also sought the advice and opinions of the wider civil society, workers in the voluntary sector and academics. This was a network that we were to get to know well and become a part of. It was a situation that was unusual in a Western European context, but perhaps not so different from other countries that were moving away from a sustained conflict.

When the disputes over parades first arose in 1995, we were in a fortunate situation. Bryan had just published research that documented the history of disputes over parades in Portadown (Bryan, Fraser and Dunn 1995) and between us we had more than ten years of research on parades and an extensive network of contacts. Surprisingly, but fortuitously for us, despite the obvious importance of parades in relation to the politics and construction of identity in Northern Ireland, little published material was available. Our initial report, *Parade and Protest*, drew on our unpublished academic work to provide some very basic information on the different types of parades and the parading organisations, and an overview of the arguments from the various parties. The report was widely welcomed and used by many of those with an interest in the issue.

The disputes were also an issue that lent itself to an anthropological approach involving first-hand observation, local networks of contacts and informants, plus a sustained and ongoing engagement over a number of years. While our approach was initially from the academic perspective of political anthropology and ritual, we were soon drawn to develop a more applied approach to issues being worked out in real time. In this we were also fortunate in that neither of us was employed in a permanent capacity; we were therefore able to target applications for short-term funding to respond to problems on the ground and issues that interested us. In this we were grateful for the initial support and assistance from Professors Tom Fraser and Seamus Dunn at the Centre for the Study of Conflict at the University of Ulster, from Janet and Alan Quilley in Quaker House and Robin Wilson at Democratic Dialogue. And when we did not have any research money, we still watched parades to ensure we kept in touch with the situation on the streets. In so doing, we quickly learnt about the importance of timing and the need to feed the research into an ever evolving context. While we were initially able to draw on our existing body of work, it was still important to present it in an appropriate format and at a time when it would have the maximum impact. If *Parade and Protest* had been published just a few weeks later (as at one time looked likely), and thus after the events of Drumcree II, our work may well have had much less impact. Again this was a different context from much anthropological and academic research which, when responding to an emerging policy problem, might take months or years to come to fruition.

We were therefore lucky to be in the right place at the right time with the right research material and the right contacts to be able to influence government policy, although we acknowledge that it was important to have a responsive politician we could engage with. Mo Mowlam was just such a person. Once appointed to the Shadow Northern Ireland position, she was keen to meet a wide range of people and get acquainted with the opinions of key people engaged with the conflict. She adopted a very different method to the more traditional, and patrician, approach of Patrick Mayhew, and while this ruffled the plumage of numerous politicians and civil servants, it also brought her respect from many within civil society. We feel that we grasped the opportunity created by our initial meetings with her. We believe that we did approach the task of trying to have a positive impact on a major social issue with energy and, we think, some imagination. It would also be wrong to ignore the sense of excitement involved, whether this was watching riots unfold or when talking with people with the power to make a difference.

When we began our work in the early 1990s, there was little interest in parades in Northern Ireland. They appeared to be the type of obscure and archaic ritual activity so loved by many anthropologists. But times changed very rapidly as peace broke out in Northern Ireland. In 1995 one of us was on BBCs 'Newsnight' with Kate Adie, and we were soon debating the issues with the Secretary of State and Chief Constable. These were extraordinary events, receiving global attention, and we were, at some level, involved. Of course the combination of a commitment to finding solutions to problems in the place where we both lived, plus the excitement of watching events on the streets, was not enough.

We did work hard. We published eight reports and numerous working papers in five years; we provided evidence and information to two enquiries; we contributed to the development of legislation, to the establishment of the Parades Commission and to the debate over the reform of policing. Throughout this time, we were working within a wider context of an unfolding peace process, with the political structures in Northern Ireland in a state of flux, and with regular visits from the British Prime Minister, the Irish Taoiseach and the US President. There are always opportunities to have an influence in periods of political transition. With the encouragement of key people around us, we were able to have a positive impact on one of the major issues in the Northern Ireland of our time. While our work did have some considerable influence, as academics our influence was limited. We helped to inform and advise, but others made the decisions. Not all of our advice was accepted. We argued for amendments to the draft Public Processions Bill that were not accepted. We did not always agree with decisions made by Mo Mowlam, or by the Parades Commission. And the resistance of the Orange Order to work within the new framework has meant that some parades have remained contentious.

At the outset some of the civil servants we engaged with were sceptical about qualitative research methods, preferring the hard facts of data to the vagueness of opinions. But over the past two decades, anthropological fieldwork methods, based around sustained engagement and participant observation, have become more accepted as an element of much of the research that has aimed to influence policy. However, such methodologies tend to have to be squeezed into policy timescales and budgets, rather than the reverse. Since the period we have described, we have both continued to work to inform and influence policy and practice in Northern Ireland. This has included a diverse body of work on such issues as public rituals (Bryan 2009), the flying of flags (Bryan 2007; Bryan and Stevenson 2009; Bryan et al. 2011), immigration (Bell, Jarman and Lefebvre 2004), segregation (Jarman 2007), forced labour (Allamby et al. 2011), hate crimes (Jarman 2012) and the flag protests (Nolan et al. 2014) as we have sought to contribute to the slow process towards a sustained peace. Over the same period, a substantial number of graduates have also sought to apply their academic research interests to the policy arena. While for some this has been a decision made on principle, for others it has been a consequence of the limited number of opportunities to pursue a career in the academy. Most that we are aware of have followed similar paths to ourselves and worked outside of the formal structures of governance, but some have pursued their interests within the civil service or with other statutory bodies.

Conclusions

Our background in anthropology offered us some important opportunities in understanding the wider contextual significance of parades in Northern Ireland. Anthropology provided us with a basic model with which to look at a range of relationships that existed in and around parades. We were able to utilise our theoretical understanding of the way that rituals work to analyse in greater depth what was taking place within and around the parades. We also took the local context seriously and drew on our disciplinary background to highlight their complexity as social events, and in particular tried to emphasise the diversity of motivations among participants in all parades. Even simply understanding the difference between a 'band parade' and a 'church parade' put us ahead of some commentators. It also helped that the British cabinet minister responsible for Northern Ireland had also trained as an anthropologist and therefore had an understanding of our approach and analysis.

Anthropological methodologies, including the practice of 'deep hanging out', as James Clifford then Clifford Geertz called it (Geertz 1998), offered us an opportunity to establish our legitimacy in an intense political environment. We were outsiders, but our intimate knowledge of parading, both in the regional and in an intensely local context, undoubtedly allowed us access to diverse groups wrestling with the problems and eventually to government. We were strong on details of who paraded, where, when and why, and we think this led to us being taken very seriously by people in some key positions who were struggling to develop responses to at times difficult and complex problems. In the classical anthropological sense, we were outsiders with a lot of inside knowledge. In this instance it served us well.

Ethnography, in this case, was the ideal methodology to understand the subject, establish contacts on the ground and stay in touch with developments. Our commitment to the field site allowed us to react very quickly to an ongoing crisis. This also meant getting close to sites of contention, which at times created risks, but also helped to affirm our credibility by allowing us to talk to people who were engaged with the issues at all levels, from the street to Stormont Castle. We were independent researchers, and were largely accepted as such by most people we engaged with, and this proved vital in terms of creating trusted lines of communication with the marching orders, protesters and band groups, with NGOs and, to our surprise at the time, senior politicians, civil servants and police officers.

When we initially began to work in an applied manner, it felt very much a poor relation to the traditional academic focus on writing for peer-reviewed journals and monographs. Policy-orientated research was a low priority and was not considered suitable for submission to research assessment exercises. However, in recent years, greater recognition has been given to research that may have an impact on the wider society and contribute to the development of policy and practice. Academics are being encouraged to think about the potential wider applications of their knowledge and to write for other audiences (Jarman and Bryan 2015). Our experiences suggest that such work can be both challenging and rewarding.

> This chapter is dedicated to the memory of Janet Quilley, who died on 19 April 2016.

Dominic Bryan is Director of the Institute of Irish Studies and a Reader in Social Anthropology, Queen's University Belfast. He is author of *Orange Parades: The Politics of Ritual Tradition and Control* (Pluto Press, 2000) and has undertaken substantial policy research on the use of symbols in public space. In 2016 he was appointed co-chair of the Commission on Flags, Identity, Culture and Tradition, as part of the peacebuilding process in Northern Ireland.

Neil Jarman is a Research Fellow at the Senator George J. Mitchell Institute for Global Peace, Justice and Security at Queen's University Belfast, and director of the Institute for Conflict Research, a not-for-profit, policy research and training organisation.

References

Adang, O., and C. Cuvelier. 2001. *Policing Euro 2000: International Police Co-operation, Information Management and Police Deployment.* Ubbergen: Tandem Felix.

Allamby, L., J. Bell, J. Hamilton, U. Hansson, N. Jarman, M. Potter and S. Toma. 2011. *Forced Labour in Northern Ireland.* York: Joseph Rowntree Foundation.

Bell, K., N. Jarman and T. Lefebvre. 2005. *Migrant Workers in Northern Ireland*. Belfast: Institute for Conflict Research.
Boyd, A. 1987. *Holy War in Belfast*. Belfast: Pretani Press.
Bryan, D. 2000. *Orange Parades: The Politics of Ritual Tradition and Control*. London: Pluto Press.
Bryan, D. 2006. 'The Anthropology of Ritual: Monitoring and Stewarding Demonstrations in Northern Ireland', *Anthropology in Action: Journal for Applied Anthropology in Policy and Practice* 13(1–2): 22–31.
Bryan, D. 2007. 'Between the National and the Civic: Flagging Peace in, or a Piece of, Northern Ireland?', in T.H. Eriksen and R. Jenkins (eds), *Flag, Nation and Symbolism in Europe and America*. London: Routledge, pp. 102–114.
Bryan, D. 2009. 'Negotiating Civic Space in Belfast or the Tricolour: Here Today, Gone Tomorrow'. Working Paper No. 13 (refereed), Conflict and Cities and the Contested State Project. Retrieved 15 September 2016 from http://www.conflictincities.org/workingpapers.html.
Bryan, D., T. Fraser and S. Dunn. 1995. *Political Rituals: Loyalist Parades in Portadown*. Coleraine: Centre for the Study of Conflict, University of Ulster.
Bryan, D., and N. Jarman. 1998. 'Monitoring Parades and Monitoring the Peace: A Report for the Parades Commission'. Unpublished working paper, December.
Bryan, D., and N. Jarman. 1999. *Independent Intervention: Monitoring the Police, Parades and Public Order*. Belfast: Democratic Dialogue & Community Development Centre.
Bryan, D., and C. Stevenson. 2009. 'Flagging Peace: Struggles over Symbolic Landscape in the New Northern Ireland', in M.H. Ross (ed.), *Culture and Belonging in Divided Societies*. Philadelphia: University of Pennsylvania Press, pp. 68–84.
Bryan, D., C. Stevenson, G. Gillespie and J. Bell. 2011. 'Public Displays of Flags and Emblems in Northern Ireland Survey 2010'. Office of the First and Deputy First Minister. Retrieved 15 September 2016 from http://cain.ulst.ac.uk/images/symbols/bryan0510.pdf
Committee on the Administration of Justice (CAJ). 1996. 'The Misrule of Law: A Report on the Policing of Events during the Summer of 1996 in Northern Ireland'. Belfast: CAJ.
Curtin, C., H. Donnan and T. Wilson. 1993. *Irish Urban Cultures*. Belfast: Institute of Irish Studies.
Curtin, C., and T. Wilson. 1989. *Ireland from Below: Social Change and Local Communities*. Galway: Galway University Press.
Donnan, H., and G. McFarlane. 1997a. 'Anthropology and Policy Research: The View from Northern Ireland', in C. Shore and S. Wright (eds), *Anthropology of Practice: Critical Perspectives on Governance and Power*. London: Routledge, pp. 261–81.
Donnan, H., and G. McFarlane (eds). 1997b. *Culture and Policy in Northern Ireland: Anthropology in the Public Arena*. Belfast: Institute of Irish Studies.
Farrell, S. 2000. *Rituals and Riots: Sectarian Violence and Political Culture in Ulster, 1784–1886*. Lexington: University of Kentucky Press.
Geertz, C. 1998. 'Deep Hanging Out' *New York Review of Books*, Vo. 45 No.16, October 1998.

Hadden, T., and A. Donnelly. 1997. *Legal Control of Marches in Northern Ireland*. Belfast: Community Relations Council.

Hamilton, M., N. Jarman and D. Bryan. 2001. *Parades, Protests and Policing: A Human Rights Framework*. Belfast: Northern Ireland Human Rights Commission.

Heymann, P. (ed.). 1992. *Towards Peaceful Protest in South Africa*. Pretoria: HSRC Publishers.

Jarman, N. 1997. *Material Conflicts: Parades and Visual Displays in Northern Ireland*. Oxford: Berg.

Jarman, N. 1999. 'Regulating Parades and Managing Public Order: Parade Disputes and the Peace Process 1995–1998', *Fordham International Law Journal* 22(4): 1415–1439.

Jarman, N. 2004. 'The Marshal Training Programme in Northern Ireland: An Evaluation for the Parades Commission'. Unpublished report.

Jarman, N. 2007. *Towards Sustainable Security: Interface Barriers and the Legacy of Segregation in Belfast*. Belfast: Community Relations Council.

Jarman, N. 2012. *Criminal Justice Responses to Hate Crime in Northern Ireland*. Belfast: Northern Ireland Association for the Care and Resettlement of Offenders.

Jarman, N., and D. Bryan. 1996. *Parade and Protest: A Discussion of Parading Disputes in Northern Ireland*. Coleraine: Centre for the Study of Conflict, University of Ulster.

Jarman, N., and D. Bryan. 1997. 'A Critical Analysis of the Independent Review of Parades and Marches'. Unpublished working paper, February.

Jarman, N., and D. Bryan. 2000. *Stewarding Crowds and Managing Public Safety: Developing a Co-ordinated Policy for Northern Ireland*. Belfast: Community Development Centre.

Jarman, N., and D. Bryan. 2015. 'Beyond the Academy: Applying Anthropological Research. A Case Study of Demonstrating Impact in the UK 2014 REF', *Anthropology in Action: Journal for Applied Anthropology in Policy and Practice* 22(2): 36–41.

Jarman, N., D. Bryan, N. Caleyron and C. De Rosa. 1998. *Politics in Public: Freedom of Assembly and the Right to Protest*. Belfast: Democratic Dialogue.

Jarman, N., and M. Hamilton. 2009. 'Protecting Peaceful Protest: The OSCE/ODIHR and Freedom of Peaceful Assembly', *Journal of Human Rights Practice* 1(2): 208–235.

Joint Committee on Human Rights. 2009. 'Demonstrating Respect for Rights? A Human Rights Approach to Policing Protest, Seventh Report of Session 2008–09'. London: The Stationery Office.

Marks, M. 2005. *Transforming the Robocops: Changing Police in South Africa*. Durban: University of KwaZulu-Natal Press.

Mowlem, M. 2002. *Momentum: The Struggle for Peace, Politics and the People*. London: Hodder and Stoughton.

Nolan, P., D. Bryan, C. Dwyre, K. Hayward, K. Radford and P. Shirlow. 2014. *The Flag Dispute: Anatomy of a Protest*. Belfast: Queen's University, Belfast. Retrieved 15 September 2016 from http://www.qub.ac.uk/research-centres/isctsj/filestore/Filetoupload,481119,en.pdf.

North Report. 1997. 'Report of the Independent Review of Parades and Marches'. Belfast: The Stationery Office. Retrieved 15 September 2016 from http://cain.ulst.ac.uk/issues/parade/docs/north97sum.pdf

Organisation for Security and Co-operation in Europe/Office of Democratic Institutions and Human Rights [OSCE/ODIHR]. 2010. *Guidelines on Freedom of Peaceful Assembly*, 2nd edn. Warsaw: ODIHR, OSCE.

Organisation for Security and Co-operation in Europe/Office of Democratic Institutions and Human Rights [OSCE/ODIHR]. 2011. *Handbook on Monitoring Freedom of Peaceful Assembly*. Warsaw: ODIHR, OSCE.

Pat Finucane Centre (PFC). 1996. *In the Line of Fire: Derry July 1996*. Derry: Pat Finucane Centre.

Patten Report. 1999. 'A New Beginning: Policing in Northern Ireland, the Report of the Independent Commission on Policing in Northern Ireland'. Belfast.

Ryder, C., and V. Kearney. 2001. *Drumcree: The Orange Order's Last Stand*. London: Methuen.

Wilson, T., and Donnan, H. 2006. *The Anthropology of Ireland*. Oxford: Berg Publishers.

Chapter 6

FROM PARTICIPANT OBSERVER TO OBSERVED PARTICIPANT
A Prison Governor's Experience

Peter Bennett

When I received an invitation from the editor of this volume to a workshop on Anthropology Beyond Academia, it was the first time in two decades that I had been asked to present as a social anthropologist. Preparation for the event caused me to reflect on issues I had wrestled with during my career as a prison governor, latterly in charge of a therapeutic community prison held in high regard internationally for its humane and highly distinctive approach to rehabilitation.[1]

The opportunity for reflection was timely because it coincided with my decision to leave the Prison Service of England and Wales after twenty-eight eventful and highly rewarding years and to move on to a position in which a qualification in social anthropology was more readily acknowledged as being of relevance.[2] My narrative is personal and serves a twofold purpose. The first is to convey how in my experience anthropological apprehension and apperception have persisted and contributed to my understanding of the world of work, as well as supporting a management style which has been described by one prison ethnographer as 'people-centred' and 'liberal-humanitarian' (Crewe 2009). I am not suggesting that my approach to prison management has been an inevitable outcome of being a social anthropologist, but I do believe my anthropological understanding has been influential in shaping the way I have managed. The second purpose is even more acutely self-conscious, or reflexive, arising from my experience of having once been a participant observer to having become a participant observed, indeed a self-observing practitioner. Reflexivity appears to have become a preoccupation during my long absence from academia as anthropologists have grappled with the problem of subjectivity in fieldwork. But it has focused in the main on those whose presence in the field has been temporary, who have never entirely belonged and who have returned ultimately to the precincts of academia. But what of those anthropologists who move on to other fields of work and yet who retain a sense of their being actors among many actors in real life dramas which are worthy of observation by others and by themselves? This latter propensity for dissociation and self-observation, seeing oneself as another embedded in a social context, a kind of intellectual levitation, has been an abiding aspect of my experience as a prison governor. It can be edifying, providing an insight into one's own behaviour, and it can lead to a better, and I believe more empathic, understanding of the behaviour of others with whom one shares the stage. The experience brings into sharper focus the impact of one's actions and the need to be mindful of the control one holds over the lives of others, particularly in a custodial setting.

Reflections on leaving academia and becoming a prison governor

Anthropological fieldwork is an absorbing and enduring experience. In the early spring of 1977, I left London bound for the city of Ujjain in Madhya Pradesh, central India. A fieldworker and ethnographer in the Malinowskian tradition, I had planned to explore social aspects of the popular devotional approach to the divine in Hinduism known as *bhaktimarga*, the path of devotion. Eventually, having begun to make sense of the profusion of traditions in this ancient centre of pilgrimage, I developed a particular interest in temple goers belonging to a sect of Krishna worshippers known as *Pustimarga*, The Path of Grace.

To feel accepted as a participant observer is a state of mind laced with subjectivity. To gain the confidence and trust of those who regard us as interlopers can be daunting and frustrating. For me it was a very real and immediate problem. For over a century, *Pustimarga* had been much maligned by journalists, reformers and indologists as 'the way of eating, drinking and enjoyment', its worshippers being dubbed 'the Epicureans of India'. A case before the Bombay Supreme Court in 1862, subsequently known as the Maharaja Libel Case after the sect's gurus known as 'maharajas', was summed up by the puisne judge, Sir Joseph Arnould, who condemned the sect's rituals for their 'loathsome lewdness' and 'debasing bondage' (Mulji 1865: 132).

The case cast an undeserved slur on the *Pustimarga* tradition and its practices, leaving its gurus and devotees with a deep suspicion of any outsiders who professed an interest in researching sectarian customs and rituals. Nevertheless, every day is precious in fieldwork, and ethnographers need to be patient. After several months, during which my presence was tolerated with circumspection, to my surprise I was summoned to the presence of a visiting guru, encouraged to take a preliminary rite of initiation and ordered to follow him to his temple palace several hundred miles away where I was provided with accommodation and access to a library of medieval devotional manuscripts. The gesture was extremely generous but had the unfortunate, and I suspect deliberate, effect of confining me to an archive far removed from the lively community of devotees back in Ujjain. Eventually, however, I managed to return to Ujjain, where I was warmly received. Recognition by a revered guru had made all the difference. I set about observing and recording the social and cultural manifestations of this devotional tradition with an attention to detail that I have not since reproduced.

Returning to the UK, I immersed myself in my fieldwork journal and sectarian texts, conveniently avoiding decisions on a future career. The eventual submission of my thesis brought with it a feeling of emptiness. I remember half-heartedly gathering information on available work and applied for a job as South Asia researcher for Amnesty International, for which I was not selected, and as an assistant governor in the Prison Service, for which I was accepted.

My choice of job was not entirely casual. The prospect of working in a prison, if only for a short time, held the fascination of gaining access to a closed, dynamic, hierarchical and conflict-ridden world. My enthusiasm was more than just academic. I was keen to engage in reform from within and in prisoner rehabilitation. Looking back, however, I suspect there was another influence guiding my decision. Delays in completing my thesis coincided with a recession between 1979 and 1982, accompanied by a rapid rise in unemployment and a dearth of academic jobs. Like many of my colleagues at that time, I suppose I was one of an age-set of anthropologists who grudgingly left academia for the world of government service.

I reported to a large adult male local prison in the West Midlands to undergo a three-month stint in uniform as a prison officer. The initial experience of the prison confirmed many of my previously held stereotypes. At that time prisoners were locked up three to a cell, sometimes for up to twenty-three hours a day. Each prisoner was in possession of a bucket; in the mornings they had to empty out the stinking contents into a recess, in a chore known as 'slopping out'. My uniform marked my initiation into a group that held considerable authority, including if necessary resort to the use of force as a means of control. I was aware that in the closed world of the prison, such authority needs close regulation lest it becomes open to abuse.

After four months I was posted as assistant governor under training to a Young Offender Institution and former Borstal in North Humberside, which maintained a more positive regime based on education and training. Early reports on my progress are telling. One of my tutors was 'a little apprehensive' about my 'approach to this period of training, anticipating an over-sympathetic attitude to prisoners, as is expected of a person indoctrinated in the sociological/philosophical thought pattern'. But evidently my initiation was going well. My tutor continued, 'the fallacy of prejudging was quickly realised ... [He] impressed as being of an open mind, prepared to amend any preconceptions that he may have held'. Another report, by a different tutor, continued to reinforce concerns about my background: 'we have had one or two tussles about his written work, which not unnaturally, tends to follow an academic pattern and pursues all possible angles in depth. He does now appreciate the need to limit oneself to the essentials in some tasks and is making valiant efforts to restructure his style'.

My overall approach and presentational style were clearly of some concern. I have no doubt that some of the advice offered by my tutors was justified. But there was also a clear message: if I was to progress as a prison manager, I would have to forgo the attitudes I had 'learnt' as a student. I recall being fearful of becoming institutionalised, particularly when my anthropological take was that avoiding this insidious threat to my identity was difficult if not impossible.

Having trained for two years as an assistant governor, I was by now beginning to enjoy working with some very dedicated staff, addressing the many and diverse needs of the young prisoners in our custody. But I still feared being overwhelmed by the role. I could always console myself with the thought that self-awareness would prevail by warding off the dangers of 'closed systems: closed minds' or the self-deception described by Sartre as 'bad faith' (1993: 167–69).

An opportunity to engage with the work in a more fulfilling and meaningful way came with a positive development in the Prison Service during the mid 1980s. Following an influential report by the Control Review Committee (CRC) published by the Home Office in 1984, moves were being made for the better management and control of long-term prisoners. The report recommended the creation of small special units for dangerous and disruptive prisoners who had been difficult to manage in high-security conditions and who were often accommodated for considerable periods in solitary confinement, a state of affairs that was costly, disruptive, inhumane and wholly ineffective as a means of encouraging prisoner engagement in rehabilitative regimes. The special units were experimental, derived from the highly innovative Barlinnie special unit in Scotland. The CRC report had set out four principles for their operation: they should be non-punitive in purpose, they should not be regarded as places of last resort, the different units should complement each other, and the Prison Service should be completely open about the establishment of the units and the way they operate.

In 1989 I was appointed manager of the recently established special unit at HMP Hull. The others were set up at HMP Lincoln and HMP Parkhurst. I was able to take part in developing a highly secure but non-punitive regime for Category A prisoners who had been difficult to manage in the high-security system. This new regime placed an emphasis on developing meaningful relationships between staff and prisoners and had a strong rehabilitative focus. Within the unit's close confines, one could observe and experience directly the therapeutic, and often confrontational, life of the unit. A dedicated staff team worked with prisoners with a range of personality disorders to make the experience a positive force in preparing men for reintegration into the mainstream prison population. At the same time, the initiative was exciting precisely because the brief was experimental and innovative. The Prison Service had set up a Research and Advisory Group in 1987 to oversee the development of the units while recognising the dearth of research on managing difficult long-term prisoners. The unit was of special interest to criminologists, providing an opportunity for practitioners and academics to engage jointly in discussions on progress.[3]

It was at this time that I returned to my earlier studies, preparing a book and several articles based on fieldwork in India (Bennett 1990, 1993a, 1993b, 1994). It was as if prison management had become a career and anthropology a pastime. But the latter was hard to sustain, fieldwork material was running out and I had become increasingly out of touch with the anthropological literature on South Asia. And yet in truth I was underestimating the degree to which anthropological apperception had already shaped, and would continue to shape, my approach to prison management.

Anthropological apperception and governing a therapeutic community prison

By 1993, having worked at Prison Service headquarters and a prison in South Yorkshire, I was appointed governor of HMP Nottingham. Becoming a 'governing governor', the term for the governor in charge, was a liberating experience. The governing governor necessarily develops a broad strategic overview of his or her prison, which includes the prison's relationship with the local community and the wider criminal justice system. By personal example, he or she sets the moral tone of the prison, maintaining a working and acceptable balance between security and the protection of the public on the one hand, and prisoner care, rehabilitation and resettlement on the other. The position brings with it an opportunity to take a lead on improving prison conditions, regimes and rehabilitation initiatives. As I progressed from HMP Nottingham (1993–98), to HMP Wellingborough (2000–02) and latterly to HMPs Grendon and Spring Hill (2002–11), I became increasingly disappointed with the statistical focus of much prison research and its preoccupation with measuring reoffending rates. Such research is essential in determining what works in achieving social reintegration, but there was also a need for good qualitative ethnographic studies that would lead to a better understanding of the social factors predisposing to offending behaviour, and hence should prove invaluable in developing interventions that could help prisoners to engage with prison regimes and play an active part in their own rehabilitation.

Anthropological knowledge and experience continued to shape my approach to prison management, in three ways in particular. First: my readiness to support, and recognise the value of, qualitative, and in particular ethnographic-based research. Second: the application of anthropological apperception to the interpretation of the dynamics operating within a prison, between the prison and the community, and between the prison and the overarching Prison Service. Third: a growing self-awareness in which the self is neither dissociated observer, nor even participant observer, but self-observing participant.

Criminologists have commented on the decline of prison ethnography. Wacquant describes how 'the ethnography of the prison thus went into eclipse at the very moment when it was most urgently needed' (2002: 385). More recently Crewe, following Wacquant, has argued that despite the considerable rise in the use of imprisonment in recent years, their 'innards have become increasingly obscured ... At a moment when it seems essential to understand what imprisonment is and what it does, research into the prison's interior life has become somewhat scarce' (2009: 1). I was concerned that it was not simply that anthropologists or ethnographers were uninterested in prison research, but that funding for such research and permission for access to prisons were difficult to come by.

I was therefore delighted when, in 2002, while I was governor of Wellingborough, Ben Crewe was given permission to conduct fieldwork in the prison. I know that Ben was reassured in the knowledge that the governor understood the nature of participant observation and could maintain a discreet and distanced support (Crewe 2009: 464). I nevertheless felt some unease. On the one hand, Ben's research would throw light on areas of prisoner society with which I was in close proximity but had little opportunity to observe first-hand. On the other hand, although the main focus of his work would be on prisoners and staff–prisoner interaction, prison managers, and inevitably the governor, would also feature. I had a sense of what it would feel like to be the participant observed, this time by another, and the picture might not be flattering.

The Prisoner Society: Power, Adaptation and Social Life in an English Prison (Crewe 2009) is an excellent analysis and will no doubt occupy a prominent place in the scanty literature of prison ethnographies. Moreover, it is through such ethnographies that we can better understand what really goes on in prisons and how best we can begin to provide the right conditions for prisoners to voluntarily engage in their own rehabilitation. My portrait as being a 'liberal-humanitarian' with 'an air of benign academic eccentricity' and a style that 'some saw as friendly and "fluffy" and others as reserved and inscrutable', grappling with the frustrations of managerialism and promoting a people-centred-approach, is not dissimilar to that described by my early Prison Service tutors (Crewe 2009: 36).

Ben Crewe had hardly begun his fieldwork at Wellingborough when I was appointed governor of Grendon and Springhill prisons. Grendon was a prison I had long admired for its therapy but had never anticipated having a part to play in its management. On top of that, it is probably the most researched prison in the Prison Service and it was from the excellent monograph by Elaine Genders and Elaine Player (1995) that I was able to get a preview of its complex dynamics.

In 1932 the Medical Commissioner, Sir Norwood East, had recommended a prison for the psychological treatment of 'willing' offenders.[4] But bureaucratic procrastination and World War II delayed such plans until 1962, when Grendon opened as 'a unique experiment in the psychological treatment of offenders', specifically for prisoners with mental disorders considered to be responsive to treatment as well as those diagnosed as psychopaths (Genders and Player 1995: 5). Until 1985, Grendon was managed differently to other prisons, maintaining a degree of autonomy within the mainstream Prison Service. However, following a report by the Advisory Committee on the Therapeutic Regime at Grendon (ACTRAG) (Home Office 1985) set up by the Home Secretary, the post of medical superintendent – the medical doctor in charge of Grendon – was replaced by a non-medically qualified governor. Thereafter, a senior medical officer reported directly to the governor.

Following ACTRAG, the appointment of a governor in charge heralded a critical change in the management of the prison, the repercussions of which have continued to this day. Genders and Player, along with many other staff and prisoners at Grendon, regarded the medical superintendent as the guardian of a medical and communitarian mode of treatment that would preserve the therapeutic regime in the face of a potentially overwhelming managerial revolution in the Prison Service. The governor and staff, having their primary allegiance to the penal institution, were regarded as being impossibly situated to protect and promote the therapy (Genders and Player 1995: 227). There is some truth in these warnings, but they are unduly pessimistic. Grendon would find a way of adapting to changes in the mainstream prison system. From this time on, the governors of Grendon have shared common experiences: on the one hand, they have had to mitigate some of the intrusive effects of the more extreme forms of managerialism with its emphases on audits, performance management and cognitive skills programmes; on the other hand, they have borne the brunt of the challenges, and sometimes vitriol, expressed by Grendon therapists and prisoners against the Prison Service, which was seen by many of them as working to dilute the therapy, or even to threaten its demise, with the ultimate outcome that Grendon would become a 'system prison'. The 'system' was a term used by many staff and prisoners to describe the encroaching organisation to which they, as 'Grendonites', felt little or no sense of belonging.

Whatever the implications of this change, a frequent topic of conversation at Grendon concerned the threatened erosion of therapeutic community principles by a 'system' that remained allegedly ignorant of, and unsympathetic to, the needs of a therapeutic institution. And in between was the governor, to be regarded either as the secular agent of Grendon's demise as a therapeutic prison or as its champion in the face of a Prison Service that had lost sight of its exceptional rehabilitative potential, never becoming one or the other but forever attempting to contrive a workable reconciliation.

Despite the threats to Grendon's existence over the decades, both real and perceived, it has shown an extraordinary degree of resilience, continuing to operate as a Category B therapeutic prison for adult males with complex needs. Unlike the majority of prisoners who are subject to a system of allocation, these inmates have volunteered to spend at least two years of their sentence addressing their offending behaviour by engaging in a highly intensive form of group therapy.

During my time at Grendon the proportion of the population serving life and indeterminate sentences increased from 50 to 90%. The majority of prisoners had been convicted of serious and violent offences, including murder, manslaughter, rape and armed robbery. Within Grendon at the time there were five therapeutic communities, each accommodating between forty and forty-six prisoners, along with an induction/assessment unit for twenty-five prisoners. One community consisted entirely of sexual offenders, although a few were dispersed among the other communities. Unlike most prisons, in which sexual offenders are kept in separate accommodation for their own safety, prisoners at Grendon generally agree to set aside their customary antipathies in the common interest of creating a safe space for therapy. The regime is based on a programme of community meetings, usually on Mondays and Fridays, attended by the whole community, specialist staff and prison officers, and small group meetings held on the intervening weekdays. The small group meetings, facilitated by a therapy specialist or a trained prison officer, cover a wide range of issues, including early childhood experiences, histories of personal abuse, incidents in the therapeutic community and the impact of crimes on victims. These groups, which include psychodrama and art therapy, report back to the community, chaired by a prisoner elected by his peers. The community functions as a democratic decision-making body within the restrictions of overall prison security, prisoners challenging and discussing one another's behaviour, voting on appointments to positions of responsibility within the community and, as a last resort, voting on a prisoner's removal from the community if he fails to engage in the therapy or breaches one of the agreed rules: no sex, no drugs, no violence. The sanction of removal is not invoked readily; rather, infringements of the rules may be seen as offence-paralleling behaviour open to challenge and further therapeutic intervention. Similarly, staff will often refrain from placing a prisoner on a disciplinary charge leading to adjudication and, if appropriate, punishment by a governor grade; rather, the prisoner's behaviour will be challenged by his peers in the community meetings. The therapy is not confined to the formal meetings but extends to all areas of prison life twenty-four hours a day, seven days a week.

By any standards, Grendon is a remarkable prison: non-punitive in its approach; a low incidence of self-harm and bullying; a scarcity of hard drugs; few serious incidents; very occasional resort to the use of force as a means of control; the absence of a segregation unit; the coexistence of sexual and non-sexual offenders; and highly positive prisoner–staff relationships. Reports by Her Majesty's Inspector of Prisons have consistently commented on Grendon as being 'an exceptionally safe prison' with 'exceptionally good prisoner–staff relationships', which is remarkable in a prison that accommodates 'a high proportion of men who are popularly known as psychopaths'.[5]

I have described elsewhere and in some detail the tensions arising from maintaining two seemingly incompatible institutions under one roof (see, for example, Bennett 2006, 2007, 2009, 2010a). My observations as a governor are bound to be subjective. But subjectivity can be a strength if our intention is to develop a greater understanding of our socially situated selves and hence of the impact of our actions on others. I can best illustrate my point by revisiting some of the observations I made during my early days as governor at Grendon, during which anthropological apperception, developing an awareness of ourselves as social beings as opposed to 'ourselves and others', was a defining discourse. Indeed, this form of awareness is what the anthropologist Louis Dumont referred to as 'the essential humanist aspect of the teaching of anthropology' (1980: 7).

On arrival at Grendon in 2002, I believed I had a reasonable grasp of its therapeutic regime. Events were to prove otherwise. Grendon was enduring what I have described as one of its periodic bouts of insecurity brought on by the escape of three prisoners from the sports field a year earlier. The investigation that followed had been highly critical of the prison's security arrangements. The event and its aftermath dealt a devastating blow to staff confidence, particularly for those directly engaged in therapy: they feared the enforcement of a much stricter degree of control, which would inevitably threaten the therapeutic principles on which the prison was based. The governor appointed immediately following the escape had moved on before he had time to respond fully to the investigation report's recommendations and there followed several months without a governor in charge who could be expected to provide clear direction and restore confidence in the therapeutic regime. The traditional emphasis on 'dynamic security' (Dunbar 1985), based on positive staff–prisoner interaction and embedded in the prison's therapeutic principles of openness and trust, had been severely tested. Politicians and the public were becoming increasingly intolerant of prison escapes. Calls for the protection of the public and the security of prisons threatened to place an increasing reliance on physical and procedural security and less reliance on prisoner goodwill and intelligence gained through close prisoner–staff engagement. A climate of uncertainty prevailed.

Unfortunately, an incident coincided with my arrival, which did nothing to help restore confidence.[6] After only three days of my induction, I went home for the weekend and returned to hear the news that a tool had been found in the possession of a prisoner. In fact, the tool had not been 'found', nor had it ever gone missing. The prisoner had been given it by a member of staff who had, with no heed for the strict security controls of a Category B prison, failed to ensure its safe return or even log its whereabouts. Before the tool's missing status had been noticed, the prisoner handed it in. On this occasion, however, the officer who received it, being mindful of the rules regarding a 'missing tool', duly expressed his concern and informed security. The details are important because they serve to illustrate succinctly the climate of uncertainty and ambiguity that permeated the Grendon regime at that time. One prison officer could consider his actions to be consistent with the demonstration of trust appropriate in a therapeutic setting; the other had remained mindful of the security arrangements appropriate to the supervision of a category B prison.

A full lockdown and search of the prison had already been planned during my absence. I had few qualms in taking over responsibility for the follow-up search. In Prison Service terminology, a 'missing tool' is a serious and reportable incident. A search of all prisoner areas would be necessary in case other tools that could be used to inflict injury or aid an escape had gone missing. In the light of Grendon's damaged reputation and its lax security, there seemed all the more reason to follow up the incident as a matter of urgency. I was told that the tool was an electric drill of the kind used by hobbyists but not normally allowed in the possession of a prisoner, at least not overnight and with no official record of its precise location. For security staff, this breach was serious, and indeed expressed by them with the utmost gravity as they revealed to me details of an implement that in the wrong hands 'could slice through cell bars like a knife through butter'.

Over the following three days, the search – subsequently dubbed 'The Big Spin', 'spin' being prison slang for a search – took on an increasing momentum as those staff less sensitive to the subtleties of therapy and more comfortable with their duties of maintaining discipline and good order used the opportunity to clear prisoners' cells of precious bits and pieces which they had accumulated over many months. For most prisoners the cell is a highly intimate space in which every effort is made to make it more homely, often in the form of minor decorative features and almost invariably centred on an 'altar-like' arrangement of precious possessions and a few photographs of family and loved ones. At Grendon, many prisoners had scavenged for bits of furniture, carpet tiles and makeshift tablecloths, behaviour that had been mostly ignored by prison officers in the relaxed regime of the wing communities. The prisoners, as well as many staff, were outraged at what they believed to be an unnecessary invasion of personal space by operational staff, and complained that the carefully cultivated climate of trust and safety nurtured by the communities had been destroyed. The winter edition of the prisoner magazine *Feedback* (2002–03) reported the dramatic events: 'over a few dark days in September Grendon was locked down as teams of officers conducted a search of cells. It sent shockwaves through the community ... We were intruded upon unnecessarily ... It was payback by security ... A reminder of the system ... There's a conflict between therapy and security', and perhaps for me most telling of all, 'It seems to be connected with the new governor'.

That the prisoner in possession of the drill had allegedly been using it to pursue his hobby of carving Fabergé style eggs, which was undoubtedly the case, had all the elements of a comic farce. But it still had implications for the security of a Category B prison.

The incident revealed the tensions inherent in Grendon's complex structure arising from its hybrid status as a prison and a therapeutic community. The Big Spin momentarily stirred up emotions, fault lines, tensions and ambiguities that would have to be negotiated with care if Grendon was to move forward as a humane and effective model of good practice in prisoner rehabilitation. I now found myself playing a leading part in open conflict with those who regarded themselves as defending a tradition under attack and reinforcing the ongoing conflict between security and therapy, and where ultimately power should lie: in the operational or therapeutic line.

I reflected long and hard on the incident and my own part in its management. Given the deficiencies in security, I was not confident that Grendon was meeting the fundamental requirement of a secure prison. But I could also understand the concerns and fears of those therapists who endeavoured to preserve, in the midst of a hierarchical prison setting, a safe space for the practice of a 'democratic' form of group therapy which had shown remarkable results in reforming serious offenders and maintaining a humane prison. Neither a cavalier approach to procedural security, nor zealousness such as that shown during the Big Spin, was acceptable. The governor would have to strike the right balance. But to do so would also require a shift of role in order to find ways of encompassing security and therapy while also putting in place a management structure that would allow this to happen. Such tensions need not, and perhaps could not, be entirely overcome or resolved; but they could be understood, managed and held in balance in a positive way by achieving a symbiosis in which security was less intrusive, more consultative and geared to providing a safe space for therapeutic practice.

Within three months of my arrival I had commissioned an internal review to identify obstacles to progress and to make recommendations for overcoming them. The review did not mince its words: Grendon was an unhealthy prison and could not operate effectively as a therapeutic community prison with the prevailing level of conflict and factionalism.

Along with the review's author, subsequently appointed as Director of Therapeutic Communities, we set about revising the management structure in order to enable the resolution of conflict while simultaneously allowing the culture of enquiry, openness, consultation and challenge to continue. The key lay in the relationship between the governor and the Director of Therapeutic Communities, both of whom resolved to work in partnership, with the governor acting as *primus inter pares*. We were well aware that since the governor had replaced the medical superintendent in 1985, the relationship between the two had often been an uneasy one, sometimes manifest in open conflict or even mutual avoidance. The integration of the operational and therapeutic lines at senior level was to set a powerful example of consultation and cooperation, which could be emulated and reproduced at all levels of the management structure.

The change provided the necessary stability for the senior managers to set about securing a clear strategic place for Grendon within the wider Prison Service, while asserting Grendon's distinctive role and the requirements of therapy. In particular, the accreditation of the therapy was essential in a world where cognitive skills programmes were in the ascendancy, and measurable outcomes were the required indicators of performance. We had no doubts that Grendon would continue to struggle if it continued to oppose new initiatives in risk assessment, resettlement, education, security, audits and performance management. It was clear that for the prison to thrive as an alternative treatment regime, it had to demonstrate its willingness to engage in an overall strategy of offender management. Grendon had cherished its autonomy but in doing so had failed to establish a clear strategic position in a national initiative for the treatment of offenders with complex and mental health needs.

The only prison entirely devoted to group therapy, Grendon has always been something of an anomaly within the mainstream Prison Service, being all the more reason for a need to prioritise research as a means of proving its worth. But research would not only be restricted to measuring reoffending rates, important as it undoubtedly is, but would also focus on positive aspects of the regime: its exceptional prisoner–staff relationships, its reputation as an exceptionally safe and humane prison, its high levels of prisoner engagement and the example it sets for reforming prisoners and for prison reform (see Bennett 2010b and other chapters in Shuker and Sullivan 2010).

One anthropologist I was keen to welcome at Grendon was Lorna Rhodes, who had conducted research on maximum security prisons in the USA (2004). Rhodes' research reveals Grendon to be the antithesis of maximum security prisons with their punitive regimes and regular resort to prisoner isolation. Grendon provides an alternative model for managing high-security prisoners and stands out as an example of good practice worthy of emulation. Rhodes 'shared with Grendon residents an initial experience of disbelief at the prison's egalitarian and informal atmosphere', but later concluded how 'Grendon has evolved a way of using institutional practice itself to address the harm done by institutional practice' (2010: 215).

In a similar vein, Genders and Player originally anticipated that their task would be to reveal Grendon's 'inner agenda' of penal control, only to find that the 'issue was not whether custody and treatment are antithetical, but how these unconsenting bedfellows were being accommodated within a single institution' (1995: 17). It is interesting that the comments of the above observers would seem to mitigate, at least in the case of Grendon, the pessimism expressed by Foucault on penal institutions (Foucault 1979). In Foucault's terms, the idea of the therapeutic prison would appear to be yet another form of coercive control: an extension of the carceral society. While I do not take direct issue with Foucault's thesis, I have argued against his absolutism as I have worked to reconcile security as an extension of the 'system' and the need to maintain a safe therapeutic space: although security dominates and encapsulates the other, it nevertheless can adapt its authority to enable the practice of a distinctive kind of rehabilitative therapy in which participants work together, not to change the world, but to maintain a space where things are done differently (Bennett 2010a). The trick has been how to allow this therapeutic space to be maintained in a prison setting, ensuring that operational procedures do not trespass unnecessarily, and to support therapists in maintaining a space good enough for a form of rehabilitation which accommodates, and is accommodated by, the restrictions that threaten to overwhelm it (2010a: 48). Managing this dynamic, and restraining the intrusive tendencies of enthusiastic security staff, has been a constant struggle but still an achievable goal.

Trespass of therapy boundaries happens from time to time. Sometimes it is necessary in the overriding interests of security, in which case I have insisted that the decision to do so should only be made by the governor in charge of the prison, and wherever possible by first consulting with the Director of Therapeutic Communities. In addition, every effort is made to set up a consultation process between operational and security staff, and with prisoners, explaining and justifying the need for intervention. But if intervention occurs unnecessarily, and without appropriate permission from the governor, there is always a danger that therapeutic integrity will be harmed, with the result that prisoners will feel less inclined to share with staff and colleagues their innermost thoughts – a prerequisite for progress in therapy.[7]

Concluding remarks

Special units and therapeutic communities are exciting because they are experimental, they encourage us to question penal orthodoxies and, by doing things differently, provide ideas and opportunities for wider prison reform. Having managed a special unit and a therapeutic prison, I have often been struck by the resemblances between these closed institutions and religious sects, my original focus of research. I have compared the tensions existing between the heterodox sect and mainstream religious orthodoxy with those between the 'democratic' therapeutic community and the encapsulating Prison Service. On the one hand, there is the sect, which is typically egalitarian, often recruiting from the deprived and oppressed, promoting the removal of priestly hierarchies and valuing the participation of all adherents in a tightly knit community of the faithful, whose members are volunteers who remain suspicious of the outside world and who prefer spontaneous devotion to conventional ritual. On the other hand, we have the therapeutic community, which aspires to 'democratic' principles, recruits from those considered to be disruptive, dangerous or even untreatable, encourages the participation of prisoners as equals in community meetings, whose members, including staff engaged in therapy, often describe the overarching Prison Service as inhumane and ineffective as a means of rehabilitation, who share a distrust of mainstream authority and who articulate their feelings with an eloquence and spontaneity which is highly ritualistic. Indeed, many members of sects and of therapeutic communities describe a similar revelatory experience: an intense, often highly emotional and life-changing feeling amounting to conversion. I have often listened to the highly charged life-changing testimonies of Grendon prisoners and been reminded of the devotional outpourings of sectarian saints.

I have tried to understand organisational dynamics, respecting the views, complaints and fears of staff and prisoners, and playing the part of broker, striving to achieve an adaptation to, as well as a compatibility with, the wider Prison Service, reaching beyond mere compromise to a position where the therapeutic community is accommodated within the wider penal structure while preserving its integrity as a unique therapeutic prison. My understanding of my role as a participant, indeed as a self-observing participant, is bound to be subjective. But I do believe that anthropological apprehension and apperception have provided the conceptual wherewithal to enhance my understanding of my role in prisons and helped me to understand the views, feelings and behaviours of those with whom I have worked. I have described this experience of thinking both 'role-free' and 'in-role' as a kind of intellectual levitation, perceiving oneself as an actor embedded in the thick description of one's own ethnography. By thinking in this way, day to day frustrations are better understood, tolerated and managed, being placed in a context that renders one's own actions and the actions of others more meaningful (Bennett 2006: 134).

I have focused on Grendon at a time of crisis. But I would not wish to convey the impression that conflict has continued to such a damaging degree throughout the past decade. Dispute and challenge are endemic, being a positive and necessary part of the fabric of therapy. But as I have shown, there is always the danger that things can get out of hand. A report by Her Majesty's Inspector of Prisons in 2009 praised the prison for its 'remarkable achievements with some of the system's most dangerous and difficult prisoners', with 'the needs of security and therapy ... appropriately balanced'. But the report also expressed concern over 'the threat to its future from continued financial cuts' and called for 'a national strategy to guide appropriate referrals to Grendon'. Despite its therapeutic focus, it has in the later years managed to achieve 'good' audit ratings for its security and the highest level 4 rating for its overall performance as a prison. And most encouraging of all, it was awarded the highly prestigious Longford Prize in November 2008; the citation reads 'Grendon's therapeutic culture, supported throughout the prison by staff and prisoners together, has produced results in terms of reducing reoffending and promoting a humane, safe regime which offer a beacon of hope'. But as the Director of Therapeutic Communities constantly reminded me, Grendon is 'a work in progress'; its inherent ambiguities will always call for sensitive management.

Peter Bennett is a former governor in HM Prison Service and a former Director of the International Centre for Prison Studies (UK). He is now working as an independent consultant on international prison reform.

In 2016 the Royal Anthropological Institute awarded him the Marsh Award for Anthropology in the World.

Notes

1. The author was governor of Her Majesty's Prison Grendon and Her Majesty's Prison Spring Hill in Buckinghamshire from September 2002 until October 2011. Spring Hill is a Category D open prison for adult males. Grendon, adjacent to Spring Hill, is a Category B therapeutic community prison for adult males which is unique in being the only prison in the UK entirely devoted to group therapy.
2. The author was Director of the International Centre for Prison Studies (ICPS), a partner of the University of Essex, from 2012 to 2014. In November 2014, ICPS merged with the Institute for Criminal Policy Research (ICPR) based in the School of Law, Birkbeck, University of London. The author is now self-employed as a consultant on international prison reform.
3. See, for example, a contemporary collection of conference papers on the special units written by academics, prison specialists and governor grades (Bottomley and Hay 1991).
4. For information on the origins of Grendon, see Stevens (2010).
5. See HM Chief Inspector of Prisons (HMCIP) reports (2004, 2007 and 2009).
6. I have described this incident and subsequent events in detail elsewhere; the following paragraphs on the search or 'Big Spin' are a summary of the article mentioned (Bennett 2007).
7. See Bennett (2010a) for examples of the impact on therapy caused by boundary trespass.

References

Bennett, P. 1990. 'In Nanda Baba's House: The Devotional Experience in Pushti Marg Temples', in O. M. Lynch (ed.), *Divine Passions: The Social Construction of Emotion in India*. California: University of California Press, pp. 182–211.
Bennett, P. 1993a. *The Path of Grace: Social Organisation and Temple Worship in a Vaishnava Sect*. Delhi: Hindustan Publishing Corporation.
Bennett, P. 1993b. 'Krishna's Own Form: Image Worship and Pusti Marga', *Journal of Vaisnava Studies* 1(4): 109–34.
Bennett, P. 1994. 'Guru, Mantra and Tradition: An Account of Vallabhacarya's Foremost Disciple, Damodardas Harsani', *Journal of Vaisnava Studies* 2(2): 99–125.
Bennett, P. 2006. 'Governing a Humane Prison', in D. Jones (ed.), *Humane Prisons*. Oxford: Radcliffe Publishing Ltd, pp. 129–39.
Bennett, P. 2007. 'Governing Grendon Prison's Therapeutic Communities: The Big Spin', in M. Parker (ed.), *Dynamic Security: The Democratic Therapeutic*

Community in Prison. London and Philadelphia: Jessica Kingsley Publishers, pp. 203–12.

Bennett, P. 2009. 'Reform From Within: The Grendon Example', Criminal Justice Matters 77: 14–15.

Bennett, P. 2010a. 'Security and the Maintenance of Therapeutic Space: A Grendon Debate', Prison Service Journal 187: 48–52.

Bennett, P. 2010b. 'Introduction', in R. Shuker and E. Sullivan (eds), Grendon and the Emergence of Forensic Therapeutic Communities. Oxford: Wiley-Blackwell, pp. 3–5.

Bottomley, K., and W. Hay (eds). 1991. Special Units for Difficult Prisoners. Hull: Centre for Criminology and Criminal Justice, University of Hull.

Crewe, B. 2009. The Prisoner Society: Power, Adaptation and Social Life in an English Prison. Oxford: Oxford University Press.

Dumont, L. 1980. Homo Hierarchicus: The Caste System and its Implications. Chicago and London: The University of Chicago Press.

Dunbar, I. 1985. A Sense of Direction. London: Her Majesty's Stationery Office.

Foucault, M. 1979. Discipline and Punish: The Birth of the Prison. New York: Vintage Books, Random House.

Genders, E., and E. Player. 1995. Grendon: A Study of a Therapeutic Prison. Oxford: Clarendon Press.

HM Chief Inspector of Prisons. 2004. HM Prison Grendon: Report on a Full Announced Inspection, 1–5 March 2004. London: HM Inspectorate of Prisons.

HM Chief Inspector of Prisons. 2007. Report on an Unannounced Short Follow-up Inspection of HMP Grendon, 31 October–2 November 2006. London: HM Inspectorate of Prisons.

HM Chief Inspector of Prisons. 2009. Report on an Announced Inspection of HMP Grendon, 2–6 March 2009. London: HM Inspectorate of Prisons.

Home Office. 1984. Managing the Long Term Prison System. The Report of the Control Review Committee. London: Her Majesty's Stationery Office.

Home Office. 1985. First Report of the Advisory Committee on the Therapeutic Regime at Grendon. London: Her Majesty's Stationery Office.

Mulji, K. 1865. History of the Sect of Maharajas or Vallabhacharyas in Western India. London: Trubner and Co.

Rhodes, L. 2004. Total Confinement: Madness and Reason in the Maximum Security Prison. Berkeley: University of California Press.

Rhodes, L. 2010 '"This Can't Be Real." Continuity at HMP Grendon', in R. Shuker and E. Sullivan (eds), Grendon and the Emergence of Forensic Therapeutic Communities. Oxford: Wiley-Blackwell, pp. 203–16.

Sartre, J.-P. 1993. Essays in Existentialism. New York: Citadel Press.

Shuker, R., and E. Sullivan. 2010. Grendon and the Emergence of Forensic Therapeutic Communities. Oxford: Wiley-Blackwell.

Stevens, A. 2010. 'Introducing Forensic Democratic Therapeutic Communities', in R. Shuker and E. Sullivan (eds), Grendon and the Emergence of Forensic Therapeutic Communities. Oxford: Wiley-Blackwell, pp. 7–24.

Wacquant, L. 2002. 'The Curious Eclipse of Prison Ethnography in the Age of Mass Incarceration', Ethnography 3(4): 371–98.

Chapter 7

IDENTITY AND APPROPRIATION IN APPLIED HEALTH RESEARCH

Rachael Gooberman-Hill

Introduction

Healthcare policy and practice shapes the daily lives of all citizens at times of health and illness. Increasingly, research evidence is used to underpin decisions about such policy and practice in a process often described as 'evidence-based medicine'. Evidence-based medicine has been characterised as 'a movement, a practice, a paradigm, a methodology, an innovation and a regulatory system' (Lambert 2006), highlighting the complexity of the notion of evidence and its interface with decisions about policy. Processes by which evidence influences health and healthcare are numerous, but in the UK, the National Institute for Health and Care Excellence (NICE) is perhaps the most obvious example of a structure that explicitly draws on research evidence to influence practice. NICE uses 'best available scientific evidence' to develop and publish guidance that is widely applied in clinical practice. The way in which evidence becomes guidance within structures such as NICE and the subsequent implementation of guidance are interesting areas in their own right (Brown and Calnan 2013; Spyridonidis and Calnan 2011; Davies, Wetherell and Barnett 2006), but before evidence can be harnessed to develop guidance, research studies must be designed, funded and conducted. It is this process that is the subject of this chapter.

To produce the growing corpus of research evidence, large numbers of researchers must ply their trade, securing funding and generating evidence. In health research, such researchers now hail from numerous disciplines including clinical specialties, epidemiology, statistics, health economics, psychology, sociology and anthropology. Often working in multidisciplinary teams, researchers design, conduct and deliver research findings using approaches such as randomised trials, cohort studies, qualitative and ethnographic studies of health, illness and healthcare use, and evidence synthesis. Health research and evidence-based medicine do not view types of evidence produced by these varied approaches as equal. Instead, formal evidence synthesis is usually seen as the method that produces the most reliable and robust form of evidence, while randomised controlled trials are viewed as producing reliable findings ripe for synthesis. Often described as situated lower down on a 'hierarchy of evidence', research findings based on non-randomised approaches, such as qualitative research or cohort studies, are seen as valid but less robust and more subject to flaws such as various types of bias (Lambert 2009).

Elsewhere I have suggested that the relatively low status of research findings based on participatory research and their conflation with 'public involvement' has the potential to challenge the importance afforded to anthropological knowledge (Gooberman-Hill 2014). Despite this risk to the status of anthropological knowledge, and possibly because of this risk, I firmly believe that anthropologists have much to offer in the kinds of research that influence health policy. Conversely, anthropologists (and anthropology) stand to gain from engagement in applied, multidisciplinary health research (Gooberman-Hill 2003). There is a need to ask how anthropology and anthropologists interact with applied health, and whether any potential for mutual gain is tinged by inequity in the face of policy-making processes that value evidence emanating from particular types of research. To explore these questions, this chapter scrutinises the minutiae of my own experience within health research as a part of the practice of evidence-based medicine in the UK today. This tells us something about the relationships between everyday working habits, identity as an anthropologist and an anthropologist's appropriation of concepts from outside the discipline of anthropology.

Anthropologists in applied health research

To deliver health research in the UK, partnerships between universities and the National Health Service (NHS) are explicitly encouraged by Department of Health (DoH) funding processes. Establishment of the DoH's National Institute for Health Research (NIHR) in 2006 created a new structure to fund and support research in the UK. The prioritisation of research to inform healthcare was further bolstered by the 2010 White Paper *Equity and Excellence: Liberating the NHS*, which stated a commitment to 'promotion and conduct of research as a core

NHS role' (DoH 2010: 24). Before these initiatives, many research-active universities and NHS healthcare providers already worked with each other to deliver research, but the inception of the NIHR engendered further collaboration at organisational and individual levels. Staff employed by universities and the NHS now engage widely in collaborative research, with many research-active staff holding contracts in both types of organisation. Together, universities and NHS providers also provide the structures through which these staff can design projects and apply for research funding from a variety of sources.

It is difficult to obtain information about the numbers or precise location of anthropologists working in applied health research, partly because of the often fluid nature of such employment, but also because next destination surveys of PhD graduates do not provide this level of detail (e.g., see Hodges, Metcalf and Pollard 2011). Furthermore, although some anthropologists working in health research are based within universities and NHS organisations, others work in think tanks, charities, non-governmental organisations (NGOs) and commercial organisations. The presence of large numbers of health researchers within formal networks of anthropologists – such as the Association of Social Anthropologists' 'Apply' Network – provides indication that anthropologists working in health comprise a large, or certainly highly visible, proportion of anthropologists who would identify as working in 'applied' settings. This said, those who use the terms 'applied' or 'engaged' to describe their work do so in awareness of the artificiality of any clear or necessary divide between applied and theoretical anthropology (Strang 2009), and some would probably not use these terms at all.

My own journey into health research starts with a conventional background: I possess an undergraduate degree and PhD in social anthropology. For the latter I spent over a year conducting ethnographic fieldwork in the Solomon Islands. Based on this, my PhD research explored class, kinship and ethnicity, but since finishing the PhD I have been working within a Faculty of Health Sciences at a UK university (see Gooberman-Hill 2006 for a description of this transition). Over the years, my role has changed from postdoctoral employment on a project designed by others to designing and running my own projects with a small team of staff. Although my job is within an academic institution, I do a relatively modest amount of teaching and supervision. Much of my work is oriented towards research and involves engagement with patients and health professionals within the NHS and with researchers and methodologists who are not anthropologists.

I have found it constantly stimulating to work within UK applied health research. My current job is varied but always busy, as I juggle project and staff management with research, committee and panel roles, teaching, grant writing, budgeting and peer review. Planning and designing research takes a sizeable portion of my time, and my role in this type of activity provides a vehicle to illustrate key themes relating to my position within an applied multidisciplinary setting. The following two vignettes are composite examples from my day-to-day work serving to highlight key themes relating to anthropological identity within multidisciplinary contexts.

Vignette 1: meeting to discuss developing a research project

Meetings form a considerable part of my workload, and many of these focus on development of new research projects and associated grant applications. While a small amount of my time is explicitly allocated to do this kind of work through the NIHR-funded Research Design Service, on many occasions I am not acting in this capacity. My input into project development meetings is usually similar, and here I provide an account of a typical meeting.

At a meeting to design a research project, a group of research methodologists and research-active healthcare professionals came together with the shared aim of establishing how to design a grant application centred on a particular health condition. We hoped that the project might eventually lead to better treatment for that condition, and to achieve this aim we thought that we would eventually need to conduct a randomised controlled trial comparing treatment options. In that randomised trial we would need to quantitatively assess patients' outcomes after treatment. In general terms, the desire to conduct randomised trials is driven by the value placed on this type of research design within evidence-based medicine, as policymakers consider findings from randomised trials – which include information about cost-effectiveness, and which can be systematically collated and subjected to meta-analysis – to form an appropriate basis for decisions about healthcare provision. There is often a sense that funding decisions take this view into account, and our team was working on this basis at the meeting, with brief discussion of the most appropriate potential funding body for the project.

We also discussed existing research literature about the health condition and agreed that there was a need for improved interventions and a lack of evidence from randomised trials. We then had to consider whether our team was ready to design a trial, or whether there was a need for more development and background work first. Such development work typically includes a synthesis of existing research literature followed by, or in tandem with, identification or creation of an intervention that could be evaluated. Contributing to the discussions, I volunteered a view about a need for additional feasibility work. We discussed how the project could assess whether patients and practising healthcare professionals thought that a proposed or newly developed intervention was 'feasible' and 'acceptable'. I also suggested that research using qualitative interviews could help to identify 'barriers' and 'facilitators' to implementation of the intervention in future practice, should the trial show that the intervention was effective.

All randomised trials must include outcome measures to assess whether the intervention under investigation brings about any benefit (or harm) to participants. In health research, these are usually standardised quantitative assessments, often in questionnaire format, and many of which are subject to copyright and used under licence. In consideration of the outcome measures that our trial might contain, I suggested that our work to assess feasibility and acceptability of the intervention could be augmented by work with patients to identify which 'outcome measures' they thought most appropriate. These could then be included in the design of the trial. Finally, I raised a question about the sort of design that the randomised trial should have, since there are several possible variants. Nothing about my comments would suggest that I was an anthropologist, let alone clearly identify me as one.

Vignette 2: using qualitative research methods

I work across several projects as the lead or advisor in qualitative research methods. Although my role varies, many of the projects employ similar sets of methods. Recently I have led several projects focused on joint replacement surgery. Joint replacements are increasingly common operations for management of certain types of arthritis, and involve removal of the joint – such as a hip or knee – and its replacement with an artificial joint. Previous research shows that although these operations are common, they are not without issues. For instance, the decisions that lead up to them are not always clear and there can be serious medical complications and long-term consequences.

One of the projects that I have been involved in focused on decisions about operations, and included observation and interviews. By observing appointments between patients and surgeons, and through interviews with both parties afterwards, the team hoped that the project would provide meaningful insight into decision-making processes and have the potential to influence practice. My role was to lead the bid for research funding, manage the project, adhere to good research practice and facilitate dissemination of findings. All of the work would be done, as it so often is in applied research, as a team effort with a researcher employed specifically for the research project.

In the first vignette, we saw how project design was driven by awareness of the need to deliver robust research evidence palatable both to funders and policymakers. In the second project, we also considered the need for a robust research design that would address the research topic and the importance of designing and describing a project with maximum appeal to potential funders. While achieving the first of these rested on bringing methodological expertise into play, the second required us to tailor the project appropriately and to describe it in particular ways. When developing the proposal, the team carefully produced it in the knowledge that the majority of the funder's peer reviewers and decision-makers were unlikely to have social science backgrounds and that some would be healthcare professionals more used to assessing studies using quantitative rather than qualitative methods. Therefore, in the proposal sent to the potential funder, we took care to include clear specification and strong defence of the study's 'sample size', consent processes, 'data collection' methods, including topics that would be asked in interviews, and a detailed description of data analysis with citation of appropriate methods literature. The project was funded and the team then employed a similar strategy in our description of the study for presentation to an NHS Research Ethics Committee. All research involving NHS patients must receive approval from such a committee, and production of the documentation for this is a major task including completion of a lengthy online form alongside submission of a study protocol, patient information material, consent forms, all proposed correspondence with patients, and a list of questions or topics that would be asked during research interviews.

This precise specification of methods is standard practice in applied health research, and is considered essential to success in securing funding and NHS research ethical approval. The precision required can present challenges when a research project requires some fluidity. To address the possibility that the areas of focus in the interviews could change as the project progressed, we were pragmatic and honest with the committee: we took care to pre-define the interview topic guides but also stated that these were simply guides that would be subject to change depending on the answers given and the progress of the study. The ethics committee was satisfied that this was appropriate and asked that if the area changed substantially, then we should return to them for a further view. Related to this, the research entailed observation of practice, which can also be unpredictable and seemed not to fit easily into the expectation that we would define the project in advance and in detail. To account for this, we took care to refer to guidance from the Association of Social Anthropologists about good practice in ethnographic research, as anthropological research so often involves observation (Association of Social Anthropologists of the UK and the Commonwealth 2011). Citation of this guidance and statements about our intention to adhere to the guidance helped us as a research team to show that we were aware of the challenges of observational research, to highlight the potential unpredictability of this method of information collection and to demonstrate understanding of the research team's responsibilities to research participants.

With the project finally underway, the project researcher observed appointments between surgeons and patients at which they discussed the possibility of surgery. The researcher audio-recorded appointments, wrote brief field notes and interviewed surgeons and patients. Audio-recordings were transcribed, the researcher applied 'codes' as a way of categorising sections of the transcribed data, and the team as a whole worked together to discuss and develop interpretation. Between us we presented findings at medical conferences and published them in two journals targeting healthcare professionals and researchers. In writing up the research, we echoed the approach taken in the proposals to the funder and the NHS Research Ethics Committee. We took care to defend the sample size, to use phrases such as 'saturation' to explain adequacy of the sample, and described the teamwork used in the analysis process as a way of showcasing the 'rigour' of the research.

Conducting the project involved the researcher meticulously collecting and organising information. Research findings indicated that people (patients) vary in their threshold for surgery, that some people come forward for surgery before their hip or knee problems become any worse rather than waiting until symptoms are unbearable, and that patients altered their style of communication to echo that of health professionals. However, as a qualitative project, these findings would not have the same potential to influence policy as the planned randomised trial in the first vignette.

In the design of this project, I was well aware of the potential to design a more truly ethnographic study involving long-term fieldwork. Instead, we chose only to include observation of appointments and interviews for two reasons. First, we thought that interviews and observation alone would provide sufficient information to address the topic. Although I considered that in-depth, long-term ethnographic fieldwork might generate additional and fascinating insight, I also thought that it may not produce enough extra detail to warrant the time and energy required and would take too long given finite resources and the need to deliver findings relatively quickly. Second, it seemed likely that a detailed ethnographic study would not appeal to the potential funder, as they had no track record of support for such work, and I had no desire to martyr the project in an attempt to convince them of the value of ethnographic research. Although it is impossible to gauge the outcome of such a submission, I did not want to take the risk, which seemed too great. I therefore did not raise this possibility of long-term ethnographic fieldwork with the rest of the project team. Since the completion of this project, I have worked to design other projects involving an ethnographic slant. Increasingly these may be described as 'process evaluations', and although involving a considerable amount of depth in fieldwork and interpretation, they still require a degree of pre-specification and rapidity. However, at this point in time, I am heartened that the value of ethnographic approaches appears to be increasingly acknowledged across applied health research.

Interpreting practice

The two vignettes are intended to serve as exemplars of my daily work. Although illustrating different types of activity, both raise questions about the extent to which anthropology informs my work, how I represent my research to suit the expectations of particular audiences and how anthropologists appropriate the modes of other disciplines. In turn, this might show us something about how anthropology sits within the processes of applied health research.

Where is the anthropology? Appropriation at work

In both vignettes, I refashioned some of the techniques and skills that I learnt in previous ethnographic fieldwork into something altogether more palatable to a multidisciplinary and clinical research community. This included use of appropriate terminology, discussion of sample sizes, lists of interview topics and transparent descriptions of analysis with emphasis on rigour. This imperative to describe qualitative or ethnographic research in an accessible fashion, whether in reports of research or in introductions to methods, is now widely apparent in clinical journals. This brings with it the potential to reach new audiences, but also means that descriptions of methods are pared down to the bare essentials (e.g. Gooberman-Hill, Fox and Chesser 2010; Gooberman-Hill 2012, 2015).

It could be argued that my current practice, which involves extraction of 'skills' learnt in anthropology, leans towards generic qualitative research. In some ways this is positive: an anthropologist in this type of role can engage with practitioners from different disciplines and learn to understand what is meant by analysis informed by processes such as grounded theory, sample sizes based on a desire to claim either theoretical or data saturation, and the reasons for pre-definition of topic and interview questions. In my role I have adopted some of the language and concepts from wider qualitative approaches, using them to justify research design to potential funders, ethics committees and journal editors. I also use language that I hear in health research to provide rationale for inclusion of qualitative approaches within studies, for instance referring to 'barriers' and 'facilitators' when introducing the potential to explore acceptability of an intervention. Rather than worrying that this compromises the integrity of such research, I have made the decision that this strategy still enables appropriate research to take place, and may bolster the chance that it will be funded and meet with approval of relevant audiences.

However, I also think that my work also benefits from my background as an anthropologist. First, in practical terms, I find it immeasurably helpful to balance my statements about sample sizes and interview topics with reference to publications about anthropological approaches that clearly explain the importance of flexibility in research, the value of long-term commitment and centrality of researchers' ethical responsibilities to participants. This is where citation of anthropology's guidelines on good practice becomes useful when I draft applications for research funding or for ethical approval (Association of Social Anthropologists of the UK and the Commonwealth 2011). Second, more fundamentally, I believe that the process that anthropologists use to make sense of long-term fieldwork provides a sense that interpretive freedom in the analysis process has value. This acts as a counterpoint to the increasing codification of analysis and reporting processes in qualitative research, which has led to and is bolstered by the growth of circumscribed and potentially constraining approaches to quality assessment and reporting of qualitative research, such as the CAS-P and COREQ checklists (Tong, Sainsbury and Craig 2007; Chenail 2008).

Although I use transparent methods of 'coding' and thematic categorisation to analyse data in my current work, I consider this as only one part of the way in which I understand and interpret research material. However, this view may be at odds with those of other practitioners of qualitative research when there is the perception that validity checks can ensure rigour and reliability in qualitative research. As an anthropologist, I see creativity and intuition as key parts to the process of interpretation in research, and consider that this is connected to the embodied and intersubjective experiences of fieldwork. The notion that interpretation can be grounded in experiential knowledge does not sit terribly easily in an environment where analysis is often done in teams to ensure 'rigour' and where auditable trails of process are considered crucial. I would also consider reflexive engagement to be the norm in anthropology. In applied health research, reflexivity is certainly acknowledged, but may appear as brief descriptions of researchers' professional backgrounds, and explanations about how the potential 'bias' brought about by these was addressed and mitigated. I now tend to keep quiet about creativity, intuition and reflexivity but firmly believe that the experience of long-term fieldwork and interpretation of research material has given me the confidence to value rather than fear these aspects of research.

It is perhaps useful here to think about the nature of anthropological skills. Although its style has changed over time, long-term ethnographic fieldwork remains central to the labour of anthropology. Its conduct is usually considered crucial to the making of anthropologists, and ethnographic fieldwork serves as an embodied method of training (see, for instance, Watson 1999). It is well recognised that fieldwork is a fluid process that can take a researcher in unexpected directions: although an anthropologist might set out to study a certain topic, this may change during fieldwork for any one of a number of reasons. Furthermore, unlike applied health research in which some form of teamwork often happens, anthropological fieldwork has often taken place through a lone-worker model, regardless of whether the field site is geographically close, distant or multi-sited. Creating an ethnographic text depends on an anthropologist's meticulous use of field notes and other materials (see, for instance, Emerson, Fretz and Shaw 1995), but is also considered a reflexive enterprise drawing on the embodied experience of the fieldwork experience (Unnithan-Kumar and De Neve 2006). The processes by which experience informs written accounts in anthropology have of course been debated and discussed, but there is seldom any suggestion that this aspect of the production of knowledge in and from fieldwork conforms to any uniform step-by-step process.

Anthropologists working in any multidisciplinary environment may face the misconception that they largely conduct research in 'remote' or 'exotic' settings. Anthropologists do not frame their discipline in this fashion (see Marcus 1998; MacClancy 2002), but this is not always the perception of others looking in. For instance, in a popular qualitative research methods textbook, now in its third edition and regularly updated, contributors (non-anthropologists) portray anthropology as a discipline that focuses on faraway 'tribes' (Silverman 2011). This is a challenge because it is precisely this type of book that colleagues in other disciplines are familiar with, and it may sometimes be their only exposure to information about anthropology. Of course, colleagues with whom I engage on a daily basis see that I work in an environment that is geographically close, which they encounter every day and that they might view as mundane. They also know that I am an anthropologist, but the understanding is that as an anthropologist, I know about how to design and do qualitative research.

Positioning anthropology

If the ability to undertake fieldwork and to produce a textual account is the mark of a fully fledged anthropologist, how does that core skill translate into research environments such as those in applied health research? The two vignettes in this chapter show how applied health research uses models of data collection that do not easily accommodate long-term ethnographic fieldwork and associated methods of interpretation. I have suggested above that UK health research is an environment in which projects are pre-defined to the level of sample sizes and interview questions, where research involves teams, and in which information comprises 'data' for which interpretation privileges systematic analysis processes. It could be argued that when anthropologists like me make decisions about presentation of research to comply with these norms, we not only make assumptions about what funders and ethics committees expect, but we reinforce rather than challenge those expectations. An alternative view is that occupying a seat at a table rather than looking in from outside makes it possible to drive change and diversity from within. In my own work, I have taken the latter stance and have decided that it is useful to be positioned inside research that influences policy and practice. From that position anthropologists can most easily introduce observational approaches and interpretive methods of analysis, and can introduce anthropological approaches to ethical research practice. Furthermore, although not readily apparent in the vignettes described above, anthropologists' deep-seated concerns with equity and participation in research may be relevant in the processes of decisions about how best to design research that will have an influence on healthcare.

Additionally, it is important to remember that anthropology cannot proclaim sole ownership of fieldwork or ethnography. Other disciplines also have long since considered fieldwork and the production of ethnography as part of their canon, albeit with acknowledgement of the key roles of Bronislaw Malinowski and anthropologists as originators of participant observation. In relation to health and illness, anthropologists have of course produced myriad ethnographies, but practitioners of other disciplines make ample use of ethnographic strategies and tools. Most notably, sociologists employ techniques that they describe as ethnographic (e.g. Somerville et al. 2008), and are also adept at producing manuals explaining how to conduct ethnographic fieldwork (see Brewer 2000; Hammersley and Atkinson 2007). When I write proposals for research funding or submissions to NHS Research Ethics Committees, and if I need to cite a straightforward text that describes observational research methods, these are the ones that I use for lack of anything equivalent from anthropology. However, unlike anthropology, which sees fieldwork – in any of its forms – as central to disciplinary practice, sociologists are more able to see ethnographic fieldwork as just one of a range of possible approaches. This enables the mobilisation of other methods that fit more easily with the norms in applied health research, such as studies based solely on collection and analysis of interview material. Anthropologists, on the other hand, must unpick fieldwork and ethnography and find out what elements of their practice are transferable, can be translated well and can deliver research findings in a short time frame.

Finally, while anthropologists like me are busy appropriating models and language that may be most acceptable to colleagues, funders or Research Ethics Committees, it is worth considering the extent to which anthropological input in applied health research is itself appropriated, defined or redefined in ways that anthropologists may have little control over. The imperative to secure research funding, approval from Research Ethics Committees and publication may be key drivers in anthropologists' appropriation of dominant models, but there may be risks in this. For instance, we might wonder if this type of engagement simply serves to bolster the current dominance of evidence-based medicine (see Lambert 2006, 2009), as anthropologists assist in the design of randomised trials and perhaps collude in confirming the lower status of qualitative research on the evidence hierarchy. If we claim that short-term observational work performs nearly the same role as longer-term ethnography, and if we suggest that transparent coding processes improve rigour, is there a risk that long-term and interpretive anthropological approaches will be deemed irrelevant or unnecessary? While applied health research provides funding opportunities, although it is satisfying to see the impact of research on policy and practice, and while intellectually stimulating, it may also be more crucial than we realise to define and maintain some disciplinary uniqueness for anthropology and anthropologists who are engaged in this way.

Acknowledgements

Thanks are due to the research staff and research participants with whom I am lucky to work. The vignettes shown here are semi-fiction composites based on projects that I have been involved in over several years.

Rachael Gooberman-Hill is Professor of Health and Anthropology within the Faculty of Health Sciences at the University of Bristol, UK. She publishes applied health research for clinical audiences, is a member of a sub-panel of the National Institute for Health Research's Programme Grants for Applied Research and leads research into long-term conditions, healthcare and service delivery.

References

Association of Social Anthropologists of the UK and the Commonwealth. 2011. *Ethical Guidelines for Good Research Practice*. Retrieved 12 February 2016 from http://www.theasa.org/ethics/guidelines.shtml.
Brewer, J.D. 2000. *Ethnography*. Buckingham: Open University Press.
Brown, P., and M.W. Calnan. 2013. 'NICE Technology Appraisals: Working with Multiple Levels of Uncertainty and the Potential for Bias', *Medical Health Care and Philosophy* 16(2): 281–93.
Chenail, R.J. 2008. 'Learning to Appraise the Quality of Qualitative Research Articles: A Contextualised Learning Object for Constructing Knowledge', *The Weekly Qualitative Report* 1(9): 29–61.
Davies, C., M. Wetherell and E. Barnett. 2006. *Citizens at the Centre: Deliberative Participation in Healthcare Decisions*. Bristol: Policy Press.
Department of Health. 2010. *Equity and Excellence: Liberating the NHS*. White Paper. London: Department of Health.
Emerson, R., R. Fretz and L. Shaw. 1995. *Writing Ethnographic Fieldnotes*. Chicago, IL: University of Chicago Press.
Gooberman-Hill, R. 2003. 'How Multidisciplinarity is Good for Anthropologists and Anthropology', *Anthropology in Action* 10(3): 28–34.
Gooberman-Hill, R. 2006. 'Among the Crowds: Learning Anthropology and Learning Multidisciplinarity', in M. Unnithan-Kumar and G. De Neve

(eds), *Critical Journeys: The Making of Anthropologists*. Aldershot: Ashgate, pp.117–28.

Gooberman-Hill, R. 2012. 'Qualitative Approaches to Understanding Patient Preferences', *The Patient: Patient-Centered Outcomes Research* 5(4): 215–23.

Gooberman-Hill, R. 2014. 'Defining Evidence: Involvement and Participatory Approaches in Applied Health Research', *Anthropology in Action* 21(2): 31–36.

Gooberman-Hill, R. 2015. 'Ethnographies of Pain: Culture, Context and Complexity', *British Journal of Pain* 9(1): 32–35.

Gooberman-Hill, R., R. Fox and T. Chesser. 2011. 'What Can Qualitative Approaches Bring to Trauma Outcome Research?' *Injury* 42: 321–23.

Hammersley, M., and P. Atkinson. 2007. *Ethnography: Principles in Practice*, 3rd edn. London and New York: Routledge.

Hodges, V., J. Metcalf and E. Pollard. 2011. *What Do Researchers Do? Career Paths of Doctoral Graduates, Vitae 2011*. Cambridge: The Careers Research and Advisory Centre (CRAC) Limited.

Lambert, H. 2006. 'Accounting for EBM: Contested Notions of Evidence in Medicine', *Social Science and Medicine* 62(11): 2633–45.

Lambert, H. 2009. 'Evidentiary Truths? The Evidence of Anthropology through the Anthropology of Medical Evidence', *Anthropology Today* 25(1): 16–20.

MacClancy, J. (ed.). 2002. *Exotic No More: Anthropology on the Front Lines*. Chicago, IL: University of Chicago Press.

Marcus, G.E. 1998. *Ethnography through Thick and Thin*. Princeton, NJ: Princeton University Press.

Silverman, D. (ed.). 2011. *Qualitative Research: Theory, Method and Practice*. London: Sage.

Somerville, C., K. Featherstone, H. Hemingway, A. Timmis and G.S. Feder. 2008. 'Performing Stable Angina Pectoris: An Ethnographic Study', *Social Science and Medicine* 66(7): 1497–1508.

Spyridonidis, D., and M.W. Calnan. 2011. 'Opening the Black Box: A Study of the Process of NICE Guideline Implementation', *Health Policy* 102(2–3): 117–25.

Strang, V. 2009. *What Anthropologists Do*. Oxford: Berg.

Tong, A., P. Sainsbury and J. Craig. 2007. 'Consolidated Criteria for Reporting Qualitative Research (COREQ): A 32-Item Checklist for Interviews and Focus Groups', *International Journal of Qualitative Health Care* 16(6): 349–57.

Unnithan-Kumar, M., and G. De Neve. 2006. 'Being There: Producing Fields, Selves and Anthropology', in M. Unnithan-Kumar and G. De Neve (eds), *Critical Journeys: The Making of Anthropologists*. Aldershot: Ashgate.

Watson, C.W. (ed.). 1999. *Being There: Fieldwork in Anthropology*. London: Pluto Press.

Afterword

An Endnote, About How to Begin
Jeremy MacClancy

Perhaps it is best to end by engaging in an educational excursus, to propose some pedagogical propositions.

An assessor of this book thought a series of guidelines for students and their teachers a valuable signing-off. The publisher agreed. Their query was: based on the material in these chapters, could one indicate what a modern degree course in anthropology might include to make its graduates more prepared for the world beyond the ivory towers? In other words, learning anthropology as an approach to life may be splendid, but graduates need jobs. Knowing that with a degree in our subject and a couple of quid they can buy a latte sounds, for most, like a bad return on their student debt.

So, how to make taught anthropology more employment-friendly yet still just as intellectually rewarding, without sounding like a careers advisor who missed her calling? My suggestions, both generic and specific:

- Interviewees and several contributors stress the ability to write succinctly. Effective writing is a learned skill. There are several good guides on the market: choose one, read, then reread.[1] Expect to rewrite, several times. You will get better.
- If in doubt, seek out the earliest article you can find by an anthropologist whose style you admire. Chances are, it will not be impressive. The Oxford anthropologist Rodney Needham was regarded as a master essayist, albeit a highly mannered one. In 1977, one of his students, despondent at his supervisor rejecting the first draft chapter for his thesis, sought out the earliest paper listed in Needham's bibliography. 'What was it like?', asked I, eager, curious. He laughed, 'Dreadful. So clumsy! So laboured!'
- You might be able to understand dense anthropological arguments but, unless you wish to be pigeon-holed as overly academic, do not bother to reproduce these scholastic styles. The much-respected anthropologist Godfrey Lienhardt used to tell his post-fieldwork students, 'Never write a sentence about the people

you lived with if you can't translate it back into their language': a deeply testing goal but a worthy ideal to aim for.
- Persuade your teachers to set essays on contemporary topics not yet established in the literature. In other words, be ready to test your anthropological skills by applying them to subjects on which there are no, or very few articles so far.
- Successful interviewees said they had to design research projects and ways to promote them. If your course has a module on research methods, take it. If not, complain.
- Interviewees said that, thanks to extended fieldwork during their doctorates, they know how to talk to people: learning what to ask, how, to whom, when.
- For over twenty years, I have included small group fieldwork exercises in all the courses I teach. Some go well, some less well, but almost all students rate it the most satisfying aspect of my modules. The same holds true for undergraduate dissertations: chances are, one based on fieldwork will be as challenging as it is rewarding.
- Make fieldwork an integral part of your dissertation.
- You don't need deep pockets or a trip abroad. Every year several of my students turn their summer job or some aspect of hometown life into their research material. A few of the recent best were: migrant agricultural labour (she pulled pints in their local pub); male friendship (his mates); open mic nights (already her preferred Friday night out). For each, their total research cost? Zilch.
- Dare to be different, or at least strive to avoid the conventional. If your choice of topic is between bell-ringing in Bulawayo or unexpected uses of the Net in Nottingham, plumb for the latter. Far better to appear contemporary than antiquarian. You wish to be viewed as an analyst of today, not a tired seeker of the stereotypically exotic.
- Open your eyes. If you think that obvious, attend to the much-lauded Indian novelist Amitav Ghosh, DPhil:

The one most important thing I learnt from anthropology (especially fieldwork) was the art of observation: how to watch interactions between people, how to listen to conversations, how to look for hidden patterns. This has always stayed with me and has influenced everything I've done, especially my journalism. (Stankiewicz 2012: 541)

I don't know an anthropologist-civil servant who would disagree. After all, as the famed popular anthropologist of the mid

century, Tom Harrisson, put it, every fieldworker should carry earplugs, and use them methodically.
- Be as technologically up to date as possible. Even better, try to incorporate new forms of IT into your research, at all levels. One interviewee was emphatic that fluency in social media would make a candidate highly attractive to her employers. It is unsurprising that she works in counterinsurgency.[2]
- Play games. Not with your teachers, but in league with them. Government departments use role play routinely in their training exercises, so it is good to get used to them early on. The fieldwork simulation BaFa' BaFa' remains the most popular, for the right reasons, whether you play the full or a skeletal version. 'Yams!' is a strategy card game where players act as nineteenth-century Trobriand big-men vying for the paramount chieftaincy. The UK-based Digital Anthropology Resources for Teaching (DART) website has several online exercises – for example, simulate ethnographic collection, rise to the challenge of Madagascan rice farming, explore Kolkata streets as an ethnographer. Trawling the internet will bring up a host of further examples.[3]
- If you really wish to impress, think up your own anthropological game, on your own or, better, with classmates. Persuade your lecturer to incorporate it in their teaching sessions.
- Study abroad. As far as I am aware, all universities in the UK now offer exchange schemes for students to spend part of their undergraduate course in a similar department in a foreign country. Research shows that students who take advantage of this are statistically more likely to obtain better degrees and gain employment on graduation. This effect is particularly marked for those from disadvantaged or black and minorities backgrounds (Go International 2016).

On top of that, there are obvious benefits for anthropology students: learning how their discipline is understood in a different educational setting (as not all national anthropologies are the same); learning to work in an international setting within a cosmopolitan cohort; coming to appreciate the cultural distinctiveness of another way of life. All of these are eminently anthropological endeavours. On top of that, the study period abroad provides an excellent opportunity to find and research a topic for your dissertation.

I have been the ERASMUS anthropology co-ordinator at the university that employs me for the last twenty years. I have yet to meet a returnee student who regretted their decision, and I have

read a host of good dissertations based on the life of the area in which they resided.
- The methods of social anthropology are deservedly renowned:
  - learning how others view, value and act in the world. This means not simply incorporating at some stage of a research project the fact that those studied may have their own ideas; it means starting with that insight, and building from there.
  - linking seemingly unconnected data into meaningful patterns;- several interviewees stressed this. Those graduating in other disciplines may have large, well-organised data sets, but few contemplated the range and disparity of information that anthropologist colleagues were prepared to consider.
  - contemplating seriously the apparently irrational, to see what logic might be lurking there. This goes hand in glove with the disciplinary cliché that we make the familiar strange and the strange familiar. Discerning local logistics is a fundamental but particularly powerful technique. It continues to surprise me how many non-anthropologists find it hard to take this on board.
  - striving to think critically at all times, being ready to eject cherished concepts and to reflect on our own position in the process. An education in anthropology is meant both to help people challenge conventional wisdom, and to encourage a critical empathy, so we can understand better those with whom we disagree most.

These are real strengths, ones to be nurtured and defended.

One colleague, an anthropologist of education, stressed the broader benefit underlying this pedagogical development of an ethnographic sensibility: 'In an increasingly complex, globalising world, this kind of culturally sensitive, cosmopolitan, ethnographically informed worldview might not only make you a better employee, it might even make you a better person' (Patrick Alexander, pers. comm., 5 January 2016). In other words, take your anthropology training seriously, and it might not just get you a job, but also provide a position from which to face the world.

We must not over-egg the case. Anthropological techniques may be particularly powerful, but that does not mean other disciplines are bereft of comparably prestigious procedures – with their own blind spots and weaknesses, of course, but also with their own strengths. Almost every person involved in this book has had to work in interdisciplinary teams, and all felt they had benefited from it. I studied anthropology at Oxford in the late 1970s, the tail end of high structuralism. We were trained to sneer at quantitative approaches, to hoot at psychologisms and to sigh over most forms of sociology. They were, our teachers said, *so* naïve. Today I am not so sure.

*

In sum, a final checklist:
- Justify every word.
- Translate Anthrospeak into a language your parents can understand.
- Take advantage of every opportunity for fieldwork your course offers.
- Face the contemporary unstudied, then analyse it.
- As a recreation: design research projects, not drugs.
- Learn to stare.
- Leave the country.
- Scrutinise interdisciplinary texts your tutor sets: how did their authors manage to combine anthropology with other disciplines, to productive end?
- If your department doesn't offer placements yet, suggest that they do.

Of course, the most impressive rule for those who wish to benefit from this book is: *work out why and how any of the above is wrong, then act on it.*

As the official 'Working for the Civil Service' webpage prominently posts, 'We want people that think differently'.[4]

*

Now, before more theoretically inclined readers throw this book at the nearest wall, I emphasise that these recommendations are for a shift in pedagogy, not an all-encompassing revolution, though some may think that's where they lead. For without theory, anthropology becomes primarily a technical skill and little more; a box of tricks marked 'Methods'. But without extramural practice, the discipline remains an exclusively academic exercise with a restricted list of members. And that can so easily turn into elitism.

Jeremy MacClancy is Professor of Anthropology in the Department of Social Sciences, Oxford Brookes University. He is the founder-chairman of Chacolinks, a small, international charity that accompanies the indigenous Wichí of northern Argentina in the legal campaign to regain control of their ancestral lands.

Notes

1. My personal favourite is Graves and Hodge (1947). On quiet days, I consider writing one myself.
2. For example, in 2016 UCL is running, on three occasions, a five-week online course on 'The Anthropology of Social Media'. Retrieved 29 February 2016 from https://www.ucl.ac.uk/why-we-post.
3. The BaFa' BaFa' kit, both teacher and participant versions, is available from Simulation Training Systems (http://www.stsintl.com/). For information on Yams!, see http://www.yamsthegame.com/. For an example of teaching anthropology via games and game theory, see Krista Harper, 'Teaching Anthropology of/through Games', *Teaching Culture*, 15 September 2015, retrieved 29 February 2016 from http://www.utpteachingculture.com/teaching-anthropology-ofthrough-games-part-1/. Also worth checking out is 'Cards against Anthropology' on *Anthropology Games*, retrieved 29 February 2016 from http://www.anthropologygames.com/. For DART, see http://www.lse.ac.uk/anthropology/research/dart/dart.aspx.
4. Retrieved 3 March 2016 from https://www.gov.uk/government/organisations/civil-service/about/recruitment. In 2009, C-SAP, a UK centre for pedagogical development in sociology, anthropology and political science (now defunct), held a series of workshops for anthropology students who were considering jobs outside academia. Their summary of these events (which includes useful facilitator and student packs), entitled 'Anthropology at Work: Applying Anthropology beyond the Academy', is available at https://www.heacademy.ac.uk/sites/default/files/anthropology_at_work.pdf. Retrieved 24 March 2016.

References

Go International. 2016. 'Gone International. The Value of Mobility. Report on the 2013/2014 Graduating Cohort'. London: Go International.

Graves, R., and A. Hodge. 1947. *The Reader over Your Shoulder. A Handbook for Writers of English Prose*. London: Jonathan Cape.

Stankiewicz, D. 2012. 'Anthropology and Fiction: An Interview with Amitav Ghosh', *Cultural Anthropology* 27(3): 535–41.

Index

Aboriginal Australians, 83–88, 89, 95
  Homelands movements, 83
  As traditional owners, 84
Advisory Committee on the
  Therapeutic Regime at Grendon
  (ACTRAG), 153–154
Affect, 96n3
Afghanistan, 18, 19
Aidland, 47
Allen, Michael, 8
American Anthropologist Association
  (AAA), 18, 43, 47
Anthropologist-civil servants, 5–38
  Awkward Johnny, 50
  'Beard and sandals brigade', 14
  Dismissive stereotypes, 14
  Distinctive, 13
  'The new black', 16
  'Oddballs', 13, 16
  Professional identity, 32–33
  Relations with academic
    anthropologists, 28, 33–39
Anthropologist-functionaries, 5–38
Anthropologists
  Critical intellectuals, 34–39
  Marginality of, 80, 83
  Snobbery, 37
Anthropology
  Activist, 82, 94
  Action-oriented, 40
  Anti-discipline, 38
  Applied, 51, 79, 84, 85, 94, 95,
    99n28, 118
  Backyard, 40, 48, 120
  See also Kedia and van Willigen
  Definition (Malinowski), 10
  Development, 104
  Dialogic character, 95
  Engaged, 51

Future, 50–52
Government, *see* Government
  anthropology
Medical, 53n12
Metropolitan, 6
Military, 18–20
Non-academic, 1
Practical, 7
Plural, 8, 51
Pragmatic benefit, 38, 50–52
Prescriptive delimitations, 8
Pure/applied, 2
Sister discipline to philosophy, 38
Software, 40, 48
Surveys, 46
Apperception, 147, 151–152, 162
Applied health research, 166–172,
  174–176
Apprentice Boys of Derry, 127, 131,
  136–137, 138
Ardener, Edwin, 7
Ardener, Shirley, 7
Armed conflict, nature of, 15
Art therapy, 155
Ashante, 6, 7
Asquith, Herbert, Prime Minister, 4
Association of Social Anthropologists
  (ASA), 13, 28, 33–34, 36, 37, 167
Asymmetric adversaries, 62
Australian anthropologists, 37, 54n17

'Bad faith' (Sartre), 150
Bands, 127, 133
Behavioural Insights Team, 48, 53n8
Belfast, 126, 130, 134
Bennett, Peter, 41–42, 49
Bhaktimarga (the path of devotion),
  148
Bill, formulation of, 23

Bombay Supreme Court (1862), 148
Bryan, Dominic, 40–41, 48, 124–146
'Bull-roarer cult', 7
Bureau of Ethnology, USA, 4
Bureaucracy,
 Anthropology of, 47
 Weight of, 26
Buzz, 26

Cabinet Office, 10, 24, 41, 48, 49, 63–64, 73
Cambridge, 5, 7, 8
CEAUSSIC, 19
Centre for Aboriginal Economic Policy Research, 84
Centre for the Study of Conflict, University of Ulster, 124, 127, 128, 140
Chamberlain, Joseph, Colonial Secretary, 4
Chambers, Robert ,12
Cheevers, Tommy, 134, 136
Civil Contingencies Secretariat, 63–64
Civil rights, 128, 129
Civil Service, British, 9–38, 80, 83, 88–93, 95, 98n20, 98n24
 Code, 28, 48
 Generalists/specialists, 32
 Promotion, 24
 Recruitment to, 88
 'Typical day', 30–32
Civil Service Stabilisation Unit, 20
Civil society, 125, 129, 130, 139, 140
Clifford, James, 45
Cognitive skills programmes, 159
Collaborative work, 50
Colonial anthropology, 3–8, 45–47, 50
 Administrator-scholars, 5
Community, 101–102
Community development, 103
Community development worker, 104
Comparative work, 138
Conlin, Sean, 11, 14
Consultancy, 84, 89, 94
Control Review Committee (CRC), 150–151

Counter-terrorism, 10, 33–34
Crewe, Ben, 147, 152–153
Crossman, Richard, 35–36, 49
Cultural relativism, 68
Cultural translation, 73–74
Culture
 'A hotch-potch', 7
 Instrumentalist approach, 20

Defence (*See* Ministry of Defence)
 Cultural assessment tools, 17
 Defence Cultural Specialist Unit (DCSU), 19–20
 Introductions to local cultural ways, 17
Defence Evaluation and Research Agency (DEFRA), 15
Defence Science and Technology Laboratory (DSTL), 16–17, 26, 27, 29, 32
 College of academics, 17
Degeneration, 3
Democratic deficit, 125, 139
Democratic Dialogue, 127, 132, 134, 140
Department for Business, Innovation and Skills, 51
Department for International Development (DfID), 11, 20, 24, 25, 26, 27, 32–33, 35, 48, 98n17
Department for Trade and Industry, 51
Department of Defense, US Government, 18
Depopulation, 4
Development, 104
Development studies, 2, 47–48
Disjuncture, experience of, 82, 85, 93, 95
Disorder, public, 40
Displacement, 79, 82, 83, 96, 97n7
Dissociation, 148
Drumcree, 128, 130–134, 140
Dumont, Louis, 156
Dunn, Seamus, 127, 128, 140

East, Sir Norwood East, 153

Economic and Social Research Council (ESRC), 33
Economists, 12, 21, 22
Empathy, 75
Ethics, 18, 27–28, 34–36, 81, 92
  Contrasted with ethos, 87
  See also Research ethics committee
Ethnocentricism, 81
Ethnography, 126, 142, 166, 167, 171, 172, 174–176
  Of government, 47–50
  Of prisons, 152–153, 157, 163
Ethos, 80, 90–96, 96n6
European Migration Network (EMN), 88, 98n15
Evans-Pritchard, Edward, 6, 7, 52n1
Evidence-based medicine, 165–166, 168, 170, 176
Evolutionists, 3
'Exotic no more', 38
Expert reports, 83, 86
Expertise, 85, 90

Feminist criticism, 20
Fieldwork, 79, 90, 91
  In prisons, 148, 151, 156
  Long-term, 167, 172–176
  Solitary, 29, 46
Firth, Raymond, 13, 45
Flags, 126, 133, 141
Flanagan, Ronnie 128
Foreign and Commonwealth Office (FCO), 11, 20, 23, 24, 26, 33
Foreign Secretary, 26
Foucault, Michel, 49, 160
Freud, Sigmund, 99n28
Frisson, see Buzz
Fuller, Chris, 5

Garvaghy Road, 130–132, 134
Garvaghy Road Residents Coalition, 123, 130
Gender analysis, 12
Genders, Elaine, and Player, Elaine, 153–154, 160
Genocide, 68, 69
Gold Coast (Ghana), 5–6

Golden Stool, 7
Goldstone Commission, 135
Gooberman-Hill, Rachael, 42–43, 48, 165–178
Government, work of, 80–82
Government anthropology
  In Cameroon, 44
  In Canada, 54n16
  In China, 44–45
  In Germany, 54n16
  In Mexico, 43–44
  In Norway, 44
  In Turkey, 44
  In USA, 43
Government Social Research (GSR), 88, 89, 98n17
Governance professionals, 15
Great Yarmouth, 107
Green, Maia, 8
Grendon, (HMP Grendon and Spring Hill), 41–42, 49, 152–162
  Director of Therapeutic Communities, 159, 161–162
  Medical Superintendent, 153–154, 159
  Reports on Grendon, 155, 162
  Search, the 'Big Spin', 157
Gregory, Robert, 39, 48, 101–122
'Guerilla strategies', 11–13, 48
Guiart, Jean, 8
Guggisberg, Sir Fredrick Gordon, 5

Haddon, Alfred Cort, 4
Hallsworth, Michael, 48
Hills, Mils, 41, 48, 61–78
Hodson, T.C., 7
Holy, Ladislav, 40
Home Office, 3, 10, 23, 24, 26, 89, 95
House of Commons, 23
Hull (HMP Hull), 151
Human rights, 128, 129, 135, 137, 138
  Committee on the Administration of Justice, 129
  Northern Ireland Human Rights Commission, 129, 138
  Pat Finucane Centre, 139

Human Terrain Teams (HTTs), 18–20, 36
Humanitarian issues, 13
Hutton, J.H., 7

Identity
  Slippery nature, 40
  multiple, 17
Imperial anthropology, 3
  Ethnographers, 5
  Justification, 3–4
Indian Civil Service, 5, 7
Indicators of success, 112
Indirect rule, 7
Indigenous rights, 53n12
Inequality, 12
Information Operations, 62
Information Warfare, 62
Interdisciplinarity, 16, 22, 26
International development, 10, 11–15
Influencing others, 119
Iraq, 18, 69, 70, 71
IUAES, 44

Jarman, Neil, 40–41, 48, 123–146

Kedia and van Willigen, 105
Kirke, Charles, 46–47

Land claims, 83–84, 86–87, 93, 97nn11–13
Landman, R.H., 2
Lawrence of Arabia, 20
Leadership, 119
'Lefties', 14
Lévi-Strauss, Claude, 82
Lewis, Ioan, 6
Litton, Ian, 40, 48
Local government, 101, 110
Lombroso, Cesare, 3
Lugard, Lord, 5

MacClancy, Jeremy, vii–ix, 1–60, 80, 93, 179–184
Maharaja Libel Case, 148
Mair, Lucy, 45
Malinowski, Bronislaw, 6, 80, 92

Management, 88–89
Marching season, 124, 127, 131, 133
Mauritius, 41, 61–62
Mayhew, Patrick, 129, 131, 140
McFate, Montgomery, 19
Mead, Margaret, 82
Meek, C.S., 6
Melanesia, 6
Merry, Sally Engle, 19
MI5, 53n8
Migrant workers, 107
Minister for Overseas Development, 11
Minister of Defence, 62, 63, 77n1
Ministers, governmental, 90–92
Ministry of Defence (MoD), 10, 15–18, 19–20, 24, 25, 27, 29, 33, 35, 36, 37, 41, 46, 53n6
  Cultural modelling programme, 17
Ministry of Justice, 24
Ministry of Overseas Development (ODM), 11
Monitoring, 136, 137, 138
Moral indignation, 72
Mosse, David, 47, 49
Mowlam, Marjorie, 'Mo', 124, 135, 140, 141
Müller, Max, 4
Murray, Sir Herbert, 5–6, 7

National Health Service, UK (NHS), 42–43, 166–168
National Institute for Health and Care Excellence (NICE), 165
National Institute for Health Research, 166–168
'Need to know', 8
Negotiation, 84–85, 90–91
Neo-liberal institutionalism, 15
Neighbourhood management, 110–111
Networks, 91, 92
New institutionalism, 15
New Hebrides (today Vanuatu), 8
New Labour, 105
Nigeria, 5–7

Non-Governmental Organisations (NGOs), 83
North Report, 131, 132, 136
Northern Ireland, 40, 123–146
Nottingham (HMP Nottingham), 151–152
Nuer, the, 52n1

Offence paralleling behaviour, 155
'Old colonials', 14
Operational researchers, 22
Orange Order, 123, 136, 141
Overseas Development Administration (ODA), 11
  Permanent Secretary, 14
Oxford, 4, 8
'Oxford school of government anthropology', 6

Papua, 5–6
Parades, 127, 130
  Notting Hill Carnival, 135
  St Patrick's Day, 135
  Twelfth of July, 126, 130
Parades Commission, 126, 135–138, 141
Participant observation, 141, 152
  Participant-observer, 147–148, 152
  Self-observing participant, 162
Participatory
  Approaches, 111
  Budgeting, 115
  Democracy, 112
Partnerships, 91
Patten Report, 125, 137–138
Peace process, 123–125, 134, 135, 139, 141
People-first agenda, 11
Policing
  Belgian Gendarmerie, 137
  Police Service of Northern Ireland, 125
  Royal Ulster Constabulary (RUC), 123–125, 128–130, 136, 138
  South African Police, 137
  See also Patten Report; Public order
Policy, 124–127, 129, 132, 140–143

Anthropology of, 47–50
Crafting of, 23, 27, 113
Development of, 46
Health, 165–166, 168, 171, 175, 177
Interventionist, 66, 67
Migration and asylum, 88–90, 98n15, 98n19
Policymakers, 83, 88–89, 91–93, 98n18, 98n22,
Political scientists, 21, 22
Portuguese migrant labour, 39, 107–109
Practice
  Healthcare, 177
  Theory of, 38, 51
Praxis, 38, 53n13
Pressure, in workplace, 30
Prime Minister, 41
Prison
  Category 'B', 157–158
  Reform, 161
  Relationship with community and Prison Service, 152, 154
  Special units, 150–151
  'System prison', 154
Prison governor, 151, 154
  Assistant governor, 150
  As broker, 162
Prison Service, 49
  Research and Advisory Group (1987), 151
Prisoners
  Category 'A', 151
  Long-term, 150
  Resettlement, 152
  Sexual offenders, 155
Psychodrama, 155
Psychopaths, 156
Public order, 136, 137–138
Pustimarga (the Path of Grace), 148

Qualitative research, 166, 169–176
Quilley, Janet and Alan, 123, 124, 127, 140

'Race', British, 3

Radcliffe-Brown, Arthur Reginald, 5, 7
Randomised trial, 165–166, 168–169, 171, 176
Rattray, Robert Sutherland, 6
Redistribution, 13
Reflexivity, 84, 147
Rehabilitation, 149, 152–153
Research, prison
 measuring offending rates, 152
 statistical focus, 152
Research ethics committee, 170–171, 173, 175–176
Research, Information, and Communications Unit (RICU), 53n8
Research methods, 80, 88, 96n6
 Agile, 40
 Disaggregation, 12
 Ethnographers of organisations, 20
 Holism, 21
 Multi-methods, 16
 Participant-observation, 42
 Respecting others, 21
 Social relations, 22
 Unpacking own biases, 36
 See also Skills, non-anthropological; Teamwork
Respondents, 80–81, 83–87, 95, 96n1, 97n7
Rhodes, Lorna, 160
Rioting, 128, 130, 132
Risley, Sir Herbert, 4
Royal Anthropological Institute (RAI), 4, 34, 36, 37

Salisbury, Lord, Prime Minister, 4
Security, in prisons, 152, 156
 On balance between security and therapy, 158, 161–162
 Dynamic security, 156
Security anthropologist, 77
Security concerns, 8, 29, 49
Self-censorship, 27, 29
Self-observation, 148
Seligman, Charles, 5
Sexism, 10, 20

Sharp, Dame Evelyn, 35–36
Short, Claire, MP, 11, 26
Skills, non-anthropological
 Delegation, 22
 Development of, 80, 84, 88–91, 98n17, 98n20
 Management, 24
 Networking, 21
 Quantitative skills, 23, 88, 89, 99n26
 Writing style, 23
Skill sets, 109, 118–119
Smith, Benjamin, 36, 42, 48, 79–100
Sociability, 73
Social change, 115, 120
Social Development Advisors (SDAs), 11–15, 25, 26, 28, 48
Social field, 82–83, 86, 91–92, 95, 96n6, 96n7, 97n13
Social researchers, 22
Society for Applied Anthropology, 37
Socialism, 13
Somalialand, British, 6
South Pacific, 8
Spencer, Jonathan, 34
Stabilisation, 71
State, the, 82–87, 90, 92, 96, 97n7
Statisticians, 22
Stewarding, 127
Stocking, George, 6, 7–8
Strathern, Marilyn, 51
Subjectivity, 81, 91, 96n5, 147–148, 156
Sudan, The, 5–6, 52n1
Taliban, 71
Taussig, Michael, 97n6
Teamwork, 16, 22, 29
Temple, Sir Richard Carnac, 4
Thatcherism, 13, 38
Theory vs. practice binary, 51
Therapeutic community, 155–156
Therapeutic prison, 154, 161–162
Therapeutic space, 160–161
Therapy (at Grendon), 154, 159
Thomas, Northcote, 5, 13
Troubled families, 116–118
'Truth to power', speaking, 34–35, 48
Ujjain, central India, 148–149
UK Border Agency, 42, 88, 93

Ulster Volunteer Force, 130, 134
Unique selling points, 72–76
United Nations, 13
University of St Andrews, 40
'Vailala Madness', 46
Victorian anthropologists, 3
Wacquant, Louis, 152
Weapons of mass destruction, 69–70
Weiner, James, 80, 96n6
Wellingborough (HMP Wellingborough), 152
Williams, Francis, 6, 7, 46
Wolfe, Thomas, 78
Writing, 114
World Bank, 12
'Yes, Minister', 35
Young Offenders' Institution, 150